The Eleven Eternal Principles

The Eleven Eternal Principles

Accessing the Divine Within

CARMEN HARRA, PhD

CROSSING PRESS
Berkeley

This book is dedicated to the memory of my wonderful husband Virgil. It is also for every-one wishing to evolve in life and those striving for a true connection with the Divine.

Acknowledgments

I have to thank my agent, Lisa Hagan, whose commitment and dedication was simply outstanding. I have to mention my superb editor, Veronica Randall, who did an amazing job with the manuscript and for believing in the concept of the book. And last but not least, this project would never have manifested into reality without the help of my dear friend, Nancy Peske, whose amazing talents have changed the lives of so many people.

Library of Congress Cataloging-in-Publication Data

Harra, Carmen.
  The eleven eternal principles : accessing the divine within / Carmen Harra.
    p. cm.
  Includes index.
  1. Spirituality. I. Title.

  BL624.H325 2009
  204—dc22

2009024444

ISBN 978-1-58091-197-9

Printed in the United States

Cover and interior text design by Katy Brown

10 9 8 7 6 5 4 3 2 1

First Edition

CONTENTS

INTRODUCTION

I couldn't deny the facts the doctors had laid out for us. My husband's x-rays and CT scans showed he had stage IV lung cancer. A large tumor in his bronchial tube made it extremely difficult for him to breathe, and he was emaciated and barely able to eat. Virgil was paying the price for years of smoking cigarettes, a habit he'd begun as a teenager when his mother was suddenly killed by a truck while walking across the street. The brakes had failed, the driver felt terrible, and there was no one to blame for this senseless accident. Virgil was in such tremendous pain and shock that he turned to cigarettes to help him feel a little better, and began a habit he would struggle with for decades, never able to break it until now, when he was too weak even to raise his head off the pillow and could only speak in a whisper.

It was Thanksgiving of 2007 and the doctors all agreed that by Christmas, my beloved husband of twenty-five years would be gone. I had arrived here from Romania as a young woman, knowing no one in the United States. A few weeks after my plane landed, I'd not only fallen deeply in love with the man of my dreams but become engaged. Our marriage allowed me to emigrate from a country run by a cruel dictator, the notorious Nicolae Ceausescu, who prevented Romanians oppressed by his regime from escaping to freedom and who stifled the economy, creating widespread poverty and despair. Virgil made my dream of living in America come true, and together we had raised three beautiful daughters. The doctors must have assumed that I was in shock or denial when I told them firmly, "No, he's not going to die."

They didn't know what to say to that. I didn't try to explain why I knew my husband would defy all the odds and soon leave New York's St. Luke's-Roosevelt Hospital with a medical record that showed the unmistakable evidence of a miracle. I'm used to having people think I'm crazy because I communicate regularly with the realm of the Divine, which has its own rules. I've told women in their late forties who'd given up on having a baby, "You're pregnant right now." I've told people with very little money, "You're going to buy a house very soon," and even described the rooms and the back-yard. They've smiled at my delightful but "crazy" predictions, then come back to me and said, "You're not going to believe this, but. . . ." I always have to laugh when they say that. Of course, I believe it—I've seen miracles hap-pen again and again.

And I knew my husband and I were about to experience one.

I prayed from morning until night, asking God to spare my husband, if not forever, then at least for a while. You never know when God will sud-denly change the course of destiny. I prayed to solidify my faith and because I needed to feel the presence of God. I prayed for courage. We human beings are not in charge of what happens, and sometimes God reminds us of that in dramatic ways. If God had any other reasons for putting us through this horrendous suffering, I don't know, but I knew my job was to let go of resis-tance, let go of any beliefs that I could fix my husband, and let the Divine take over. The doctors weren't going to pull a miracle out of a hat. They were physicians, not magicians.

When Virgil's test results came back after Christmas, the doctors were astonished. The chemotherapy had worked beyond what they could have imagined. The tumor seemed to be gone. The blood tests showed no sign of the cancer. My husband had been brought back to life from the brink of death. All the assumptions about this particularly deadly form of cancer had been altered. All of the doctors were shocked.

But I wasn't. For karmic reasons that I trusted but didn't fully under-stand at the time, I knew that Virgil was not meant to die yet. And I would have my precious husband with me for nearly two more years. I knew what the future held because I was given a great gift as a small child. I nearly drowned in a river while at a picnic, and took a short trip to the land beyond our senses, where beauty, grace, and love were so powerful that I didn't want to come back. I returned to life sputtering and looking up into the frightened eyes of my father, who had revived me. But after that day, the doorway to the glorious realm of God never closed again for me. My intuitive abilities were awakened, and I could see into the future and the past and communicate with those who have passed. I knew I'd become a famous singer, travel the world, and get to America somehow.

As I grew up and this "crazy" dream of mine began to manifest, other people flocked to me to find out what lay ahead for them. They recognized my abilities and wanted to know their futures so that they could have some sense of control. They longed to hear that they would find love and happiness and enjoy good health, and that everyone they cared about would be okay.

That's not always what their future held, and I was careful about what I said when I knew they were headed for disappointment or loss. I always explained that we have free will and can exercise some control over our future, but that ultimately it is determined by God, who has His own plans. Sometimes those plans make sense to us years later, and in some cases we never understand why things happened as they did.

After I moved to America, I quickly developed a large base of clients, some of whom were very wealthy, famous, and influential. But I knew my purpose was to do more than tell them about what I foresaw in their future. I could see that they were wrestling with karmic, psychological issues that were causing them to suffer. I went back to school and eventually earned a PhD in psychology, as well as one in hypnosis. I also studied the ancient divination arts of numerology and astrology, and combined these with traditional therapy techniques and my intuitive abilities to help guide my clients.

As I continued to educate myself, reading about mystic traditions and great prophecies, I began to understand why people suffer so much. I learned about the divine laws, which are often in contradiction to our man-made laws. I could see that all the religious traditions were rooted in the greatest prophets' understanding of these Eternal Principles. Religious leaders who function at a lower level of consciousness often distort these laws, interpreting them incorrectly because of the limitations of their understanding of the Divine. Religious dogma often contradicts the divine laws. But the Eternal Principles have stood the test of time throughout every civilization.

I began to recognize that whenever I applied the divine laws to my own life, I experienced well-being, tranquility, joy, vitality, and even better health. I knew that my purpose on earth was to help people understand and work with these Eternal Principles so that they could free themselves from depression, addiction, anger, jealousy, and fear. I wanted to help them change their karma and break the patterns of thinking, feeling, and acting that were causing them great pain and hurting the people around them. And I learned that because of the Law of Totality, each person who raises his awareness and aligns his actions a little more closely with God's laws changes not only his life but also the lives of others. Eventually, enough people will awaken to a higher consciousness that the entire world will change dramatically, saving humanity from the suffering we are headed toward.

The Coming Upheaval

The Mayan and Hopi calendars, Nostradamus' predictions, and the prophecies encoded on the walls of the Great Pyramid of Egypt reveal that we are at an ending point in human history when great astrological changes will occur in the cosmos. Some believe this means that the human race is destined to sustain tremendous losses, and may even become extinct. I believe we are on the verge of a major shift in the human experience, but it doesn't have to be a destructive one. It is frightening to see the polar ice caps melting, the increase in terrorism around the globe, the humanitarian crises, and the collapse of our banking systems. There are days when it seems the whole world is falling apart and going mad. But we hold the key to changing our destiny. We can awaken to the signs that we have to change the way we live and evolve.

God not only wants us to survive, God wants us to return the earth to a state of paradise. To do that, we have to understand that we exist in two separate realities at once, the visible, physical world of the senses, and the invisible, metaphysical world of the Divine.

Divine Reality

Our minds are wonderful tools for understanding the world, but we use them in a very limited way. We've convinced ourselves that the world of our senses, where we suffer pain and illness and watch our bodies grow old, is the only reality, but it isn't. There's a larger reality that operates according to a very different set of rules; it is the realm of God.

To help us understand the two worlds, visible and invisible, man-made and divine, God gave us two sides of the brain. The left hemisphere is involved in most of our thinking and reasoning, while the right is the seat of intuition and the area where dreams are created. Our left brain understands the world of the senses, while our right brain allows us to perceive that there's more to reality than we can see, hear, feel, smell, or touch.

Each of the two worlds, man-made and divine, has its own set of rules. We've all woken up from a vivid dream and wondered how our minds could have created such a strange story. Dreams defy the rules of logic, which are laws of our ordinary reality. When we dream, we might be able to fly or be suddenly transported from a mountaintop to a city bus. In our dreams, someone who died long ago may be alive or we may find that we are small children again. Whatever happens in the dream world seems to make perfect sense until we awaken. The realm of dreams is a very different reality. We live according to its rules when we are there, and we return to the laws of the physical world in the morning when we open our eyes.

In our everyday lives, we follow many rules that make perfect sense to us and seem to provide us with order and security. When we encounter the laws of the divine reality, we can become confused because these Principles often contradict our man-made laws, perceptions, and recipes for success and happiness. How can we attract what we desire (which is the promise of the Eternal Principle of Attraction) without working hard to achieve it? How are we supposed to believe that our lives are filled with riches (which is true, according to the Eternal Principle of Abundance) when we struggle to pay our bills? How can we love our enemies (which we must do according to the Law of Love) and, instead of judging and punishing them, forgive them (which we must do, according to the Law of Karma and the Law of Love)?

The Eternal Principles, or divine laws, confuse us because we don't understand them. We were taught the rules of this world: Don't steal or you will be punished, hard work and perseverance always pay off in success and happiness, and so on. Because we are ignorant of the divine laws, we are blind to the realm of God. We feel lost, alienated, and disconnected from the Sacred. We fear death and suffering and want desperately to believe that if we do everything right, playing by the rules we've created, we'll be okay. Then a crisis comes along, and it's like an earthquake beneath our feet. We lose our sense of security.

To make the world a less frightening and unpredictable place, we've invented rules, religions, dogma, and laws to protect ourselves. These laws seem to work fairly well much of the time, but they create a world that is far inferior to the paradise we could be living in, if only we would operate in alignment with the sacred Eternal Principles. We have to stop thinking that we can do a better job of organizing reality and creating harmony and beauty than God can!

If we knew about the divine laws, and obeyed them, using them as the basis of our man-made laws, we could change our reality. We could end much of the terrible suffering in the world, and let go of the fear that our short, human existence is the only one we'll ever experience. We would see that we are all eternal souls taking human form for a brief time, and that our spiritual selves are our real selves. We'd understand that heaven, the world of God, is our true home.

We have to bridge the gap between the visible world and the invisible world in order to bring the light of divinity into our everyday reality. When Jesus said, "The kingdom of heaven is at hand," he didn't mean that we would die and go up to the clouds where angels play harps. He meant that we can begin to pull aside the veil between this world and the other world, and allow paradise to infuse our lives like sunshine streaming through a window.

The Eleven Eternal Principles of the Divine Realm

While there are many divine laws, this book will focus on the eleven that are most helpful for changing our lives and our world for the better. In numerology, eleven is a master number. Ten is the number of completion while one is the number of beginnings, so eleven represents the time of change, when something is dying and something else is being born. It's the number of rebirth and spiritual enlightenment, marking the connection between endings and beginnings.

At this point in history, the planets are moving into the eleventh house, and we are entering the Age of Aquarius, the era of great change. We can suffer and continue on our path toward global warming, large scale disasters, and widespread distrust and unrest as we go through a time of great upheaval—or we can use our free will to choose transformation. Although the problems in the world may seem overwhelming, each one of us who decides to work at aligning with Divinity plays a crucial role in helping all of humanity to live better lives and create a more loving world.

The eleven laws of the Divine, or Eternal Principles, are as follows:

1. The Law of Totality
2. The Law of Karma
3. The Law of Wisdom
4. The Law of Love
5. The Law of Harmony
6. The Law of Abundance
7. The Law of Attraction
8. The Law of Evolution
9. The Law of Manifestation
10. The Law of Dharma
11. The Law of Infinite Possibilities

The Principles are beautifully simple, yet they can frustrate us because we find them hard to apply to our lives. We're so completely immersed in our physical reality that it's difficult to believe we don't have to struggle, negotiate, accumulate wealth and security, fight to defend ourselves, suffer losses, work hard to regain lost ground, and eventually leave all that we've valued and acquired behind us when we die.

Many people pride themselves on being pragmatists who understand how the "real world" works, and they scoff at "foolish" dreamers. Pragmatists believe in man-made rules about how to create lasting happiness, not realizing that happiness cannot be a permanent state. They don't understand that they're dreamers too. By choosing to ignore a much better reality that we can experience anytime and align ourselves with, they're dreaming a nightmare.

Because we are convinced that our harsh "survival of the fittest" world is the only reality, we try to find rules we can live by that will make life flow more smoothly. If the old rules don't work, we end up having to discard, tinker with, or rewrite them. We continually alter the man-made rules to meet our new needs, or to be in alignment with our new perceptions. For years, our laws concerning the mentally ill were based on the idea that they were dangerous, incurable, and even possessed by the devil. As we came to a deeper understanding of mental illness, we changed our laws.

We also change our laws to solve new problems. Then we have to come up with a way of enforcing them and punishing the law breakers. We call this system "justice." But divine justice and divine law work very differently, as you will see.

All the Eternal Principles work for everyone, in every part of the world. They work no matter what the culture or what the era in history. They always have and they always will. Follow them and you will experience divine justice. You will get exactly what you deserve: tranquility, joy, health, abundance, and love. This is your birthright, and you can reclaim it by living according to the Eternal Principles.

The Split between the Realms

If divine laws work so well, why did we ever stop obeying them? The answer lies in the origin of humankind.

When we were first created, our souls lived according to the laws of the Divine. By choosing to create the human experience, a choice we made with God, we separated out from the Sacred Creator. The new, physical reality we experienced was so different from our experience as nonphysical beings that we developed a sort of amnesia about our true nature. We forgot that we helped to manifest the natural world, including our own bodies. We started to become aware of our mortality. We had a sense that after death, some part of who we were would survive, but death became a great mystery to us.

Archaeologists discovered in Iran the remains of a very early ancestor of modern man, called Neanderthal, which revealed our early awareness of death and the afterlife. The skeleton of a man about forty years old, whose arm had been cut off and whose eye sockets indicated that he had been blind, was found buried with several types of wildflowers covering him. These primitive, ancient people may have been unlike us in many ways, but they must have observed that flowers seem to die in the winter, but come back to life again in the spring. By retaining this disabled member of their clan who could no longer hunt or gather berries, the Neanderthals acted out of compassion and love. Instead of abandoning him, they embraced a reality beyond that of the survival of the fittest.

When we are facing death, we sense that the physical world is only one realm of existence. Unfortunately, most of the time we forget that truth and operate from the belief that we have to fight each other and try to create enough security to stave off our fear of death. We forget that physical death only destroys the body, not the soul, which is eternal and always a part of the Divine. As the British Victorian poet Lord Tennyson said, "That each, who seems a separate whole, should move his rounds, and fusing all the skirts of self again, should fall remerging in the general Soul." We are but performing some dutiful "rounds" while in the flesh, only to sink again into that eternal Soul after death.

Our focus on the survival of our physical body is hardwired into our brain. We are programmed to fear death and to snap ourselves into survival mode whenever our physical safety is threatened. But we forget to use that part of our brain capable of remembering our eternal nature. We forget that physical death is merely a passageway back into our existence as energy beings rather than as souls interwoven with a physical body.

The Origin of the Man-Made Realm

The story of Adam and Eve in the Bible is a metaphor that explains what happened when, as energy beings existing in perfect harmony with the Divine, we chose to create the visible world and consequently forgot about our eternal connection to the loving force that is God. It is a tale that reveals what happens whenever we create the illusion that we are disconnected from the Sacred.

Adam and Eve lived in harmony with all the creatures of the earth, and they never suffered from lack or want. They weren't afraid of death because in this paradise, there was no suffering and no death. Then Eve, and later, Adam, chose to disobey God's one admonition: to never eat the fruit from the tree of knowledge of good and evil. To do so would be to perceive separation and disharmony instead of unity and harmony. The moment they ate from the tree, Adam and Eve destroyed their ability to remain in paradise. They were forced to take up residence in the physical world, where they would toil, struggle, experience pain, and die. They stopped living according to divine law and began creating man-made laws.

However, we can go back to the Garden of Eden, so to speak, by understanding and obeying the Eternal Principles. The closer we come to that ideal place, the closer we come to transcending the limitations of our physical nature.

The Wisdom We Have Lost

By having rejected the Eternal Principles, we've lost the wisdom and knowledge that would make our world far more hospitable for all. Thousands of years ago, our lives were primitive by today's standards, but our wisdom was much greater than we can imagine. We were more in touch with our divine selves and able to communicate with God more easily. Because of this, we were able to defy the laws of physics and science. Today, we look at the Great Pyramid and the obelisks of Egypt and scratch our heads wondering how ancient man could possibly have constructed these amazing structures using only their primitive technologies. We are in awe of the ancients' ability to travel thousands of miles over treacherous lands and seas and trade ideas and objects with each other. Our ancestors were also able to travel easily between the visible and invisible realms, and had access to knowledge that remains unknown to us.

We know that our mental and emotional states affect the health of our bodies. Imagine being so filled with love, so free from negative emotions and worry, that the cells of our bodies would create even healthier new cells whenever they replicate. At every moment, you are growing new cells—the old liver, lung, skin, and bone cells are dying and being replaced by new ones. Why shouldn't your new cells be strong and healthy? Why shouldn't you be able to grow a new heart, new bones, and new, supple skin? Someday, all of us may be able to do this.

If we were to experience joy and peace as a result of living in alignment with the Eternal Principles, we wouldn't have to manifest illness and we could slow down the aging process. All the pollution and toxins that affect our bodies would not be manufactured and put into the air, water, and earth if we weren't focused on our own immediate needs but gave priority to the needs of all of humanity, now and in the future. If we lived according to Eternal Principles instead of out of a fear of suffering and death, we could live in harmony with the earth, nurturing it instead of mistreating it.

We are meant to be like trees, living for hundreds of years, interacting with each other and our surroundings in the web of life. We speak of the "tree of life" and chart our family trees. We build houses of wood, and intuitive people understand that wood is the only substance that carries human vibration. Walk into an old home with lots of woodwork and you might feel that others have lived there before because you're picking up on their vibration, which has affected the wood. An old superstition says that when you speak of illness, you should knock on wood; some think you should do this to ward off evil spirits, others say you do it in order to touch the positive spirits that live in wood. In the Bible, it is wood that saves us from destruction when Noah builds his ark. Jesus was a carpenter who worked with wood, and He died on a wooden cross, giving up his life so that we could be freed from suffering. And the Kabbalah says the body is the tree of life. Wood has always been an integral part of our human experience.

The part of ourselves that remembers our true nature whispers to us that we should connect with trees and wood in order to be reminded that our nature is similar to that of the trees. We're meant to touch the earth and the sky, to remain in our physical existence while stretching toward the heavens and Divinity.

As long as so many of us live according to man-made laws, ignorant of how the divine realm works, humanity will suffer. We're all interconnected, so that what one individual does affects not just him and the people closest to him, but the whole of humankind. It doesn't always feel this way, but that's because we are so caught up in the world of our senses. If we look closely, we can see evidence of just how much one person can affect the whole, or how much a small group of dedicated, loving people can change all of society. We can address the problems in the environment or in our community, or create art that moves people's hearts, but we also affect the whole on a purely energy level. We change the vibration in our corner of the energy matrix (or grid) whenever we align ourselves more closely with Eternal Principles, as you will come to see.

You can begin transforming your life and the world today by understanding and applying the Eternal Principles to your life, but first you must come to understand your spiritual nature as a being of light. Only then can you truly grasp God's laws and begin using them to lift yourself out of fear and suffering, up into a higher state of being.

UNDERSTANDING YOUR
SPIRITUAL NATURE

Like everyone and everything, you are made of light. We are not just physical beings living in a physical reality, but light-energy beings living in a realm of energy.

Your physical body is made up of four elements: hydrogen, oxygen, nitrogen, and carbon. The atoms of hydrogen, nitrogen, oxygen, and carbon are made up of the very smallest bits of matter, called particles. These particles are constantly moving around: What appears to be solid or liquid is just a lot of space and a very few particles vibrating within that space. In fact, if you pushed all the particles in your body together so that there was no space between them, the amount of matter left over would be a microscopic pile!

While these tiny particles are matter, they often behave like waves, or units of light, so even that microscopic pile of "stuff" is actually a cluster of light. We see ourselves as solid beings, but to understand the Eternal Principles and how they affect us, we have to remember that in essence, we are light beings.

At a physical level, you have a body that is separate from other people and your environment: this book, your chair, the ground you walk on, and so on. But at an energy level, you have a light-energy "body" that is woven into the grid of energy that makes up the universe. You are part of God and God's creation in the same way that you are part of life on earth. Gaze at a picture of a large crowd taken from a distance, and it looks like one mass made up of many dots of color. Your mind knows that each dot is a separate person, but looking from this perspective, you see one, not many. You see unity, not separateness. Similarly, while a prism will split light into rays of many colors, all the separate rays of light come together in that prism. Your light body is intimately connected with all other light bodies, and all energy, at all times. The nature of our light bodies' relationship to the energy of the universe is summed up by the Law of Totality, one of the Eternal Principles you will learn about in this book, and one of the divine laws that we need to understand and respect.

If you are very sensitive to energy (that is, you are intuitive), you can perceive the light energy of other beings. Have you ever felt that you are not alone in a building, even though you don't hear or see anyone? Or, have you ever looked up because you sensed someone was standing in the doorway looking at you? You knew someone was there because your senses picked up on subtle signals, but also because you sensed a change in energy, or vibration. It's unfortunate that in America, we are skeptical about intuition because we can't control or replicate it in a laboratory. Science teaches us to value logic and reason. So, if we have a "funny feeling," we'll often push it aside or laugh it off as just a quirky experience, but intuition is very real.

Doctors can measure the energy of a person in many ways: CAT scans, MRIs, EEGs, EKGs, and so on. You might not be able to tell that someone is lying, but a lie detector will pick up on subtle changes in breathing and heart rate that occur when that person isn't telling the truth. The heart's magnetic energy extends outside of the human body. Blood, too, has energy; my blood is likely to have a different vibrational speed, or frequency, than does your blood. When my mother received a blood transfusion, her mood and attitude shifted dramatically afterward. I'm certain this happened because she received blood that had a higher vibratory rate than her own did. (In fact, Jehovah's Witnesses do not allow blood transfusions because they consider blood to be sacred and not to be shared with other people.) Psychologist Paul Pearsall, in his book *The Heart's Code*, wrote of patients who received organ transplants and acquired the personal characteristics and memories of the organ donors. Patients reported strange dreams that, it turned out, were actually memories of how their organ donors had died. Our memories and energy are embedded in the tissues of our hearts, lungs, kidneys, eyes, and other organs. Someday, scientists may develop technology sensitive enough to allow everyone to perceive other people's magnetic fields and auras.

People, thoughts, and feelings are all made up of energy, vibrating at various rates. The higher a person or object's vibration, the more that person or object is in tune with the Divine. As light-energy beings, we are capable of raising our rates of vibration at any time. If we create a feeling of joy, perform an act of compassion, and live in accordance with the Eternal Principles, our vibrations will increase. If we give in to fear, anger, hatred, and jealousy, our vibrations will decrease. Our light-energy bodies will dim, becoming darker, denser, and heavier. We will become vulnerable to dark, negative energies that will connect with us and cause us to think selfish, destructive, and even evil thoughts.

From a psychological view, sociopaths lack empathy and suffer from disturbances in the brain. Energetically, they are light beings vibrating at such a low rate they are completely unaware of their divine nature and their connection with God. Their negativity manifests as anger, violence, manipulation, and narcissism. To a lesser extent, you may have felt your own vibration lowered when you spoke in a sarcastic tone, judged others harshly, cheated "just a little," or gossiped. When we dismiss that small voice that says, "I shouldn't do this," we act in contrast to God's will, and lower our vibration.

Each of us can experience the Divine in every single moment and choose to raise our individual, and collective, vibration, making ourselves lighter and more luminous as the dark, heavy, polluting energy falls away. When we do, we become more aware of our divinity, our connection to God. The more we feel connected with the Divine, the more we are able to access divine wisdom, love, and compassion and feel energized, enriched, and vitalized. Doing good makes us feel light, buoyant, and united in love with all of humanity. The higher our vibration, the more we feel drawn to create even more joy and love.

If you apply the laws of the Divine to your life, you will live in a sacred and holy way and feel yourself lifted up as your vibration rate increases. Even when tragedy occurs, you will feel the presence of God comforting you because you will have awakened to your divine connection to the Sacred.

In that moment when we do good, we experience God and vibrate at a very high rate, but we may not realize the importance of what we are feeling. We may think, "That felt good, but now I have to get back to my To Do list." Our days are filled with chores designed to bring us security in the physical world: shopping for groceries, making phone calls, going to doctors' appointments, and so on. We rarely devote our time to the most important activities, such as loving fully and forgiving those who have harmed us. Too often we tell ourselves we are just too busy to do what matters most to us, but what we are really doing is making our fears of suffering and death a priority over what is most important. If you were to die, today, you wouldn't say to yourself as you left this earth, "Oh, but I didn't finish putting my bills on a spreadsheet!" We concern ourselves with the most insignificant and unimportant things and take for granted that we'll have plenty of time to do that which we say matters most to us.

When we recognize our eternal, divine nature and our relationship to Divinity, our thoughts, feelings, and actions easily fall into alignment with what is divine and eternal instead of being aligned with the fear of death, loss, and suffering.

Our Relationship to the Invisible World

Science, math, logic, and traditional physics have helped us create technologies that have increased human longevity and improved our lives. Medicine, sanitation, aqueducts, electricity, and similar inventions have turned out to be invaluable for our survival and quality of life. And ever since we began to understand quantum physics, we have also come to realize that what we think we know about how the universe works is nothing compared with what we *don't* know. Our understanding of light versus matter and the nature of objects can no longer be explained according to the rules of everyday reality. The universe seems to be obeying a set of laws we cannot begin to understand. What we are seeing evidence of is the workings of the divine realm, something our human minds are not yet able to comprehend, although we may be able to someday.

The Eleven Eternal Principles

We are limited in our perceptions by our current stage of evolution. We find it hard to imagine or believe in anything we have not experienced. When we get a glimpse of the way God's realm works—for instance, when we discover dark matter in space, or learn that a wave of light sometimes acts like a tiny particle of matter, and vice versa—we have no idea of what to make of it. However, these discoveries open us to the possibility that there is another reality we interact with, an invisible world operating independently from our own.

People who have had near-death experiences are often forever changed because they have experienced this other, invisible world. They not only have faith in an afterlife, they have an experience of life after the physical body has ceased to function. They do not need to be convinced that they are eternal beings. By recognizing their eternal nature, they are able to let go of the fear of death and suffering. They know without a doubt that all pain is temporary and death is merely a passageway into a new existence.

I learned this lesson when I was five years old and wandered away from a family picnic to explore the nearby river. I fell into the water and was swept under the surface by a strong current. I remember everything going dark and quiet, and suddenly, I was in a beautiful, lush valley, surrounded by loving, gentle beings. I was so happy there I wanted to stay, but was told I had to leave. Instantly I felt myself thrust back into my body, and I began coughing up water. That day, I discovered my eternal nature. I also opened doors in my mind, waking up dormant sections of my brain, and ever after I have had intuitive abilities that cannot be explained by scientists.

If you have never experienced the other world, you might find it hard to imagine a reality that you can't see, feel, hear, taste, or smell. Yet, you probably have no difficulty believing in the existence of another reality called the Internet. The World Wide Web cannot be located in time and space. You can interact with it, but you cannot see it or touch it. You can only see evidence of it when you look at your computer screen. How would you describe the Internet and its nature to someone who had never seen a computer? You might say, "It's a place, like an information super highway that you can't drive on, but it exists. And you can connect to it very easily, at any time, with the proper equipment. You can communicate to people all around the world instantaneously." Try to imagine how strange that description would sound to someone who has never seen a computer, and yet, it's accurate. The invisible world can be described in a similar way.

If you have experienced or sensed the realm of the Divine, beyond time and space, and beyond mortality, you might have pushed that memory out of your mind. Maybe when you talked about this other reality to others, you were told that that you were crazy or that your imagination was running wild or you experienced a trick of the mind. Unfortunately, most of us have been taught to quickly dismiss anything we don't understand.

Many children still retain their ability to communicate with this other reality that they were a part of so recently, before they were born into human form. My goddaughter, Elizabeth, was born two months after my grandmother Anna died. When Elizabeth was two, she saw a picture of my late grandmother, pointed to it, and said, "Anna," then she pointed to herself and said, "Me." She did this several times—"Anna, me. Anna, me." She is now eight years old and has a personality just like my grandmother's. A woman I know used to insist as a little girl that there was a man who lived in her house. She claimed this man would watch her and smile at her as she played in the afternoons while her siblings were at school. Her mother told her to stop making up stories, but many years later, when the girl had grown up and moved away, she got a call from her mother, who said, "Remember that imaginary friend you had as a little girl? What did he look like? Because I've seen him hanging around the house and he's angry, and pointing to the driveway." The city was ripping up the end of the driveway to do work underground. When her mother described the man—grey hair, high-waisted pants, and a red plaid shirt—the daughter said, "That's him. That's exactly what he looks like." The two of them did some investigating and learned that this spirit was that of a man who had died in the driveway of their home many years before. They realized that he was upset by the changes being made to his space. He stopped appearing after the mother told him he needed to go away because he didn't belong there. (If yourself ever see a lost soul such as this, recognize that he's confused about being dead and tell him to go toward the light. This will help him to leave the physical world and reach his eternal destination.)

Accessing the Divine Realm

You don't have to have psychic abilities to be open to communication from the invisible world. God is there, ready to listen to you at all times. The Latin verb *vocare*, meaning to call or summon, became the English cognate "invocate." And indeed you can summon God with the invocation: "God, I need help." But to hear the answer, to feel the presence of the Sacred, you have to banish the millions of tiny distractions cluttering up your mind. If you are frantically trying to figure out how to solve your problems, you won't be able to hear God's response. You must become quiet and still. If any thoughts arise, imagine they are only words projected on to a screen and watch them fade away. You have to stop creating thoughts about your thoughts and getting caught up in the distraction of all the thoughts and feelings your mind wants to create.

Pay attention to your breathing as you let your thoughts become mere background noise. "Breath" is an etymologically fascinating word, believed to have been introduced into human speech around 1,000 B.C.E. as the Indo-European word *speis*, a word that mimics the sound of blowing or breathing out. From there it developed into the Latin *spirare*, meaning "to breathe." But *inspirare* in Latin means literally "to blow into," such as the action of breath transferring sacred wisdom into a physical being. This is how the Bible describes God as having created man: "The Lord God formed man of the dust of the ground, and breathed into his nostrils the breath of life; and man became a living soul." (Genesis, 2:7). Interestingly enough, *spes* (very close to the Indo-European *speis*) is the Latin noun for "hope," or "faith." The root words of "faith" and "breath" are thus very much alike. Similarly, the acts of breathing and finding faith complement one another: we inhale divine inspiration and gain calming faith with each long, meditative breath.

When you want to feel your connection to God, let God blow hope into your soul. Feel yourself inhale, welcoming in the oxygen that nourishes every cell within your body. Feel yourself exhaling all the toxins, anxieties, and fears that have been accumulating in your light body like sediments in water. Imagine breathing all of that dark energy out of you, and filling yourself with the light of the Divine as you breathe in again. Don't pay attention to the time and start thinking, "Okay, okay, already, I'm quiet, I want my answer!" That's like hanging up the phone on God! Be patient and keep the lines of communication open as you focus wordlessly on your breathing. You will feel the agitation inside of you settling down. Tranquility will replace your worries, and you will feel lighter, because you will have raised your vibration and opened yourself to allowing God's light to rush in and fill you with joy, creativity, and wisdom. As the great German theologian and philosopher Meister Eckhart said, "The spirit of God, like a divine wind, a breath of living fire, blows through living beings, through the world and the cosmos, from eternity to eternity. . . . The divine wind blows through the inmost essence of all beings." In fact, the very name for the Almighty may be associated with respiration: In the Hebrew testament, God is referred to as Jahweh. This name is said to have derived from the ancient Hebrew verb *hawah*, which means both "to be" and also "to breathe." Some have even said that the tetragrammaton JHWH (just Jahweh without vowels, the original four-letter Hebrew word) parallels the sound of a full inhale-exhale breath; think of a baby's first startled breath, or the heavy breath one draws after surfacing from underwater.

While you're performing this placid exercise of breathing with awareness, remember that God may not answer right away. It may be that you are meant to learn something else before you have clarity, but it's important to be open to what the Divine has to tell you. And sometimes, just feeling the peacefulness that comes from reconnecting with God is enough to make it easier to move forward and deal with all the challenges in your life, even if you're not always sure you're making the right decisions. If you connect with God regularly, you will return to this harmonious state more quickly each time you begin focusing on your breathing, and you will discover that you don't become upset as quickly as you used to. Answers to your questions will start flowing into you, sometimes quite unexpectedly, and you will feel stronger and more courageous.

God Speaks to Us through Our Physical Bodies

Our bodies are designed in such a way as to remind us of our connection to the cosmos and to each other. God doesn't want us to forget our true nature. Our ten fingers and ten toes reflect the fact that we experience cycles of ten years throughout our lives. Babies complete their first cycle, from conception to birth, and enter their tenth month as complete human beings. Our ten digits also remind us of the ten planets, including Eris, because we are supposed to recognize that we are made of the same material as the cosmos, and that we are a part of it. The lines in our palms reflect our karma and destiny, which our soul knows about but which is hidden from our conscious mind. Our hands were designed to be conduits of God's energy. The hands have an enormous number of nerve endings, so they're exquisitely sensitive to touch and temperature, as well as to energy. We can receive and distribute energy through our hands, using "healing hands" to cure illness and heal injury. In meditation and prayer, the hands are used to draw in and send out energy, whether the palms are held upward toward heaven or pressed together in order to create a circle of completion, sending vital energy back into the body. When someone is suffering, simply holding her hand or touching her hand can be enormously comforting, because you are actually sending positive energy from your light-body into her own.

The human body is 80 percent water, which is a conduit of energy. If you constantly generate negative energy in the form of angry or envious thoughts or feelings, you will pollute your body, sending toxic energy to the tips of your fingers and the tips of your toes. Eventually, those toxins may create disease, weakening your body's ability to fight poisons from the environment. When the body is threatened by an infection, it generates mucus and white blood cells, and uses its fluids to try to flush out the infection. When tissue is inflamed, plasma loaded with white blood cells rushes to the site where the pathogen is located in the hope of preventing it from further harming the body. Life-giving, healing water can restore health, but when it is tainted by negative energy, it can't do its job properly. This is why it's extremely important to rid yourself of dark, heavy thoughts and feelings.

As a light-energy being freed of the physical body after death, you won't experience dark emotions like anger, fear, or sorrow. Those feelings are created in the human brain and are experienced as physical phenomena (neuroscientist Candace Pert, Ph.D., has shown that emotions are actually neuropeptides in the body, that is, they take a biochemical form). When you feel angry or sad, the fluid in your body moves in response to this emotion, and you cry in order to wash out the dark feelings. Fear causes your sweat glands to activate and your heart to beat faster so that your blood flows through your veins and arteries more quickly, moving toxic energy through all the areas of your body. Hundreds of years ago, physicians thought that to cure illness, you should cut into a patient and drain some of his blood. They understood that the blood carried poisons, but they didn't understand that blood and other bodily fluids could be cleansed instead of removed.

Each part of the body is connected to the other parts, physically and energetically, just as each individual human soul is woven into the fabric of the Divine. A friend of mine had minor foot surgery and thought she could go back to work the next day without any problems as long as she took some mild painkillers, but was surprised by how difficult it was for her to concentrate. She told me, "I don't understand why I'm so tired. It's just my foot that's injured, not the rest of me." In the West, we think of our bodies as machines made up of separate parts that can be individually fixed or replaced, and that the rest of our self can operate just fine even if one part of the machine is in need of repair. Every cell in the body knows when the foot is suffering, just as the Divine feels the suffering of every soul, because we are all connected together in the body of God.

Once we understand our spiritual nature, we can begin to understand how the reality of souls and divinity operates. It has its own order and its own laws, which can be difficult to grasp in the face of so much pressure to believe that our man-made laws are logical and practical. Comprehending how much wiser and better the divine laws are, we can begin changing our lives for the better.

THE FIRST
ETERNAL PRINCIPLE:

The Law of Totality

All people and all creatures are
one, united with the Divine.

Our light-energy bodies, or souls, are united with all other creatures, the trees, the stones, the ponds, and the mountains in the energy grid called Divinity. Because we are connected, we are all continually influencing each other and the world around us. Every action we take affects others as well as ourselves. The idea that we can go about our business living however we like, without creating consequences for ourselves and others, comes from the false perception that we are separate beings. It's true that at the physical level, you and I can't occupy the same space and we have different bodies. But in the Divine realm, which is not limited by our rules of time and space, individuality is an illusion.

As humans, we have a collective mind. Our unconscious is aware of this, but unfortunately, living in the physical world distracts us from this inner knowledge. Your ego, which is your mind's awareness of yourself as an individual, refuses to recognize what your subconscious knows. Even if you do see signs of your connection and influence on others, your ego will dismiss them as unimportant. Our separateness seems so real that most of us mistakenly believe it's the only reality instead of just the reality that the ego perceives.

All of us go through basically the same experiences in life: the passages of birth, adolescence, marriage or partnership, parenting, getting older, and death. We all feel sorrow when someone we care about is hurt and become angry when we see an injustice. We have similar thoughts, too. Yet we tend to focus on our differences instead of our similarities. We create divisions between people in order to serve the needs of our ego, which wants to see itself as unique, special, and extra important. The ego is afraid of what will happen if we identify with the whole of creation instead of as an individual. It's the aspect of our awareness that's rooted in the more primitive part of our brain, the limbic brain, which evolved to ensure that above all else, we survive as physical beings. The more evolved part of our brain, the neocortex, recognizes that our individual existence on this planet is neither who we truly are nor is it as important as our small but crucial part of all creation.

When we meet someone who doesn't look or act like we do, the ego can take charge and we quickly give in to the primitive emotion of fear.

This fear may be mild (for example, feeling shy when entering a room full of strangers) or intense, causing the heart to beat rapidly and breathing to become shallow. We are actually programmed to instantly sum up and categorize people and situations so that we can act promptly in case of danger. However, if we don't use our more evolved brain and use our higher awareness to judge a situation, we can become immediately suspicious of anyone who seems a little different, causing us to become further isolated and out of alignment with the Law of Totality. It's true that there will be actual threats to your personal safety in the physical world. Difficult and dangerous situations serve as a mirror, reflecting back to you all the issues your soul needs to work on; this is the Law of Karma. But the real danger is not death or harm to your individual self. The real danger is in never resolving your karmic issues, so that you are always subconsciously creating suffering for yourself, in lifetime after lifetime.

We often fear something terrible and unexpected happening, but there are no accidents, good or bad. All is a part of God's plan. A car crash, a flood, and an unexpected health crisis are the physical manifestations of thoughts and emotions that must be processed so that we can learn the lessons they have to teach us.

In the West, we give ourselves too much credit for influencing the physical world. No one person is responsible for all that happens to him. No one is that powerful! The ego likes to think it's in charge, but because of the Law of Totality, we are all influencing each other, all the time: Somewhere in Singapore, someone's actions are influencing you. What you did yesterday is affecting somebody, somewhere. Our connections to each other are much closer than we thought.

In quantum physics, there is a theory called the butterfly effect, which states that the fluttering of a butterfly's wings alters reality in a tangible way, perhaps even causing a storm on the other side of the world. The interconnectedness of everything in the world of the senses is not just an abstract concept. It is actually part of science.

The global banking crisis began to awaken many people to this truth on a physical level. Who knew that a house in Cleveland was owned by people in Singapore, Germany, or Orlando, Florida? Yet that is what happened, when the derivative financial products that were created were bundled, sold, rebundled, and sold again, spreading risk and obscuring who owns what. When the banks in Iceland failed, police officers in England suddenly had their operating funds slashed because their pension money was invested in Icelandic banks. People were shocked to learn that we were all so interconnected financially.

The Law of Totality weaves our lives into others' in ways we often can't understand or even perceive. We are not only connected to other people and creatures, such as animals, but also intertwined with the Divine, whose plans affect all of us. Our collective mind, in conjunction with God, manifests our world. Imagine a sphere made of light that is your soul. That sphere shines outwardly and overlaps with other spheres of light. Where two spheres come together, you are both influencing the physical world with your energetic interaction. God is the sphere of light that encompasses all light.

When a light-energy body vibrates at a high rate of speed, its light is very bright. When it vibrates more sluggishly, its light is dulled. Those whose souls vibrate very quickly affect the world around them by creating positive, generous feelings and thoughts that manifest positive situations. When they face a challenge, these positive people recognize it as a lesson— as an opportunity to learn something, develop a new skill, or deepen their understanding of the world. They are able to find good in every situation because they live in alignment with the Law of Totality and recognize their responsibility to heal their small corner of the energy grid.

Then there are people who always seem to be in self-destructive mode. People who struggle with addictions constantly spar with others over one drama or another. They feel taken advantage of or victimized. Unaware they are unified with the rest of creation, they feel disconnected from other people, from God, and from their own souls. Drugs, alcohol, and obsessive thoughts, as well as dark feelings such as jealousy, anger, and resentment, or sadness and hopelessness, cloud their minds. Every challenge is evidence that the world is a harsh place. They believe they have to depend on themselves to survive because no one else can be trusted.

When someone is vibrating at a low level, their darkness affects everyone around them. You can actually feel their heavy energy draining you of your sense of vitality because they're so needy and unhappy, or angry and pessimistic. It's as if they are standing in a dark room longing for any sort of illumination, even if it's just a tiny candle flame. When someone is so engulfed by darkness, he can't even see the light switch on the wall next to him. There's never a power shortage when it comes to Divine energy, but if someone can't see that light switch and has never used it and has no idea that it's there for him, he remains stuck in that dark, lonely room.

When you recognize the Law of Totality and its enormous power, your thoughts, feelings, and behaviors will change, and you can let go of man-made fears and loneliness.

The Energy of Our Environment

Hints that this Divine light switch exists can be found within our bodies and the environment. God gives us many clues that we can call on Divinity at any time!

Vibrational energy is something we can sense if we are open to it. If you feel uncomfortable in someone's presence and don't know why, it's probably because they're vibrating at a low rate. You might feel repulsed or drawn to a person or a home because you're picking up on its energy. If a situation feels right to you, if someone seems to radiate trustworthiness, pay attention. Intuition is never wrong, although intuition works best if your subconscious isn't clouded with a lot of unresolved karma. Your subconscious desire to attract problems will allow you to work through your issues but can crowd out your intuition.

It's important to take seriously any unexplainable emotions, thoughts, or sensations in yourself and in others. It's possible your intuition is picking up on physical clues, which are registering in your subconscious mind but not your conscious mind. Sometimes, intuition is an energetic awareness that something is going to happen, or that something is happening far away from you. For example, you might find that you're expecting the phone to ring just before it does, and before you look at the Caller ID you know who is calling. One of my clients recently tossed and turned all night, seemingly for no reason, and learned the next morning that her sister, several states away, had died during the night.

In America, people are often very dismissive of the way human energy interacts with the energy of other people. They mistakenly believe that negative energy won't affect them and that they don't need to replenish themselves by connecting with positive energy. They'll watch violent movies and television shows, laugh at comedians who have a mean-spirited sense of humor, or listen to music that reflects the hatred and prejudice in the world. We shouldn't deny the existence of darkness and brutality, but we need to protect ourselves from these types of energy. It's too easy to be influenced by them. Listening to uplifting music or watching inspiring movies raises our vibration. For instance, the symphonies created by Bach or Verdi stand the test of time because anyone listening to them can feel the incredible positive energy they generate. The high vibration of art and music influences our own vibration, because we are connected to that energy in the realm of divinity. The Victorians knew this and created beautiful public parks, such as New York's Central Park, so that even the poor could feel uplifted by being in a lush, green, natural, and visually delightful space.

To understand how our energy influences others and vice versa, it can be helpful to think of all of creation as a vast, endless expanse like an ocean. When the sunlight shines on the water, it infuses it with light energy and heats it up. The ocean's surface is warm and sparkling, but a few feet down the water is dark and cold because the sun hasn't penetrated that far. In fact, when you swim in a lake you might notice that suddenly, you've come across a cold spot. This is how light energy works: there are some places where it's darker (colder) and some places where it's lighter (warmer), but they're all a part of the same large body of light. If you stay in a cold, dark spot, your body's warmth will seep out into the water and eventually you will become cold unless you keep moving to generate heat. If you are around depressive, angry people, you will have to keep generating positive feelings, thoughts, and energy to stop yourself from sinking into darkness along with them. You are influenced by others' energy just as they're influenced by yours.

We're also influenced by the energy of a place, which is influenced by what happened there in the past or the natural energy of the land or the buildings. There are sacred spots in the world, such as Sedona, Lourdes, and the Himalayas, which carry a great deal of healing energy. There are also areas where so much hatred and violence have occurred, the energy is very dark, making it difficult for the people in those areas to remain in the positive energy state they generate.

If you pay attention, you will be able to pick up on energy that connects you to other people and the past. A few years ago, there was a fire in the apartment building where one of my clients lived. When we talked about it afterward, she told me she'd always felt there was a negative energy in the building. People seemed to engage in a lot of squabbles and disagreements. The building was said to have been haunted, and my client swore she sometimes saw the figure of a young man out of the corner of her eye but when she looked in his direction, he was gone. We later learned that the building on 9th Avenue and 60th Street had been erected on the site of a graveyard. The troubled souls whose bodies had been buried in that spot were still wandering around the space where the building was situated. Their dark, heavy energy had been affecting the residents and I believe was responsible for the fire (the physical cause of it was never discovered).

Our Collective Mind

Although we may think we have no connection to strangers who died long before we were born, or to people around the world that we've never met, we actually have much in common with them and are intertwined with them energetically. Humans share a collective mind filled with memories and wisdom about the human experience. When we are able to tap into this collective mind, we can be stunned by what we find there. It makes no sense in the man-made world. How can I recall memories of living in Egypt thousands of years ago? I can remember what I looked like and what my home was like; I can tour it in my mind's eye.

Sometimes, people experience synchronicities that defy logic. A friend of mine was at a political gathering about an hour from her home in the Midwest, and when she started chatting with the person standing next to her, she realized that the woman had been born in the very same New York City hospital as her own husband. My friend turned to her husband to tell him about this strange coincidence, and he said, "And I just learned this man standing next to me lives two houses away from us!" If you talk to people who seem to be strangers, you might be shocked by what you find you have in common. It's no accident that we run into people we know in unusual places, or that we have an odd, coincidental connection to a stranger. We are meant to interact with these people and be reminded of the Law of Totality.

We also share memories and experiences with other people across time and continents. When we dream at night, our mind will often use symbols that would be recognized all over the world, in different cultures, past and present. Across cultures, a body of water often symbolizes emotions, for example, while a flower often symbolizes beauty and fertility. However, if you dream about the lake where your family went swimming each summer, or you dream about the yellow tulips you saw in a planter when you were coming out of the doctor's office last week, you have to consider how those experiences might influence the meaning of those dream symbols.

We are very much alike, and yet in our daily lives, we focus on our differences and make them out to be very important. They become a powerful part of our perception of who we are.

Our soul will deliberately choose to be born into a challenging situation in order to help us heal our issues, but also to remind us that we are all one, that there is no black or white or Hispanic, no gay or bisexual or heterosexual. There are no conservatives or liberals. These are differences we create when we are under the illusion that the physical world is all there is. We categorize and separate people into groups instead of connecting with each other's humanity.

Healing the Broken World and Achieving Wholeness

In Kabbalah and in Judaism, it's said that at the beginning of time, the world shattered into many pieces, and our job on earth is to do the work of *tikkun olam*—the healing of the broken world. We do our part to bring together what seems to be shattered and separate, whether it's our soul, or another's soul, and unite all the parts. With love, we knit together connections in the physical world, reaching out to those who are suffering, and healing our own pain by bravely facing our issues and working through them.

The word "holiness" is the Greek root *holos*, which is also the root of the word "whole." Holiness *is* wholeness. Love connects us all and is sacred and holy. It purifies us and makes us aware that we are always embraced by the Divine, always able to tap into God's holy, healing power.

Our health—physical, intellectual, moral, emotional, and spiritual— matters to ourselves, to each other, and to God because we are all connected. When one person is suffering, everyone suffers. In our world, people are starving to death, dying of AIDS, or in chronic pain, and yet many say, "That's not my responsibility." They're completely wrong. We are all each other's responsibility.

I'm not saying you personally are responsible for alleviating all the suffering in the world. No one person can take on that enormous burden. However, each of us can do something to achieve *tikkun olam*. We can't allow ourselves to feel alienated, to push the button on the remote and change the channel when we see an image of someone in pain, and to avoid feeling compassion and a desire to do something to make the world a better place. I know it can be overwhelming to look at all the problems in the world, but that feeling of depression and powerlessness lifts when we start doing our part, however small, to address them.

Everyone can serve in a different way, and what you do for others may never make the headlines or bring you attention. My father wasn't a famous or powerful man, and for a long time, we lived in poverty in Romania, but if he had money in his pocket when he was approached by someone in need, he would always offer them what he could. He knew that a coin or two wouldn't make a huge difference in their lives and might only buy a loaf of bread that would last their family for a day, but for that family on that day, it was a wonderful gift. If you are caught up in thinking, "Someday, when I'm not so busy, when I have more to give, I'll help the world out by doing something grand and important," you are not participating in the healing of the world. You are putting off this holy responsibility in order to serve your ego, which is afraid that tomorrow, you won't have any pennies in your pocket if you give a few away right now.

God doesn't expect you, personally, to discover the cure for autism or end all hunger on the planet. You just have to be open to opportunities for helping, and use them. They show up all the time, and you will recognize them when you remain aware of our unity with all that is Divine.

The Circle: The Symbol of Totality

The Law of Totality is represented by a circle, which has no beginning and no end. This symbol shows us that every ending is a beginning and every beginning is an ending. The ancient Mayans thought of time as a circle because they saw what we could not: that the events of the past show up again in our lives. The wheel of fortune turns and the past becomes the present again. The issue you didn't resolve—your feelings of inadequacy as a child, for example—comes up again, and you find yourself dealing with those same feelings in your marriage or in your relationship with your boss. What appears to be a separate and distinct event is connected to other events in your life and in the life of others.

The connections you have to the past and to other living beings are a series of circles. There is no way out of the cycle of repetition except one: through the middle. Otherwise, you will keep going around and around the rim. To find peace you must go deep into the center, into the eye of the hurricane. There you can access all the subconscious wisdom you have, and even the divine wisdom that is held in the collective mind. Then you can finally say, "Now I understand why I'm putting up with my boss's verbal abuse. It's that old feeling I have that I'm not worthy of respect. I want to get rid of that destructive belief once and for all!" What you discover in the center of the circle may be very painful—often you will become aware of a situation where you have been playing the role of a victim. Whatever the truth is, it is crucial that you find it and deal with it rather than circling around it, avoiding it all your life, and getting caught up in the wild winds of your own personal hurricane.

Three-dimensionally, a circle becomes a sphere; begin walking at any point on earth and eventually you will come back to where you started. Though the largest bodies in our solar system are spheres, the gravity of each planet or moon affects those nearby, bending their orbits into an elliptical shape. This is another reminder of the nature of the universe. We are not floating alone in the cosmos. We cannot help but affect one another, pushing and pulling each other just as the moon tugs at the ocean creating tides and the planets influence each other's movements.

When you interact with someone else's sphere or circle of energy, it influences you. Every time you talk to or meet with someone else, it's an opportunity for healing. It may not provide you with a chance to make a monumental difference in your life or theirs, but you never know. The little uplifting comment you make to someone may give her the little push she needs to do some of her own healing. The irritation you feel when someone annoys you is an opening to discover what makes you so quick to anger and what it is that you need to heal inside yourself. Be awake and ready for the possibilities that show up in your life.

We are all united in a circle of life. This circle requires many creatures, each playing a role in the elaborate dance we all perform. We're meant to work together, in unity, to bring about holiness and wholeness. On our own, we can't reproduce; we need another person in order to make a baby.

In fact, the circles and spheres in our body are reminders of the Law of Totality and our connection to other people, to creation, and to God the Creator. When pregnant, a woman's body becomes round, and the baby's head comes out a round vaginal opening. Our head is basically round, as is our brain, which has two halves that need to work together, in unity, to perform the most sophisticated tasks, such as using language or conceiving of God.

Ancient religious rituals were performed in a circle, a form that reminds us of totality, the cycle of life, and our connectedness. Later, rituals were performed beside an altar at the front of the church or temple, and the people were placed in the audience so that the priest (or rabbi) could address them as an authority figure lecturing the masses (sometimes, the priest even performs the entire ritual with his back to the people). This way of standing in relation to the congregation can make people feel alienated instead of united with each other and with God.

I've always found it interesting that around the time that the Catholic Church in Europe was amassing power at the expense of the people, and working with kings to buttress each others' power, the belief that the earth revolves in a circle around the sun changed. Many ancient people, from the Greeks to Indians, to the Europeans, Mayans, and Babylonians, had observed the sky and correctly noted that the earth is on the rim and the sun is in the center of a circle. But during the Middle Ages, the Church insisted it was the sun, the power of light, that revolved around the earth, or the physical world. Symbolically, this represented a shift in belief that power lay with man. While the Church ostensibly was devoted to God, in reality it became devoted to the power of popes and kings. God loves us and the earth, but we are not all powerful as the Divine is. We are not the center of everything. God is. The configuration of the solar system is just one of many reminders of that fact.

Astrological charts are circular. The body's cells are circular, too. Our DNA, on which is imprinted the code of life itself, is a spiral, which is nothing more than a circle that has been cut and stretched into three dimensions but still retains a beginning and an ending. Because of the circle's connection with Divinity, in the future we will be drawn to work with this powerful shape and be able to break the limitations of time and space and mortality. Airplanes will be circular or spherical and will be able to travel faster than the speed of light. We will work with the center of our circular cells to create healing, because we'll understand that to change, we have to travel to the center of a circle, every time.

Why We Feel Disconnected from God and Each Other

Despite all these signs from God that show us our relationship to Divinity, and despite all these clever reminders of the Law of Totality, our primitive part of the brain, the limbic brain, constantly creates for us the illusion of separation and limitation. We fear the connection, commitment, and togetherness our soul longs for because we don't trust others. But, we are meant to break away from this destructive, alienating belief that is rooted in the fear of our own mortality. It's completely out of sync with the Law of Totality.

The flip side of this alienation is seeking a sense of unity by attaching ourselves to a group and then deciding that our group is superior to all others. This tribal attitude feeds our ego and keeps us edging out God. It's healthy to create families and communities that we have loyalty to and who in turn can give us support. But we mustn't let our connections to the people we choose to be with distract us from the divine reality that we are united with all people everywhere. We continue to learn this lesson in a very painful manner, as people all over the world fight with each other over religion, political beliefs, and race. No group is better than another group, and the very idea that there is one group separate from another is only a man-made illusion.

Until recently, in the West we placed great trust in institutions such as the church, the government, and large companies. It didn't occur to most of us that a big corporation would fire someone just before he received his pension—or that a company would do away with pensions altogether. We never thought that presidents would conspire to break the law, and lie about it. It was unthinkable that a major church would not only hide the fact that some of their priests were pedophiles, but send them to other parishes where they could harm more children, rather than remove them from their duties. Nowadays, we tend to assume that we can't trust any large group of people. But at this time in history, as we move into the eleventh house of the zodiac, we are meant to regain our ability to trust—not blindly, but wisely.

How can we start the process of trusting the whole again, of healing it? It begins by healing ourselves. Jesus said, "How can you remove the sliver from your brother's eye when you have a log in your own? First take the log out of your own eye. Then, you can see well enough to take the sliver out of your brother's eye." He also asked John to baptize or purify him before he began his work. When he admonished his followers to, "Love your enemy as you love yourself," Jesus was trying to help people understand that while it is noble to want to help the world, we must first cleanse ourselves of any impurities and become a vessel of love. You can't help others when your soul is clouded with the dark energy of self-hatred. You can't trust others if you are untrustworthy yourself. Bring out of the shadows the ugliness you find there, and shed light on them. Light, or love, will heal you and purify you. Then you can embrace your purpose, which is to further heal yourself even as you are healing the world.

Feeling Our Connection to All of Divinity

In the United States we tend to value individuality over community. We act as though we are responsible for our own lives and no one else's. But we are all connected in divine love. Refresh your heart's memory of this link to others by traveling to other communities and cultures, or by reaching out to people in your community that you normally think of as unlike you. As these actions take you out of your comfort zone, you may find yourself tempted to let your ego take the wheel and to start pontificating about what you think is important. Resist that urge and instead ask questions, and then listen to the answers you receive. Listening is much too rare these days. Try to find common ground with others to remind yourself, and them, of the Law of Totality.

Celebrate your family. When you have guests over for a meal or just to have fun together, don't feel you have to go all out in order to win them over. What people want most is not a fancy party but to feel listened to and valued. There are people who own huge, expensive houses that are always empty, because the homeowners' priorities are out of place. When you get together with others, forget about what your home looks like. What's most important is to share food and memories, not to impress people and make them think you're important. If you feel you have to "wow" them, you need to take a look at your insecurities and address them.

Don't forget about the importance of community that extends beyond your old friends and your relatives. Say hello to your neighbors, smile at them and strike up a conversation. Invite them over to meet your family and friends. This is a very loving way to remind yourself and everyone else that life is about compassion and kindness, and reaching out to others. Block parties are a wonderful way to get to know who lives across the street instead of awkwardly turning your gaze away when you make eye contact because you don't know who they are.

Learn about history, and, if you can, travel to important historical sites and open yourself up to the energy that is there. Let yourself feel what it must have been like to experience what the people there felt. We are connected to those who came before us because of the Law of Totality. Allow yourself to experience that sense of connection.

Find ways to meet others in person instead of relying on correspondence through the Internet. Too many people spend their time in "virtual reality," text messaging each other or communicating through the Internet, especially through social networking sites. Virtual communication is better than no communication, but it is very different from the experience of traveling on a bus or train and talking to someone about who they are, how they came to be traveling, and what they're thinking and feeling. You can't pick up on people's energy and feel your energetic connection to them over the Internet (unless you're very skilled at working with energy to begin with). You can't even be certain that the person you're corresponding with is who he says he is. He could be anyone, and lying to you about all his personal details. If you have children, encourage them to take the iPod out of their ear, put away the cell phone, and actually interact with other people even if it feels a little uncomfortable at first. Teach them good conversation starters, and if you don't know any, learn and practice using them yourself.

Again, it's very important to pay attention to serendipity and coincidence and your intuition. Value and respect the information that comes to you. Examine it and see what you can learn. Pay attention to your dreams. Think about the symbolism and messages your subconscious mind is generating for you. Dream symbols can come from the collective mind as well as your own mind, and you might learn something incredibly important from your dreams. You may have a precognitive dream or realize you or someone you love has a medical condition that requires attention. It used to be that whenever I had a dream that I'd lost a tooth or teeth, someone in my family died soon afterward. Making these connections may not allow us to change the future, although we can try, but they can allow us to emotionally prepare for what is destined to happen.

When we align ourselves with the Law of Totality, we align ourselves with the Divine and therefore we find ourselves content with whatever comes. Life starts to make sense. When something terrible occurs, we'll naturally feel sad, angry, or upset, but a part of us will be aware that there's a reason for it, even if we don't know what it is at the moment. The Law of Totality allows us to stop seeing ourselves as all alone in a cold world, and instead use a crisis as an opportunity to discover the lessons that the Universe is trying to teach us.

If you apply the Law of Totality to your life, you will feel less lonely. You will stop isolating yourself, because you'll open up to trusting other people. You will also stop thinking of happiness as a goal you can reach sometime in the future after you've worked hard enough and created enough security to sit back and say, "Okay, now I can retire from all the suffering in life." You will see that you can experience happiness at any time, because there's always someone to help you return to a state of joy. Even strangers will reach out to someone they see suffering, but we forget this.

I've had clients who were extremely wealthy, who had no need to work in order to live a life of luxury. Instead of enjoying all their riches, they were absolutely miserable and constantly creating unhappiness for others, too. They didn't have any sense of what was truly important in life. They saw their money as something that separated them from ordinary people. I'll never forget the wealthy client who asked me to come over to her apartment to give her a reading and oh, on the way, would I mind picking up her dry cleaning? I laughed (and stopped taking her calls), but this false sense of entitlement that causes people to treat others as if they were inferior comes from a sense of separateness. When you feel alone in the world, you want to build up a feeling of power and importance so that you don't feel scared and alone.

The Divine will provide everything you need and will heal your pain if you focus on remembering that your job on earth is to participate in the healing this world badly needs. You have an important task as a part of the larger whole. When you extend compassion to another, or do something, however small, to help the environment or serve your community, you are healing a corner of the web that weaves together all of life and all of creation.

Awakening to Our Totality

Fortunately for the human race, people everywhere are beginning to awaken to the Eternal Principle of Totality. We're noticing connections we hadn't seen before. Americans are realizing that what they buy in the grocery store was grown or manufactured somewhere else, and transported into their neighborhoods. They are thinking about the origin of everyday objects, and the consequences of their decisions and actions. For instance, food that was sprayed with heavy pesticides in another country can cause health problems to the people who work with the produce thousands of miles away, and to the person who eats the food as well. Transporting that food a long distance creates pollution that adds to global warming. Not long ago, the number of people who thought about these connections was very small. Often, our waterways are polluted by medications people have flushed down the toilet. Fortunately, some communities have wisely decided to establish collection points for toxic chemicals and for prescription drugs so that they can be disposed of properly.

The banking crisis has been a major force awakening us to totality and interconnectedness, as has global warming. If we pay attention and change our perspective, we can still save our planet. We can't settle for simply changing a few lightbulbs and think that will fix everything. I saw a television show recently about "green decorating" that informed viewers if they felt like changing their home's look, they could buy new green products like flooring and paint. But the reality is, the truly green way to decorate is to not change anything if you don't have to, to avoid generating pollution from manufacturing and transportation, and dumping the old flooring and appliances into landfills! We still have a long way to go before we truly understand just how far reaching our actions are, and what we have to do to live in a sustainable way. Each of us can change our behavior in small ways, and because of the Law of Totality, as we change our behavior we will affect the whole.

The challenges facing us are enormous, but each time one person wakes up to the Law of Totality and the other Eternal Principles, and begins to align with the divine order, the world starts to change. It only takes a few people to create a tipping point, when the whole world changes and masses of people change their thoughts, feelings, and behavior. The Law of Totality reminds us of how much power we have collectively and how important it is to use our individual power.

The Lesson of the Law of Totality:

Grace is divine, for we are all connected, in divinity, at all times. Feeling disconnected from each other and God is man-made.

Ego is the awareness of one's separateness and one's need to survive as a creature on this earth. The ego's concern is not divinity but individual survival and individual power.

When you only experience your ego rather than your connection to all that is Divine, you are unable to experience grace. Grace is a state of beauty and serenity, as well as a state of loving and feeling loved. Lucifer, the angel who fell out of God's grace, did so because of the sin of pride, which is a form of arrogance. Pride is something we experience when we only see the world through the eyes of the ego. Fearing for our survival, we focus on building up our power, influence, and reputation. Because we can never completely conquer the fears of our ego—that we won't have enough for tomorrow, that we are inadequate, that someone might take away all that we've worked so hard to acquire—we are always in denial of how little control we have over the circumstances of life. We think of reputation, power, and fame as safety nets, and convince ourselves that we are more important than this person or that person, but we are only fooling ourselves. I once had a client who was enormously wealthy and well-respected. The man came from a famous family and had a solid reputation in his career and millions of dollars in assets. He was considered a tremendous success and in the prime of life. One day, when the man went to the dentist to have a tooth pulled, there was a problem with the anesthetic and he died of cardiac arrest before the paramedics arrived. No amount of security we build for ourselves in this world is enough to keep us alive if it is our time to go. Yet we want to believe we are so indispensable that God wouldn't dream of calling us home!

People who are in denial of how little control they have over fate generally are mesmerized by the power they've attained in this world. Not long ago, a politician who made his career investigating and prosecuting others for wrongdoing was caught breaking the law. In fact, he was caught because of oversight laws that he himself had pushed to pass! This man was completely caught up in his ego and greatly overestimated his power in the world. Like the rest of us, he was not invulnerable, even though he'd tried very hard to create that feeling for himself.

We fall from grace and lower our vibration whenever we try to take all the credit for our blessings in the physical world, saying, "I'm so proud of myself for creating all my wonderful successes!" We forget about God's role and the role of others who have assisted us in bringing about our good fortune. No one can become successful without the help of other people. Sometimes, those who are most helpful are people we don't even know. Too often, we take for granted opportunities we have, overlooking the influence of ordinary people whose names have been forgotten to history, brave souls who died to make sure that future generations would have those very opportunities.

When you recognize the enormous power of the Divine, you can't help but feel awestruck, humble, and very small by comparison. However, while we shouldn't become enslaved by pride, God doesn't want us to feel utterly powerless and inconsequential, either. In the Bible, Jesus tells us that God has counted every hair on your head, and that God is like the shepherd who will search high and low for one lost sheep even though he still has the rest of the flock. We're meant to recognize that each individual, including ourselves, is very important. To align with divine law, we have to get our ego out of the way, let God into our awareness, and experience our oneness with divinity and each other.

THE SECOND
ETERNAL PRINCIPLE:

The Law of Karma

What we do and what happens to us are
the result of our soul's choice to come
to earth to learn the lessons
we need to learn.

The Law of Karma is perhaps the most important Eternal Principle to understand. If we don't have a good grasp of it, then even if we align ourselves with the other ten Eternal Principles, peace and joy will elude us. Karma is extremely powerful. Whenever we ignore it, we become trapped by it.

In the ancient language of Sanskrit, *karma* is defined as actions, thoughts, and deeds. It is the collection of the memories of everything you have ever felt, thought, experienced, done, or suffered. These memories are imprinted upon your soul. You bring them with you from lifetime to lifetime until your karma is fully resolved.

Reincarnation and Karma

Inherent in the idea of karma is the concept of reincarnation. Unlike Judeo-Christian theology, which teaches that we experience only one lifetime on this earth, Hinduism, Buddhism, and other ancient religious traditions hold that our souls transmigrate, that is, they reincarnate into human form, return to the invisible world after the death of the body, then reincarnate on earth, again and again. The Greek philosophers Socrates and Plato, both living 2,400 years ago, also supported the philosophy of reincarnation. According to the Platonic doctrine of reminiscence, "all our knowledge is a remembrance of what we have known only before we are born." Socrates said, "We must have received our knowledge of all realities before we were born. Our souls existed formerly apart from our bodies and possessed intelligence before they came into man's shape."

Even in the New Testament, we find evidence for reincarnation. Jesus' disciples asked him about a blind man, questioning who had sinned that he should have to suffer from this condition—was it the blind man or his parents? Jesus responded that neither was the case, and that the condition of blindness came from a previous life (John 9:2-3). Jesus also said that John the Baptist was a reincarnation of Elijah (Matthew 11:14).

Why We Reincarnate

The purpose of reincarnation is the purification of the soul, the shedding (that is, the resolving) of negative karma so that only good karma may remain.

In the nonphysical realm, where souls reside between incarnations on earth, we are unable to work through the karmic issues that we carry around like psychological baggage. Your soul lugs that suitcase into the other realm, but to express your issues, explore them, and let them go, you have to be in the human realm—on the other side, you cannot even open the suitcase.

Here on earth, we can deal with our karma in two ways: through suffering fruitlessly or by courageously choosing to experience love, forgiveness, and acceptance, even it when it is very difficult to do so. When we are compassionate and loving, we create positive karma that erases the negative karma and we gain wisdom. Rather than get upset about challenging situations, we can choose to look at them as opportunities to be more loving and compassionate toward ourselves and others, and to learn our lessons so that we can stop attracting hardships and difficult people.

Aligning ourselves with all of the Eternal Principles reduces our suffering. There will always be pain in the material world, but we don't have to make it worse by fighting against Divine Law! Sadly, our egos often cause us to try to fight our way out of suffering, and this only causes us further pain and struggle. Going to war against the Universe is exhausting and futile. When we accept how the Universe works, learning from it and working with it, aligning ourselves with its Principles, we begin to resolve our karma. But to do so takes a great deal of love for ourselves and others.

Once a soul has let go of all its negative karma, which can take many, many lifetimes, it is able to achieve nirvana, or perfection. In nirvana, we are at the highest state of consciousness, aware of our complete union with Divinity. The soul who has reached nirvana does not have to return to earth unless it chooses to incarnate in order to help heal the world (this is what the Buddhists call a *bodhisattva*).

Jews and Christians teach that we only have one lifetime, and after we die, God will either punish or reward us depending on how we behaved on earth. The Universal Law of Karma says that we have many lifetimes and are always involved in the process of healing ourselves so that we don't have to be punished with suffering. The reward we receive for creating good karma and resolving negative karma is joy and peace in this world and in the next.

When we look at our lives and wonder, "Why did that terrible thing happen to me when I'm a good person?" or when we see someone else suffering, we need to remember that all pain has a purpose, and that these tragedies and troubles occur because of karma. In the other realm, a soul who is about to incarnate into earthly form may deliberately choose to be born into a severely dysfunctional and impoverished family or a war-torn country. When we are outside our physical form, we forget just how agonizing our suffering can be while we are in human bodies. We also forget how difficult it is to control our experiences in the moral realm. This amnesia is somewhat like the amnesia of childbirth: a woman prepares herself for the pain of labor, is surprised by how much more intense the experience is than she expected, recognizes that she has to surrender to the experience because she can't control it, then, later, forgets just how painful and difficult it was!

Because the soul's purpose is to put itself in situations where it has the opportunity to work through its karma, it might make the same choices even if it could remember just how hard it is to live on earth. In ancient Greek mythology, the concept of a soul's amnesia is rightly explained through the existence of Hades, or *the underworld*; the ancient Greeks did not believe in Heaven and Hell, but in a land where all the dead went until they chose to come back to human form. Hades had many rivers, one of them being Lethe. Lethe was known as the "river of forgetfulness," and souls drank from it so as to forget their physical history on earth. Thus, a soul could not remember its past in the tangible realm, the many different shapes it had taken, the constant troubles it had endured while in a body susceptible to pain and illness. Interestingly, there also existed a river named Mnemosyne in the land of Hades. This second river contributed to a soul's memory and returned to it a whole host of recollections from previous corporal encounters. Certain souls chose to drink from this river instead of Lethe, so that they might remember their past lives. Mnemosyne was also the name of the Greek goddess of memory, and indeed, our very own modern word "memory" developed from this ancient Greek deity and mythological river (it was adopted by Latin as the word *memoria*, then found its way into the English language).

Having forgotten just how difficult life in this realm can be, however, we reincarnate in order to fulfill our purpose, even though we recognize that suffering will be a part of our existence. From a human standpoint, addiction and disease are terrible aspects of life. Addictions can cause us to feel deep depression and pain, and even destroy our relationships. Disease can ravage our bodies and force us to deal with the horrible prospect of leaving behind those we love and the life we've come to cherish. But the soul sees these afflictions as powerful opportunities to end all the suffering that it experiences lifetime after lifetime. Though we have the choice to face our challenges with love and compassion for ourselves and others, if we choose to deny our addictions or treat disease as simply a physical problem with no emotional or karmic cause, we suffer in vain. We need to remember that whatever suffering we undergo, our job is to learn and grow from it. Then, eventually, we can stop reincarnating into a world of pain, war, and sadness.

Karma Is Just

Karma is not a punishment but a form of justice. It ensures that those who do wrong will suffer not because of payback but because they are out of alignment with Divine Law and not learning the lessons they came to this world to learn. When you do wrong, you must face the uncomfortable consequences, whether you do so in this life or the next. There's no escaping the consequences!

The other side of karma is that those who do right will reap the benefits of their actions. It makes a great deal of sense, and explains how we free ourselves from the curse of original sin (a doctrine in Judeo-Christian theology). It may seem that good people suffer while bad people thrive and flourish because karma is not instantaneous. It can take time for it to play out in our lives. Once the seed of karma is sown, however, it will sprout and grow, whether in this lifetime or the next.

In fact, karma is so powerful that unchecked, it will grow like a weed. If you have good karma, created by treating others well, being grateful and loving, and generously giving to the world, it will increase like a carpet of lovely violets. However, if you create negative karma, it will become like a cancer, rapidly multiplying. You can't ignore it forever. Negative karma, left unresolved, will lead to disease and disaster.

The pain you experience as a result of your karma serves a purpose: it wakes you up to what you need to address in your life. If you step on a sharp stone and cut your toe, your body's healthy neurological system goes into action and causes your brain to create the sensation of pain. This pain draws your attention to your foot and helps you to notice the wound, clean it, and care for it so that it can heal. If you didn't experience that pain, you might not have known that your foot was in danger of becoming infected, which is a far worse situation than having a small cut. Similarly, the pain in your life is meant to wake you up to your negative karma so that you will resolve it rather than remain ignorant of it and let it accumulate and get worse, drawing you further and further into anger, depression, envy, or greed.

Unresolved bad karma doesn't make you a bad person. All of us have unfinished business and lingering negative thoughts and feelings surrounding actions and events. While you may not think much about it in the present, you may still have negative feelings about a friendship that ended a couple of years ago, leaving you wary of becoming close to someone again. Your negative thoughts and your hurt feelings created negative karma that you still carry and will continue to hold on to until you can learn from that experience and no longer feel angry when you're reminded of it.

Resolving Karma

Karma's purpose is to help us achieve harmony and balance so that we can be united with the Divine and escape suffering. It steers us toward achieving perfection and purity as a soul over the course of many lifetimes on earth. In this life, karma helps us mold our character and develop courage, love, and compassion. It helps us learn our lessons through love instead of pain. When we are conscious of our issues, feelings, thoughts, and actions, we can choose to take a different perspective and create good karma instead of bad.

We address, or resolve, karma by taking the negative charge out of it. We start by acknowledging our unfinished business: the unprocessed, negative feelings and thoughts we created when we intentionally gave in to our darkest emotions and acted in ways that hurt ourselves and others. After acknowledging what we've done, we forgive ourselves for not being perfect, learn from the situation, and consciously try to change how we behave in the future. In doing so, we shed a light on that dark energy of negativity and transform it.

Intentionality is a key part of karma. If you harm someone accidentally, you don't create karma. My husband's mother was killed by a driver whose car malfunctioned causing him to plow into a crowd of people. Although several pedestrians were killed, and the man felt terrible about what had happened, he did not create karmic obligations, just feelings of guilt or sadness in himself. My husband, who was a very young man at the time, didn't feel anger or resentment toward the driver, because he understood that his mother had been the victim of a random accident and that the driver wasn't at fault. By not responding with anger and hatred, or holding on to his sorrow, my husband ensured that he did not create bad karma for himself.

Understanding intentionality helps us do the right thing and create good karma, as well as minimize our bad karma. In a past life, the Buddha was once told that a certain man was going to sink a ferry carrying five hundred people. He prayed and reflected on what to do. Should he kill the man to save five hundred lives? Or should he remain nonviolent, but allow those five hundred people to die? Finally, he chose to kill the man, but not just to save all those lives. He killed the man for the man's own sake, to save him from the karma of committing five hundred murders. He created good karma by committing murder with the best of intentions. He did not create feelings or thoughts of guilt, which would have created bad karma, but acted with intention and compassion for all: the five hundred men, the would-be murderer, and himself.

This Buddhist teaching story reminds us that we are not always aware of our true intent. We can be in denial of what our subconscious mind desires, which could be in conflict with what our conscious mind desires. You might think you want to create a lasting, loving relationship that leads to marriage and children, but your subconscious mind may want to resolve karma from your childhood or a past life. Its intention may be for you to become emotionally involved with someone who will help you face your issues about trust and betrayal. If your partner cheats on you, it isn't a punishment for something you did wrong. It is the natural consequence of your karma. You can resolve the karma by acknowledging what is happening, letting go of your emotional response, and learning from the situation. Being aware of your fears and anger about incidents in the past where your trust was betrayed allows you to see more clearly and accept that the person you want to marry isn't ready for a monogamous commitment. It allows you to be honest about all the signs that this isn't the person for you, unless you want to get stuck in the old karma and cause yourself to suffer.

Present, Past, and Accumulated Karma

Each day, your actions and thoughts create karma, good or bad. The more you are aware of your past karma, the easier it is to change your present karma and to shed the accumulated karma. When you let go of anger, hatred, jealousy, resentment, negativity, and despair you begin to think and behave in a more positive way. These three types of karma—past, present, and accumulated—can all be resolved by creating good karma and learning the lessons from your past so that you are able to finally let go of the negativity you've been carrying with you.

It's only natural that we experience grief at a loss, or anger when we feel betrayed. But the moment we realize that we are experiencing a negative emotion, or creating thoughts that perpetuate negative feelings and actions, we need to stop ourselves in order to avoid creating unwanted karma. Accumulated negative karma makes it very difficult to change our patterns, but we must.

Discovering Our Karma

There is no escape from karma. We are stuck in the karmic wheel, going round and round, experiencing birth, life, and death over and over again until we release ourselves from the wheel by shedding all our bad karma and moving inward to the stable center where we are one with God and in eternal peace. The first step in getting off of that karmic wheel is to discover what your karma is, that is, what negative patterns you have and what you have done in the past that has harmed yourself and others. Only by recognizing your karma can you begin to resolve it.

Several years ago, my close friend bought a lovely condominium in a new development. He got along beautifully with the other people in the building, made several friends, and always had pleasant interactions with the condominium association, until one day, when a new woman took over the management. This woman became convinced that the properties weren't generating enough money, so she doubled the maintenance fees and started charging for all the extra services. My friend left town for several months and came back to find that his bicycle, which he'd kept in the parking garage for years, had been thrown away. The new association president said she had cut the lock and put the bike in the trash because he hadn't paid the new bicycle storage fee that had been instituted. She even presented him with a bill for the months of storage for the bicycle that had been confiscated! The association president brought in so much toxic energy that the condominium owners began to sell their homes, and those that stayed refused to pay the new fees and stopped recommending the place to their friends who were looking to buy a home. As a result of her quest to make every cent she could, the condominiums were left vacant and unsold, and thus, the building lost its charm and became run down. This woman had brought about the very scenario she'd most feared. This is how karma works: it causes us to operate from fear and create the very scenarios we most want to avoid, and which our soul knows are most likely to wake us up. The association president needed to wake up and face her issues about money and scarcity or she was going to continue to collect less and less money.

When things are going badly despite your best efforts, pay attention and ask yourself, "What am I challenged to learn here?" A karmic lesson is before you, but if you focus on creating a tale of woe, telling yourself "I can't believe this is happening to me! I don't deserve it!" you may miss the lesson, and then you will have to suffer even greater pain and loss in the future.

Repeating patterns in your life are the result of karma as well: You divorce an alcoholic, meet a fantastic new man, fall in love, and discover that he's an alcoholic. What you have to accept is that subconsciously, you chose to get involved with another heavy drinker so that you could work through your issues around addiction and alcoholism. You are not to *blame* for making poor choices. Your conscious mind might not have been aware that you were dating an alcoholic for the second time, or it might have pushed aside all the signs. But if you don't face your role in *subconsciously* choosing the situation, you will end up in the same boat again and again and again. Let go of any guilt or blame, and accept that you are face to face with a karmic issue that needs to be resolved.

Ways to Discover Our Karmic Challenges

Most of us don't remember our past lives and experiences in which our bad karma was created. They are buried in our subconscious along with long-forgotten memories from this lifetime, but sometimes they seep out into our dreams or express themselves in our desires or phobias. Hypnosis can bring these memories to the surface, allowing you to understand that your fear of airplanes is the result of having died in a plane crash in a previous life, or that your attraction to military life is due to your having been a soldier in many lifetimes.

These memories, the record of your karma, are also kept in the book of records on the akashic plane in the invisible world. The akashic plane can be reached if you practice achieving a certain level of consciousness, or you can tap into it spontaneously. If you've ever had a precognitive dream, it's because while you were sleeping, you were able to reach this timeless plane and take a peak into the book and read about the future. In the akashic plane, all events, past and present, are happening simultaneously.

Undergoing a past-life regression or hypnosis can be very helpful for discovering your karma. You can also learn what your karmic challenges are through your destiny code. I wrote *Decoding Your Destiny* specifically for this purpose. Your destiny code is based on your birth date, because your soul chooses to enter your physical body at a precise moment when the stars are aligned with the very issues it wants to address in this lifetime. Your issues may include the loss of a mother and difficulties with mothering, while others may struggle with stubbornness and egotism, to having difficulty achieving emotional intimacy in relationships.

You can also discover your karmic challenges through therapy, which will teach you how to face your karma and accept yourself as you are, right now, rather than to deny your weaknesses. It is important to be patient with yourself and accept that you have a long way to go before you can achieve perfection. Some souls are more evolved, which is why you shouldn't compare yourself with others. Comparisons are likely to make you feel bad about yourself and slip into denial about your issues in order to avoid the painful thought, "I'm not good enough" or "I'm not strong like she is." People who abuse drugs and alcohol don't feel good about themselves and are often trying to avoid facing their issues and suffering emotional pain, but this only prolongs the process of resolving karma and causes them even more agony.

The Mirror Effect

One way karma plays out, which can be very difficult to recognize, is by presenting you with a situation where you take on the opposite role that you took in a previous situation where the negative karma was first created. It can be hard enough to recognize when you are working out an issue by repeating the same behavior over and over. What is really tricky is recognizing when it's the same problem but you are playing a different role, as if the scene were playing out in a mirror.

My mother had a very lonely childhood. Her mother died right after she was born, and my mother was raised by her older sister. My aunt must not have been very nurturing, because my mother often said her sister's lack of maternal love caused her tremendous emotional pain. By having children herself, my mother had the opportunity to heal this loss. Unfortunately, despite her best efforts to let go of her negative feelings connected with motherhood, she unknowingly re-created them by becoming overly protective of her own children. As my sister and I grew older, we resisted her attempts to be very involved in our lives. Our desire for independence from her pained my mother greatly. She was not able to see that by avoiding her own mother issues, she was preventing herself from finding a balance between giving her children too much attention and not enough. Her subconscious mind was gripped by fear and the misguided belief that she needed to be a part of every aspect of her children's lives, or risk being a neglectful mother. The truth behind this belief was so painful that her conscious mind insisted that she was only expressing an abundance of maternal love. According to the Law of Karma, she will have to come back in another life to heal this karma around mothering once and for all.

To help yourself discover your own karma, keep in mind that whenever a situation feels familiar or painful, you are probably caught in the wheel of karma. Do not focus on what role you are playing or how that role is different from anything that happened in the past. Instead, reflect on the situation, and notice what feels familiar. Are you once again dealing with boundary issues, financial problems? Once you identify the issue you will be able to see how your karma is playing out in your life, even if the issues show up in a different arena than they did before. If your mother was overbearing, you may be mirroring her behavior, if not as a mother then perhaps in your role as a boss. If you fear not having enough money, you may become rich but be terrified of losing it all. The goal is to recognize each issue and resolve it, preferably before you have alienated others or a long string of people have stolen from you.

Believing and Trusting in the Law of Karma

Sometimes, it can be difficult to believe in the Law of Karma. From our limited perspective, we cannot always see that the core of karma, justice and balance, is being served. We look at a newborn baby who has many physical problems and ask why he should be in pain when he's done nothing wrong. A baby hasn't had time to accumulate karma in this lifetime, which means he is probably working through karma from a previous lifetime. If you are a good person and something terrible is happening to you, it is most likely your karma playing out and you have not yet recognized what your karmic themes are.

None of us can escape the karmic wheel unless we work through all of our personal karma and are somehow able to remain free of family and global karma, too. People who do terrible things to others may seem to get away with their crimes, but they never truly do. If they don't suffer in this lifetime from their negative karma, they will carry it with them into the next lifetime.

The older you get and the more time you spend observing people, the easier it is to see the patterns of karma playing out and to recognize that people who live badly usually come to a bad end while good people usually die peacefully. We take notice when someone who is a wonderful person dies too young, but we forget about all the good people who live well into their eighties or nineties. We also don't realize that a soul may have chosen to leave this life early. Having accomplished what it set out to do, it may long to return to heaven for a rest. It's natural to feel grief at our loss. But, we should remember that the one who died is now free of any pain whatsoever and experiencing only love, happiness, and peace—and that he will continue to watch and try to protect and guide us from the other realm. The souls who have left this life hear every word we say to them, and they will help us try to resolve our karma if we'll only call on them and receive the courage they send our way.

Family and Global Karma

We not only have personal karma, we have family and global karma. The issues shared by a family, or even a nation or region of the world, will continue to be revisited in lifetime after lifetime as we reincarnate back into the same groups, playing various roles. Your father might reincarnate as your daughter, and your sister might reincarnate as your cousin so you can work together again to resolve family karma. Souls will be born into bodies in the same region of the world over and over again in order to resolve the negative karma they created many hundreds or even thousands of years earlier.

It makes sense that the same group of people wrestling with shared karma would come back to help each other out. If you are the only member of your family willing to resolve your psychological issues, to accept what is, to forgive, to change your thoughts, feelings, and behaviors, and move forward into healing, you may not reincarnate into the same family. However, you may decide to rejoin your family in another lifetime to assist them in their own healing.

There are parts of the world that are still trying to heal from the wounds they inflicted upon themselves long ago. The Middle East remains in continual turmoil because too many of its inhabitants repeat the same destructive patterns, perpetuating the negative karma that caused so much pain to so many over hundreds and hundreds of years.

It can be difficult to accept that we are responsible for the terrible things that happen to us. It's not that some people are "bad" and therefore deserve a corrupt government, or that those who lived in New Orleans during Hurricane Katrina deserved to die. That's not how karma works. Try to let go of the ideas of punishment, justice, and blame for a moment. Remember that souls have a very different perspective than our human minds do. At least some of those souls chose to be born in a particular time and place on earth in order to face their karmic issues. Those who found their courage and heroism may have been people resolving old karma, while those who died may have left this world because of their soul's desire to force the rest of us to confront the unresolved issues of poverty, crime, and exploitation. You cannot look at any particular person and know what their karma is, or why they suffered what seems to be a random tragedy.

Some people have been very upset when public figures have suggested that the tragic events of September 11 were the result of U.S. foreign policy decisions. This is an oversimplification of how karma works. Each person who died that day had his or her own personal karma, family karma, and global karma. There might have been some people who had very little bad karma to heal but who chose to be a part of that calamity so that they could play a part in healing the world. Our foreign policies certainly influenced those who attacked us, but the terrorists also had personal, family, and global karma that drove them to their deeds. If you listen to how terrorists talk about America, you can hear how their own personal and psychological issues affect their views. By creating more negative karma, the terrorists of September 11 doomed themselves to tremendous suffering in the next life.

Globally, we have many problems that cause us pain: poverty, disease, inequality, hatred, racism, genocide . . . the list goes on and on. Because of the Law of Totality, every healing act we perform, every bit of good karma we create, contributes to the healing of the world. You may feel over-whelmed and depressed by all the catastrophes, wars, and cruelty reported in the news, but everything you do that is kind, loving, unselfish, and nurturing will uplift humanity because we are all connected. We rarely see how far our actions reach, but good karma truly does spread healing like ripples stretching out across a pond after you've tossed a pebble into the water.

Interfering with the Karma of Others

Although we may want to help others heal, it's very important to work in alignment with the Law of Karma. When we intervene with someone else's karma, we risk taking on karma that doesn't belong to us, creating misery for ourselves. Our good intentions cannot change the fact that intervening in someone else's karma enables that person to avoid resolving it himself. It may even cause him to create more negative karma.

At a global level, the United States intervened with the karma of an entire nation when we invaded Iraq. To send troops to another country in order to prevent genocide is not a violation of the Law of Karma. Helping innocent people who are being tortured and killed creates good karma. However, when we go to war against another country because we do not like its leader, we are meddling in that nation's karma and creating more negative karma for everyone. If we are afraid of being attacked, then we need to deal with our own karma surrounding fear rather than strike preemptively on the chance we are in danger. If we truly wanted to help the people of Iraq—if that was the real goal—then we needed to have first healed ourselves of hatred and violence so that we could see how best to reach out to them and inspire them to heal themselves. Instead, we acted from ego and fear and started a war. We are mixing our karma with Iraq's, and we will have to pay the consequences for not letting them work through their issues of violence and hatred on their own.

In our own lives, we interfere with others' karma too. It can be agonizing to stand by and watch a loved one suffer when we feel certain that if we were to swoop in with money, a place to live, or advice, we could save him pain. When we prevent someone from experiencing the consequences of their behavior, it often enables them to continue their suffering.

It is commonly thought that an alcoholic must "hit bottom" before he is able to stop drinking and start addressing his issues, and that everyone's bottom point is different. The same is true of anyone suffering because of karma. You can offer to help someone, but if you are helping in order to not feel guilty or scared, then you need to heal yourself of your guilt and fear first. Only then will you have clarity about what you should do. Only then will you be able to avoid creating negative karma for yourself in your futile effort to "fix" their problems. Sometimes, you can do everything you possibly could and yet not be able to help another person. In fact, that person may refuse and even resent your offers of assistance. This is extremely difficult to accept, but accepting that each of us has our own karma and our own path is part of living in alignment with Divine Law. We must accept that we are not all powerful and able to "fix" others through our sheer willpower. Anger about our powerlessness only causes suffering.

One of my clients had a brother who could never seem to hold down a job and was constantly asking her for money. She rented an apartment for him because she was afraid that if she didn't, he would become homeless. But her brother ended up moving out of town with a new girlfriend, leaving his sister to pay the rest of the money due on the lease, costing her thousands of dollars. When she later asked me what she should have done, I advised her to explore her need to rescue her brother. I told her, "You can't keep doing this for him. You wouldn't take his SATs for him or brush his teeth for him. You're not letting him grow up. If you let go of your need to have him treat you well and act responsibly, and you let go of your own need to prove that you're a good sister who deserves your mother's love and everyone's admiration, then you can make the right decisions about when to help him and when to just let him do what he's going to do."

She realized that she hadn't wanted to believe she would be stuck paying her brother's rent, and she had to take responsibility for her choice to give him money when she knew his track record. While she could do nothing to fix her brother's karma, she did choose to learn from this expensive lesson and accept that she could not rescue her brother from himself. She had to offer what she felt comfortable offering and then let go of the need to see the results she wanted. After a while, she decided that the one thing she truly felt comfortable offering her brother was to find him a therapist, drive him to his weekly appointments, and pay for his sessions for three months. When her brother refused this help, she was able to accept his decision even though it frightened and scared her to think about what might happen next given how dysfunctional his behavior was. By healing herself of the need to be the good sister, she was able to stop interfering with his karma, and allow him to pay the price for his own actions.

It was a difficult decision for her because she knew how much her brother was likely to suffer. But, she kept reminding herself that his soul was making a choice to steer him toward situations that would challenge him to work through his karma. She couldn't create the "bottom" for him; he had to hit it himself.

The more clarity you have about your own issues, the easier it will be to make decisions about helping those who don't give back or thank you for your sacrifices and gifts. Healing yourself and saying "No" may inspire them to change, but it's more likely that they will continue on their path until they've suffered enough to face their karmic issues and begin the healing process. In fact, sometimes simply walking away from the situation is the kindest thing you can do because you stop feeding that person's illusion that you are the problem in their life. Whenever we choose to engage in someone else's narrative about being a victim, we enable them to avoid looking honestly at themselves, which is the first step in healing their own karma. Choosing not to play the part in their drama is good for you and for them.

Remember that when you help others, you should be aware of your own issues so you don't fall into the trap of trying to rescue them and then feeling victimized yourself. Accept that the other person is where he is on his spiritual journey, but have the wisdom to recognize what you can and cannot change, and accept the limits of your power.

We Create Our Negative Karma!

If asked, most of us would probably say that we never do anything intentionally wrong. But when we feel victimized, we can feel a powerful thirst for revenge. If we give into this low vibration, we will create negative karma. I had a client named Jean, who was in her fifties and had been happily married for thirty years. She'd recently received a disturbing phone call from a younger woman who claimed she was carrying Jean's husband's baby. Though Jean was deeply shocked and upset by the news, she urged the other woman to meet her so they could calmly discuss the situation. When they sat down face to face, the mistress spoke of the affair openly, even admitting that she had known Jean's husband was married. But it was not until Jean asked, "Why are you doing this to me?" that the second woman revealed her intentions. Two years earlier, she had divorced her own husband when she discovered he'd been having an affair. The experience changed the woman into a bitter, vengeful person, who wanted other married women to feel the same pain. She told Jean, "I don't care that this is wrong. I'm doing it because it was done to me." It seems the woman felt her behavior was justified because it had made her feel better. She may have felt smug and powerful at first, but through her actions and intentions she had created negative karma. There would be no escape from the consequence of this choice: eventually, she would suffer, because this is how karma works. It is one thing to succumb to lust or greed and make a mistake from which we learn, but it is an entirely different karmic issue when we don't take responsibility for our choices, call ourselves a victim, and use that as an excuse to deliberately harm others. Many people do this in subtle ways— they lie, cheat, or steal "just a little" because they feel they've gotten a raw deal in life. They justify their behavior by telling themselves that they are not really harming anyone, but they are. The waitress who has to pay the bill when the customer sneaks out and the person who makes a purchase and later realizes the salesperson misrepresented the quality of the item are harmed by people who acted upon the thought, "It's no big deal if I stick it to someone else." When we harm others we create negative karma for ourselves.

Healing Our Karma

We can begin healing our karma today by stepping back from our thoughts, feelings, and behaviors and reflecting upon them.

If you don't know how to step back and calmly witness your own thought processes and behaviors, cognitive behavioral therapy can help you to iden-tify your negative, distorted beliefs and to begin analyzing them. Very often, when we look at our thoughts, we see that they don't make a lot of sense. For instance, deep down, you might hold the belief that if you are a likeable person, everyone will like you. But this belief isn't true. Many people in this world have so many problems that they aren't able to treat you well, no mat-ter how good a person you may be.

When you recognize you have a habit of creating negative thoughts and bad feelings that lead to hurtful actions, be gentle with yourself. Don't sit in judgment. Be compassionate toward yourself and patient, because it takes time to break habits. Our brains are programmed to create habits, and you have to consciously choose again and again to stop yourself from going down the same old road. If you can create a new habit of correcting your thinking, creating positive feelings, and acting in a loving way, you will find it easier to break the old habit of reacting to life with anger, sadness, and frustration.

As you create good karma by healing yourself, your life will begin to flourish and you will be a like a sponge for blessings. You will find yourself giving back to the world in all sorts of ways, from caring for stray animals to driving elderly people to doctors' appointments, to being a mentor to younger people or volunteering to help in your child's school. You will have plenty to give because you won't deplete yourself by constantly giving to others in order to work through some unresolved karmic issue you don't recognize. You won't have to create suffering for yourself anymore.

The Law of Karma and the Law of Totality

Seeing that we are all connected in divinity allows us to stop looking to blame others or ourselves when things go wrong, and instead focus on what we can do to transform the situation for the better. We allow the Law of Karma to work instead of trying to rush in and fix all the problems we see around us. We treat ourselves kindly and view others with compassion even if we don't understand or like their behavior. We stop trying to be in charge all the time and align ourselves with the Law of Totality because we know that as long as we heal ourselves, someone, somewhere, will be affected at an energetic level by our healing. I have a friend who has sold many copies of her book aimed at helping people with a rare health condition, and she says that looking at her impressive sales figures doesn't move her as much as getting an e-mail from someone she has never met who says, "Thank you, because your book gave me hope and guidance." Your small, kind act toward one neighbor is an act of good karma that changes the energy of the matrix of life.

The Lesson of the Law of Karma:

Compassion is divine.
Judgment, blame, and punishment are man-made.

Negative karma causes suffering while good karma heals us and the world. The purpose of karma is not to punish us with suffering but to provide justice and bring us to our highest state of being. As a justice system, it works far better than our own man-made laws. When it comes to righting wrongs, no amount of edicts, ordinances, lawyers, judges, or prisons can ever accomplish what karma can achieve: justice, peace, and ultimately, freedom from all suffering. If we judge ourselves negatively, or judge others as "bad" or "evil," it doesn't help us to resolve karma; it causes us to create even more negative karma.

To align yourself with the Law of Karma, you need to be non-judgmental. You must have compassion for yourself and others, recognizing that each of us has different lessons to learn and that we all learn at our own pace. Just as some children learn to read faster than others do, and some will be more skilled at math while others will be more skilled at athletics, each of us has our own path, our own karma to resolve, our own amount of awareness, and our own level of ability to change. Some people do not have the strength to face their issues. Their soul overestimated what they could handle in this life. These people end up creating negative karma instead of good, and push themselves further back on the path. Their suffering will continue and worsen. There is no need to punish someone who is punishing himself at a deep, soul level. What would that accomplish?

Being nonjudgmental means forgiving people even when they have no remorse. It does *not* mean you should give them more opportunities to hurt you. We need to capture terrorists and criminals to prevent them from further harming other people—and themselves. But lashing out at them, coming down to their level by using violence or cruelty to punish them, is not in alignment with the Law of Karma. Violence is man-made. It is a misguided way of righting wrongs, because we only end up creating our own negative karma while trying to address theirs. Every time a war ends, there are soldiers who go home and wrestle with the demons of guilt for the rest of their lives. Unlike the Buddha when he had to commit violence against the would-be murderer of five hundred men, these soldiers were unable to carry out their duties with a clear conscience. This is why it is absolutely crucial that we work to prevent all wars and violence. Our man-made solutions of imprisonment and killing do not work to create harmony and peace in our world or in our hearts.

To forgive means to detach. Don't entangle yourself in someone else's karma. Love yourself enough to accept your darkest side, work toward healing it, and you will find that peace is manifesting in your life. This is the promise and the gift of the Law of Karma.

THE THIRD
ETERNAL PRINCIPLE:

The Law of Wisdom

Wisdom is recognizing what we can and cannot change, accepting our limitations, and choosing to use our suffering as a tool for learning about ourselves and growing spiritually.

One of the wisest prayers I have ever heard, The Serenity Prayer written by Reinhold Niebuhr and adopted with a slight rewording by Alcoholics Anonymous, is an excellent reminder of what we must do if we are to face our karma and begin working through it:

> *God, grant me the serenity to accept the things I cannot change*
> *The courage to change the things I can*
> *And the wisdom to know the difference*

If we try to change the things that are beyond our control, we are likely to wear ourselves out and become filled with hopelessness. If we can accept the limits of our power, have patience with ourselves, and be at peace with whatever is going on in our lives, we will find tranquility, which provides us great strength to face our challenges. Wisdom allows us to take off the blinders and understand what we are doing instead of remaining in denial and fear. With this awareness, we can find the courage to begin to address our karma and ease our suffering.

Wisdom isn't knowledge; it isn't the same as knowing a lot of facts or information. Wisdom is a way of using knowledge, and an awareness of how we can acquire knowledge and of how little knowledge you have. Life is filled with mysteries and we can't always know the answer to the question "Why?" Wisdom is a perspective that allows us to accept that some things are outside of our control. Wisdom also gives us the courage to do what is difficult and to change what must be changed in order for healing to take place. It is what helps us learn our lessons and transform the way we think, feel, and behave.

If you are unwise and avoid your karmic issues because you don't want to suffer, you are resisting what your soul came here to learn, and you will suffer even more. You will also have to rely solely on your mind, on your thinking process, to guide you. The rational, analytical mind is very useful, but it has limitations. It doesn't tap in to the infinite wisdom of the Divine. It's easily clouded by strong feelings and preconceived notions, so it resists learning and changing.

Your brain is set up to work very efficiently so that you do not waste energy trying to figure out new ways to do things you already know how to do. In some ways, this is good. You wouldn't want to have to think about how to create each of the letters in your name every time you had to write it or whether there might be a better way to write the letters. Imagine how tired you would be by the end of the day if you'd had to question and analyze every move you made, from which toothpaste to use to whether or not to pour a glass of juice before you open the blinds or vice versa. Much of the time, we are on autopilot.

The problem is that our minds can lock us into patterns of thoughts, feelings, and behaviors that are unhealthy for us. If you're in the habit of eating a sugary donut for breakfast every morning, and tossing a box of donuts into your grocery cart every week, you are not paying attention to how that food makes your body feel or how it is harming you. You are not being wise or mindful, not thinking about what you are doing or how your food choice is affecting your body. You can also have unhealthy habits of the mind that cause destructive attitudes, which create negative karma. You might think, "I don't have the patience to deal with people who aren't as smart as I am, so I'm not going to feel bad about being rude to people who are confused by what I'm saying to them." You might not even realize you think in judgmental ways, because your attitudes are so deeply engrained.

To break bad habits that create negative karma, you must become aware of your patterns and bravely admit to them. If they make you feel uncomfortable and bother your conscience, then you know what you must do: change them. It can be incredibly difficult to break a bad habit, but with wisdom, you can do it more easily because you understand the karmic consequences of your habits and you feel committed to transformation. You also understand that hard as it is to alter your behavior, you can always rely on God's help. Willpower is very useful, but feeling your connection to the Divine gives you the courage to change no matter how much pain it causes you.

Why We Need Wisdom

Without wisdom, we become trapped in our karma, struggling to make our lives work and placing too much trust in facts and knowledge. We think that if we just have enough information, we can fix all our problems. It's as if we become nearsighted, and we think that everything would be okay if the people around us would just change. Without wisdom, we are unable to accept people and situations as they are and discover what we can learn from them and how we can feel tranquil regardless of what's going on. Instead, we try to control everyone and everything. We wear ourselves out taking on the weight of the world. Wisdom means accepting what we cannot change and understanding that suffering has a purpose. If we find the purpose and learn the lesson, the suffering begins to go away, because we've aligned ourselves with the divine Law of Wisdom.

With wisdom, acceptance, and courage, you can erase your negative karma, freeing yourself of the psychological issues that you've been grappling with for years or lifetimes. Wisdom allows you to be honest with yourself and acknowledge what you are doing wrong, even though doing so may cause you to feel bad. You might feel guilty or ashamed, or angry or sad, but with the perspective of wisdom, you will be able to understand that these emotions are temporary and will subside once you change your karma. When you stop making unwise decisions that create negative karma—that is, choices that harm yourself, others, and the world—you can begin to make changes that will help you create the life you want to live.

You can manifest just about anything you desire if you are willing to acquire wisdom. Creativity develops when you are wise, because you see possibilities you were unaware of before. You let go of your mind's limitations and see that just because a situation or friendship doesn't look like it will pay off for you doesn't mean it is a waste of time. Whatever happens, you are open to the opportunities each situation may provide you, whether they turn out to be opportunities to experience pure joy or to experience suffering and learn something important.

Self-awareness also allows you to recognize when you are in a relationship, job, or project that generates suffering instead of what you want. You understand that running away from a problem doesn't solve anything, so you make a wise decision about whether to stay and work it out, or leave and *still* work it out. When you have wisdom, you recognize your own role in creating suffering.

If you leave a job because you do not feel your boss and coworkers respect you, karma dictates that you will navigate toward another situation in which you are disrespected until you face that particular issue and work through it. If you are wise, you will accept this inevitability, face your karma, and begin resolving your deep inner feelings and beliefs that continually lead you into situations that cause you to feel disrespected. You will also see the potential for resolution in each situation and come up with solutions. Whether you lose your house to foreclosure, your spouse leaves you with three small children to raise, or you develop a serious illness, wisdom allows you to be honest and resilient so that you can begin creating a better situation immediately simply by shifting your perspective.

Wisdom also causes you to see the past, the present, and the future differently. You stop obsessing about what you longed for or lost, or what you desire, and you are able to see clearly what you need to do right now, in this moment. Psychological or karmic issues narrow your lens and cause you to see yourself as a victim of life, but wisdom helps you discover your power and let go of the past and your concerns about the future. With wisdom, you can live in the present instead of always looking back with regret or worrying about what's ahead.

It is inspiring to hear stories of people who have triumphed over suffering, people who no longer define themselves by their painful childhood experiences. They are *informed* by their past, but not limited by it. They are able to discover who they are and who they might become, because they no longer think of themselves as victims or wonder who will hurt them down the road. They do not re-create their anguish by retelling the same old story of how they suffered. With wisdom, you too can break away from the old definition of yourself and triumph over suffering.

People who are wise are happy, peaceful, and powerful. You cannot destroy their spirit. The story of Jesus' death and resurrection is a reminder that people can become very afraid of the power of someone who is wise, and will try to hurt or even kill the person. But the divine soul that is wise and loving can never, ever be destroyed. Wisdom gives us the strength to transcend the ugliness and violence in the world. It is a crucial balm for us in a world that is becoming more and more turbulent. We need to make good decisions not just in our own lives, but in regard to our planet and all of humanity. Wisdom will save us all from terrible suffering.

Wisdom, Power, and Acceptance

To transform anything, we must first accept it as it is. If we resist the truth about a matter, we will not be able to see how to change it. Acceptance starts with honesty and clarity.

Wise people know that to see a person or situation clearly, they must first let go of their own ego stories of victimhood and stories of "he said/she said." They need to see things from more than one angle and have compassion and empathy for everyone involved, knowing that people think, act, and feel differently depending on the karma they carry with them. Instead of setting themselves up as the judge between who is the good guy and the bad guy, who is right and who is wrong, they let go of blame.

We sometimes think that other people's behavior is motivated by their desire to hurt us, or because they do not care about our feelings. With wisdom, we are able to see that others are often unconscious of the consequences of their actions, or are suffering so much, due to their own karma, that they cannot bear to look at how they are hurting others.

Unconscious actions occur on a global level as well. Oppressive and hurtful policies, which have angered so many around the world, aren't necessarily the result of evil men who want to harm others. Often they are the result of misguided thinking. When we are afraid we will not be safe or have enough money unless we get the better end of every deal, we can act like bullies. We cannot admit to ourselves the consequences of our actions and the true motivations behind them, because that would make us feel guilty and deeply uncomfortable. To exercise wisdom, we have to look with compassion and acceptance at our actions as a country, and at the actions of other countries. As long as people are afraid they will not get their needs met, they will strike out against others, whether by committing a terrorist act or setting up a system that leaves people hungry and poor, justifying the infliction of violence as necessary for their own safety and comfort. We cannot resolve any of these problems until we admit to the truth of what they are and see through to everyone's fear, and accept that we've got to find the courage to change what we can. When we understand and obey the Law of Karma, we stop committing acts of violence. We know that violence never solves anything and only makes matters worse.

Wisdom also means accepting that we cannot have all the answers. They may reveal themselves to us in time, and problems may resolve themselves without our having to work at fixing them. With this awareness, we find it is easier to stop seeing problems everywhere. We stop feeling frantic and trying to solve everything from how to make our teenage daughter feel better about losing the part in the school play to how to solve the health care problem in America. Compassion is important, but if you let your ego fool you into believing you can prevent or cure all the suffering you see around you, you will feel overwhelmed and depressed. If you are wise, you will heal yourself of your need to be the rescuer of everyone, because you will accept that you do not have that much power. You will understand that you, like everyone else, play a small but important role in changing the world. You can be sympathetic to your daughter and to those without health care, and then you can see what you are able to do about these situations. Maybe you can help your daughter find an acting class. Maybe you can learn a little more about health care and write to your government representatives about your ideas.

When you make these small but important efforts to change difficult situations, you stop feeling disempowered and cease being haunted by the question "Why?—Why is this happening? Why is it so hard for me to get ahead? Why doesn't my husband change? Why do I have to have health problems?" It's good to explore the question "Why?" and learn what you can, but it is easy to get frustrated because there is no simple answer. You may never know the answer, but if you are accepting, you are more likely to learn the lesson in the suffering.

Being wise and accepting also means that you don't feel the need to have everything go your way. That attitude will wear you out. You will never be able to manage your life and your experiences to the degree that you can achieve lasting happiness. Acceptance of how things already are allows you to find the joy in what is happening right this moment, and to feel grateful no matter what is going on. Wisdom lets you see that you can choose to be happy; it is not something you have to create by trying to control every situation to make it better.

The wisest woman I ever knew was my grandmother. She had no education, but she knew what she could and could not change. When the communists took power in Romania, she lost everything: six houses, all her land, and all her money. Her husband was so distraught that he died of a stroke very soon afterward, and Grandma had to move in with her daughter. She had plenty to be angry and resentful about: her losses, the lack of water and food, and living in a country where she was powerless to change the regime. But Grandma was accepting. She never panicked or complained. She lost two daughters to cancer when they were middle aged, and she didn't despair. She said, "I accept God's decision to take my children before taking me." She was always happy and joking, and never argued or focused on her aches and pains, even though she had three strokes and two heart attacks before she finally died in her sleep at age 102 soon after learning that she'd just lost her son. I believe she lived that long because of her attitude and her wisdom. Life was very simple for her, and her gratitude and faith gave her tremendous strength.

When we are wise and accepting, we do not have to struggle very much. Problems resolve themselves—we find a new place to live, we somehow put food on the table, and we get through another day. Eventually, circumstances change. In the meantime, we do not need to create even more problems by fighting life, trying to make it conform to our expectations.

Wisdom goes against our culture's attitude here in America, where we are told that if we want something to happen, we have to take charge and make it happen. Not long ago, I met a woman from India who was living in the United States. She said that while there were a lot of challenges in her home country, she felt people were wiser and more accepting of life there.

In America, she said, everyone seems to be dissatisfied, working long hours to earn money so that they can be happy and create security. Go ahead and plan for the future and work hard, but keep in mind that there is really no security in the physical world. You can have all the money in the world and everything in your life in place and still die tomorrow. So no matter what the future may bring, try to be happy today. If you *believe* you're happy, then you will find the energy to deal with life's challenges and create an even better life for yourself.

How We Develop Wisdom

Socrates said that wisdom is our inheritance, that it is a gift that lies dormant in our consciousness until it is rediscovered. After the Dark Ages, Europeans began to look back to the great cultures of the Greeks and Romans to reclaim the wisdom they had lost. For all our knowledge in the modern era, we are not very wise. We ought to be looking back to the wisdom of the ancient people in all cultures, wisdom that has been lost and forgotten.

We think that to gain wisdom, we simply have to grow older, but not everyone automatically becomes wiser with age. People with a lot of negative karma become stuck in it and do not learn the lessons that create wisdom. They get so caught up in their suffering they cannot recognize and accept the limitations of their power, or find the courage to change their karma. I have had clients who at thirty, forty, or fifty are still rebelling against their parents or obsessing over whether their mother or father approves of them. They're a long way from acquiring the wisdom that some people have as early as their teenage years.

Everyone gets angry, experiences grief after a loss, or acts out of fear at times. If you are wise, you allow those feelings to surface but you do not become hypnotized by them. You do not feel guilty or embarrassed, or deny your feelings. You face your emotions and your mistakes and look for the lesson. This is a difficult habit to establish because it seems less painful to pretend that everything's okay, but denial just causes more suffering. Recognize your difficult emotions and your tendency to think of yourself as a victim of other people's behavior, or a victim of fate or bad luck. Then, stop yourself and make a conscious decision to discard that disempowering notion. Accept what is happening in your life instead of resisting it.

Understand that often, we are encouraged to give in to blame or vindictiveness instead of accepting the situation as it is and then working to make it better if that's possible, and to learn from it in any case. The moment you recognize your negative feelings, use them as tools to discover your lessons and work through your karma. Don't use them to create a story about how you've been harmed, because that will just prolong your suffering.

To be truly wise we must also learn to tap in to the wisdom of the Divine. You can do this by listening to your intuition instead of letting your rational mind take over. The mind tends to ignore evidence that it doesn't know everything at all times. In our arrogance we move ahead and act before checking in with God. It's what leads you to make bad decisions on an impulse.

To hear the voice of your intuition, you have to slow down and become quiet, then pay attention to any unusual sensations in your body or feelings that something is not quite right. We all have an open line of communication to God, whose wisdom knows no bounds, but we are hard of hearing and quick to dismiss God's messages.

Your intuition may tell you that a present situation or relationship is all that it seems to be on the surface, or it may sense what's going to happen in the future. In the divine realm, the rules of time do not apply. When you tap into sacred wisdom, you are able to know things about the future (and past lives, for that matter). Never shut off this inner wisdom and tell yourself, "I must be imagining things." Trust it, listen carefully, and follow its directions.

You could think long and hard and not find any evidence that your intuition is right, but it is, because intuition comes from God. On the bright, sunny morning of September 11, 2001, I was driving to Manhattan after dropping my daughter off at school in Long Island when suddenly I realized something felt very wrong. I sat with that feeling and listened to hear any messages from the Divine. What I heard was the voice of my late mother, urging me to go home and turn on the television. Now, if I'd let my conscious, rational mind take charge, I would have said to myself, "What a ridiculous thought. Why would I change my plans, cancel my appointment, and go back home to Queens to watch the news? I'll just ignore that message." The very reason I am open to hearing messages from spirits on the other side is that I allow myself to access my subconscious mind and my intuition, the portal to all the wisdom in the spirit realm. Because I trusted my intuition that day, I heard my mother's message. I turned the car around, went home, turned on my television, and saw that a plane had just crashed into the World Trade Center. The phone began ringing with newscasters who knew me asking if I had any insight into what was happening— even before the second plane hit and everyone knew something was very, very wrong. I told all of them what I intuited: that there were four planes trying to attack us; one was going to the White House and one was going to the Pentagon, and that thousands would die. The message was tremendously powerful for me.

When you shut yourself off from your intuitive mind, you shut yourself off to knowledge that can be crucial, even lifesaving. You block yourself from achieving wisdom that will help you in every challenging situation.

You also develop wisdom by slowing down and paying attention. Meditating, going to therapy, and journaling all are useful tools for discovering and accepting your issues, letting go of your stories of victimhood, and finding the courage to transform your thoughts, feelings, and behaviors.

What Is Transformed When We Acquire and Apply Wisdom

None of us can progress in learning our lessons and healing our negative karma unless we have wisdom. If we achieve wisdom and apply it, we are calm and in control, creating good karma and positive energy. We raise our vibration as energy beings, and this helps raise the vibration of the energy matrix that all people and creatures are woven into.

The reason wisdom allows us to be calm is because it helps us see that it is our low level of awareness, our ego, that is dismissing all the beauty and love in the world and focusing in on the ugliness. Collectively, we project our ugliness outward and create war, famine, disease, and suffering.

When you choose to see beauty in the world and enjoy it, seeing the positive instead of the negative, you are being very wise. You will begin to feel accepting and calm, and express peacefulness in your actions, thoughts, emotions, and communication. You will respond to violence and aggression with compassion, not violence.

Acquiring wisdom is like working your muscles to strengthen them. First, you have to commit to being wise. Then, in every circumstance where you have the choice between accessing wisdom (being loving and accepting) or giving in to your ego's need to be right and powerful, you have to choose wisdom. If you make a mistake and give in to your ego, then as soon as you realize it, you must vow to be wiser the next time. You have to be determined to change your old, unwise way of thinking and operating, but you also have to be forgiving of yourself and very patient.

Patience is a crucial part of acquiring and maintaining wisdom. It's easy to become discouraged and think that you, and the world, have too many problems to ever become healed, but you have to let go of that false idea. You must find your courage and keep working on resolving your negative karma, and the karma you share with others, every single day. This is the only way to progress.

We are not very patient people. Our society is very fast-paced. We feel that we should be able to quickly fix problems and help others become wiser. Whenever you are feeling impatient, take a look at history and all the people who had to spend years helping others to become more compassionate, understanding, and just. Susan B. Anthony, the leader of the women's movement in the nineteenth century, lived to be over 100, and yet, for all her hard work to help American women win the right to vote, the amendment granting women's suffrage didn't pass until long after she was dead—but it passed. If she hadn't put forth her efforts over many decades, it would have taken much, much longer to achieve this goal. You can never know when your own efforts will pay off. Tomorrow might be the day when everything turns around. Your goal might be achieved the day after you die. You have to keep going, keep doing what you know you need to do, and trust in the timing of the Universe.

Remember, too, that it used to take hundreds of years for ideas to spread across the globe. Now, it can take seconds! It's funny how the faster information moves, the more impatient we get. We get a new computer with more processing capability and the old one that used to seem so fast now seems super slow! We have to develop the wisdom to understand how we created our problems and what we need to change. Then we have to have the patience to accept our limitations and accept the timing of things even as we have the courage to continue our healing work.

When we become wise, we inspire others—even people we've never met, who only hear about our stories of triumph, patience, and acceptance. You cannot inspire everyone. Only the people who are ready to be lifted up to a higher level of awareness will be encouraged by your wisdom. Some people aren't ready to let go of their anger and their victimhood.

Every single good act you perform, with good intention, helps heal the broken world and is recorded in heaven. Even the smallest acts of kindness, from letting someone else take a parking space that you came upon first to putting out birdseed in the wintertime, are noted. Never underestimate the healing power of kindness.

Feel gratitude. Express it. So often, people will do nice things for us, and we are in too much of a hurry to notice or say "thank you." Every day, my friend thanks the crossing guard in front of her son's school when the guard stops the traffic so that they can get across the street. I constantly tell people I love them and that I'm glad they're in my life. Creating good karma in this way heals us and the entire world a little bit at a time—and a little bit is a lot.

The moment you start to feel cynical or pessimistic, stop yourself. Look around you at your blessings, take the time to feel gratitude, and give thanks to God. Say "thank you for all you do for me" to everyone who helps you. This will make a big difference in your ability to achieve wisdom.

Wisdom, Totality, and Karma

We know the Law of Wisdom works with the Law of Totality because when we recognize our connection to all of creation, we no longer overvalue our ego or fool ourselves into believing that we can make the world conform to our expectations. We understand and accept the limits of our power, and we take responsibility for our part in healing the world.

Wisdom gives us the power to erase negative karma. We do this by practicing acceptance and courage. Tapping in to divine wisdom through intuition, we discover the karma we've been afraid to face. The little voice that says "This relationship doesn't feel right to me" is a call to recognize karmic issues and resolve them in order to avoid suffering.

Remember, wisdom isn't a collection of facts, and being wise doesn't mean that you know more than anyone else does. Wisdom is about self-honesty, acceptance, and courage. If you get stuck analyzing your psychological issues but do not use courage to resolve them, you will remain unwise and make the same mistakes over and over again. A good therapist will confront you if you continually make excuses for not being courageous or changing the way you think and act. A therapist should never reinforce feelings of victimhood. Instead, she should understand and accept how you feel but help you to change your negative thoughts and actions. Otherwise, you are wasting your time and money and perpetuating your suffering. The more you work on your patterns, the more you can tolerate the uncomfortable feelings you experience when you look honestly at what you've been doing and the distorted thoughts that have been driving you, the less pain you will cause yourself.

I have often had clients in my clinical practice who left therapy because they didn't want to change. They didn't want me to gently push them out of their comfort zone, challenging them to leave behind their stories of suffering and do the hard work of healing their karma. It's frustrating when you can see what someone needs to do but don't have the power to get them to do it. But when someone walks away from therapy because she wants to avoid facing her issues, I can only bless her. I know that the next person who walks in the door may be someone who is truly open to change, and that it

The Eleven Eternal Principles

is not my job to try to fix everyone and everything. In a world with so many problems, it can be hard to remember that truth, but I know that by trusting in and working with the Law of Karma, I am doing as much as I can to heal others and myself.

The Lesson of the Law of Wisdom:

Acceptance, courage, gratitude, and discernment are divine.
Anger, jealousy, sadness, and judgment are man-made.

God doesn't want us to suffer. We created suffering by choosing to live a mortal life and creating negative karma that had to be resolved. Every one of us has personal karma, family karma, and group karma. Together, we share global karma. This karma causes us great sadness. We feel angry, jealous, and despair because of the pain we create for ourselves and others.

If you live according to the Eternal Principles, you will reclaim your power to let go of these man-made problems and use the remedy of wisdom to heal yourself. You will stop feeling the need to blame others, or fate, for your problems, and no longer look at yourself as a victim with little power to change your life. You will be able to discern what you can change and what you cannot, and you will accept that reality.

Often, it takes many years to become wise. The ancient Chinese believed that women reach the age of wisdom after menopause because the power of the mind increases when the hormones are no longer a strong influence. Teenagers, who have many hormonal shifts in their bodies, are often confused and moody, and unable to see clearly. People with chemical imbalances can also have difficulty attaining wisdom because of the influence of their biochemistry. There are many reasons why we may have difficulty achieving wisdom, but most of us are able to gain a little wisdom each day if we align ourselves with the Eternal Principles. If tragedy strikes, we have the choice to grow from it and become wiser than we ever dreamed possible.

In most cultures throughout history, people looked to elders for wisdom. In our culture, we do not know who to turn to when so many people remain stuck in their negative karma. We've become distrusting of priests and leaders because they have too often betrayed our trust or proven to be lacking in wisdom. We have plenty of information available to us through books, the media, and the Internet but very few wise guides. If only there was a Wisdom Channel on television! After all, if we can have so many cooking and sports channels, shouldn't we have a channel devoted to the important pursuit of wisdom?

If you are lucky enough to find a wise person who can advise you and help you develop your own wisdom, that is wonderful. If not, then commit to spending regular time as an observer of your life. Notice your suffering and explore it so that you can learn from it. You can choose to stop being absorbed by your man-made, negative emotions and let go of the story of yourself as a victim with all sorts of problems. Claim your birthright as a wise and courageous person who makes good decisions, who doesn't run from pain but instead walks through it in order to find the hidden lesson it offers and turn your troubles into the soil that grows beautiful flowers.

THE FOURTH
ETERNAL PRINCIPLE:

The Law of Love

Pure, unconditional love heals our karma
and our hatred and reminds us of
our divine nature.

Let me not to the marriage of true minds
Admit impediments. Love is not love
Which alters when it alteration finds,
Or bends with the remover to remove.
O, no! It is an ever-fixed mark
That looks on tempests and is never shaken;
It is the star to every wondering bark,
Whose worth is unknown, although his height be taken.
Love's not Time's fool, though rosy lips and cheeks
Within his bending sickle's compass come:
Love alters not with his brief hours and weeks,
But bears it out even to the edge of doom.
If this be error and upon me proved,
I never writ, nor no man ever loved.
—William Shakespeare, Sonnet 116

Shakespeare eloquently captured the beauty of divine, unconditional love—the love that is our natural inheritance. Unfortunately, we turn away from the Law of Love and engage in judgment, hatred, and cruelty. When we do love others, we love them conditionally. We'll say "I love you" to our partner, and claim to love humanity, but when people disappoint us with their imperfections, we quickly withdraw our love.

We're here on earth to love one another, no matter how challenging it is to be loving. We're not here to merely survive another day. We hate, harm, and kill because of our fear that if we do not harm others, they will harm us first, and because of our ego's obsession with staying alive at all costs. Our soul is much wiser than our ego is. It knows that physical survival isn't everything. It knows that it is better to love and risk death than to survive by any means necessary. Our soul is capable not of merely loving someone we like a lot, but of unconditionally loving everyone, including those who have hurt us or who act in evil ways.

The Ways in Which We Love

Love takes many different forms: You can feel love toward your family, yourself, your community, your environment, your work, your neighbors, your pets, your fellow man, your God, your people, and so on. But pure, divine love is a natural driving force, a state of mind or consciousness that few ever really achieve. It requires an extremely high level of acceptance, courage, and faith: acceptance of people and situations, courage to do what is right even when it is painful or risky to do so, and faith that karma will ultimately provide justice so there is no need to play judge and jury in any circumstance.

Often, when we think of powerful love, we think of romance. Romantic love can inspire great kindness and compassion. When you first fall in love and the world feels magical, you find yourself acting lovingly toward everyone. However, your ego can quickly get in the way; you focus on everything you do not like about your partner and wish for a perfect relationship that runs smoothly, all the time. When you become disillusioned by the relationship, you need to take notice of your false expectations. Let go of your self-pity and commit to accepting your partner exactly as he or she is. Learn from whatever the relationship can teach you. Otherwise, your objections toward your partner will pile up and you will create more negative feelings and thoughts, dimming the light of your love.

Hard as it is to love unconditionally those who we like and enjoy, it is even harder to love and accept people we do not like. Everyone has at least one person in his life that is very difficult to love. These people are a challenge, offering us an opportunity to grow in our ability to be accepting and loving. Hardest of all, however, is feeling unconditional love for those who have harmed us. But it is our job to love them anyway.

Love, untainted by the conditions we often place on it, is incredibly powerful and healing for ourselves, for others, and for the world. Divine, authentic love isn't affected by our man-made laws. Authentic love is transcendent. It allows us to rise above our fear, anger, and sadness. It causes us to see that we should never hate anyone and that there is never any excuse for cruelty.

Love is healing. It inspires words and actions that are in alignment with divine law. When we feel genuine love, we are energized and become creative. We see solutions instead of problems, and we deepen our wisdom and understanding. We act with kindness.

Love reminds us of our connection to God and to each other, healing the pain of feeling alone and alienated and giving us the courage to reach out to others with compassion despite the risk of being hurt. Love drives out our fears and allows us to give up our need to control other people. It frees us from defensiveness and anxiety, and causes our negative emotions and thoughts to fall away.

We use the word "love" so often that we forget what authentic love is. We "love" what we see in the window of the clothing store, or "love" getting a raise at work. Again and again, I have clients insist that they've fallen in love with a man they've just met, only to tell me a few weeks later that they hate him. They wonder, "What was I thinking?"

Genuine, divine, authentic love is unconditional, never domineering or demanding. When you say things like, "I love my sister, but until she agrees with me and admits she's wrong, I'm going to stay mad at her," you are putting conditions on your love. But when you can say, "We disagree, and although I think she's wrong, I love her and I accept that she doesn't always see things my way," you are experiencing authentic love. Authentic love sends others an invitation to love unconditionally as well.

Unconditional Love versus Negative Emotions

Pure love never creates negative emotions; it heals them. In contrast, giving in to anger, resentment, jealousy, or sadness dims the powerful light of love. Imagine a clear glass of fresh water sitting in the sunlight, and then putting a teaspoonful of dirt into it and stirring. The entire glass of water becomes polluted. It loses its transparency and purity, and sunlight cannot shine through it. This is what happens to love when we foul it with dark, heavy, negative emotions.

Because we all have karma, there will always be times when we are plagued by negative emotions and are not as loving as we should be and make excuses for our mean-spirited and destructive behaviors. In online message boards or behind someone's back, it is easier to be unkind because we do not have to look into the eyes of the person we are hurting. It's a lot harder to justify our cruelty when we express it face-to-face.

To align ourselves with divine law, we have to commit ourselves to acknowledging when we are not loving others unconditionally and not acting in accordance with the Eternal Principle of Love. That's when we have to push ourselves to love more perfectly, no matter how difficult it is to do so. We cannot let our negative emotions rule us, or we will be defying the divine Law of Love.

When you love unconditionally, you do not feel anger or sorrow, you feel joy and excitement. You want to succeed, and yet you are so happy for other people's triumphs that you do not mind whether or not you get credit for what you achieve. Your ego doesn't get in the way of healing yourself and loving others. Every time you choose love over fear or other negative emotions, your love will be further cleansed of its imperfections. You will feel even stronger and more loving. Unconditional love allows you to feel a sense of well-being even when your circumstances are troublesome, and it will foster your courage and wisdom.

Why It Is So Hard for Us to Love Unconditionally

Jesus said, "Love your neighbor as you love yourself," but we often find it very difficult to do this. First, we have to love ourselves unconditionally and let go of any painful beliefs we are holding on to, such as "I'm not a good person" or "I do not deserve to be happy." Low self-esteem can only be healed by unconditional love for one's self. We have to be able to love and accept ourselves as we are, right now, in this moment. Only then can we hope to love others unconditionally.

When we forget the Law of Totality, we become self-centered or focus only on ourselves and the people around us. We forget our duty to love everyone regardless of their behavior or whether we like or even know them. Without meaning to be cruel, we are often oblivious to how our actions affect strangers we may never meet. We do not think about the children who develop asthma because of the extra air pollution created whenever we drive our cars unnecessarily. We do not feel compassion for the Iraqis who have been injured or killed, or who have lost their homes because we chose to invade their country. We avoid thinking about them because we do not like to admit that we've harmed others.

Whether we've hurt someone we know or created negative karma in the world by being selfish, neglectful, or cruel, personally or as part of a group, it is painful to consider that we have behaved badly. To heal ourselves, and others, we have to open up to that feeling of discomfort and suffering. We must be honest with ourselves about what we have done and what we are doing. Too often, we ignore the suffering we have caused in others until our karma forces us to deal with it by bringing about situations that cause us to suffer terribly as well.

What Happens When We Do Not Love Unconditionally?

When we put conditions on love, we try to control what is beyond our power to control. We may withhold our love in an attempt to make others come around to our point of view, or until they behave the way we want them to. We become judgmental and punishing and create a lot of damage in our lives, because we destroy relationships and hurt other people's feelings. Unconditional love is expansive, open, and accepting, not constricting. When you reject it, you lock yourself and everyone else in a prison and then feel hopeless about finding the key that will allow you to escape from suffering. The key is unconditional love.

When we do not love others unconditionally, we send the message that they are unlovable. These negative messages never motivate anyone to heal. Instead, they cause people to feel so awful that they increase their resistance to personal honesty, healing, and transformation. They may fight back or withdraw and hide. The only way to have any hope of bringing someone around to a more loving, healthy state of being is through love. The only cure for darkness is light. Adding more darkness to a situation only makes everything darker.

When you do not unconditionally love yourself and others, you pollute your small corner of the world. If you think of yourself as connected to all other beings and creatures in an energy grid, then every time you create darkness through unloving thoughts, feelings, and actions, you dim the power in that part of the grid, creating a dark spot.

The way we treat others and ourselves affects the leadership in the world and the actions of large groups of people. If you become angry with your neighbor because you feel he's not keeping up his house and therefore is dragging down the value of your property, you should try to talk to him. If he is completely resistant, you can calmly let him know that his inactions leave you no choice but to ask the local government to enforce the ordinances concerning property maintenance. But if you hurry over to city hall to file a complaint before talking to him you are being warlike. How can we create peace in the world when we are so quick to do battle with others? Being loving requires us to overcome our fears about confrontation and disapproval. Naturally, there are times when you should speak to someone through an intermediary for your own safety, but too often, people perceive their neighbor to be their enemy and give up on finding common ground before they've even attempted to have a conversation and work out their disagreement. You might learn your neighbor hasn't painted his porch or fixed his broken windows because he's living on a fixed income and cannot afford to do the maintenance.

Sometimes, other people aren't willing to make peace with us or find common ground. If you unconditionally love and accept someone you disagree with, despite seeing no signs that he is willing to love you back or treat you well, then you have a good chance of bringing about tranquility into your life and into your corner of the world. Ask yourself, how important is it for that person to do what you want him to do?

It can be hard to be patient and accepting when you see so much suffering and injustice all around, and when you are in pain yourself. But if you let your ego get in the way, you will prevent yourself from healing your soul and resolving your karma. You will be unable to contribute to the healing of the planet and humankind.

The ego generates impatience and arrogance. It's our inner voice that says, "If only everyone would just conform to my vision of the world, then we could have peace and harmony." It's our egos that make us want to pressure others to see things our way—for their own good! Bullying, intimidation, sarcasm, and scolding never lead to peace and harmony, but our egos drag us back into warlike behavior again and again. We use religion not as a tool for spiritual healing and growth but as a weapon against others. We insist our belief system is right and mistreat others who disagree with our ideas about God, which violates God's divine Law of Love.

Our arrogance and disrespect to others have reached the point that the earth itself is rebelling. An increase in the number and intensity of earthquakes, tsunamis, hurricanes, and cyclones is the result of our negative vibrations making the earth ill. We have to evolve in order to save our planet. I believe that if enough of us start living from a place of authentic love and acting with compassion for all that we will prevent the destruction of our planet and the human race. We must work harder at aligning ourselves with divine law instead of man-made law.

Controlling Our Emotions So That We Can Love Unconditionally

If we do not align ourselves with the Eternal Principle of Love and love everyone, including ourselves, without condition, our egos will take over, making us feel insecure and frightened. Fear leads to sin. You may not consciously want to hurt anyone, but then you convince yourself it is okay to be dishonest, manipulative, or even abusive because in the moment, it feels powerful to control other people.

We may try to justify our selfish or harmful behavior rather than admit we are doing something wrong and so we can then correct ourselves. Afterward, we feel terrible about what we've done, which makes us dislike ourselves, so we avoid the pain of our guilt by pushing that emotion back into our subconscious. The more we give in to our ego's need to be right and in control, and accept its excuses for our negative feelings, selfish thoughts, and harmful actions, the harder it is to shift back into authentic, pure love for ourselves and others.

Negative emotions are very powerful and can pull anyone away from the light of love into the darkness of fear, anger, and despair. Many people grew up in families where they weren't taught how to recognize and deal with their emotions. They act in unloving ways even if they do not truly want to harm anyone. They need guidance to learn how to stop being ruled by their feelings. Managing negative emotions is a skill anyone can learn through therapy, self-help books, and workshops if they're willing to put in time and effort.

Teenagers have an especially difficult time with emotions because their hormones can intensify their feelings. The mood swings they experience can frighten them just as much as they frighten the teenager's parents and siblings. Suddenly, the young person is angry, sad, or insecure and doesn't know why. If she's not shown how to accept and work through these feelings, and taught that all emotions are temporary and will subside, she might panic and start repressing her feelings. To ease her suffering, a teenager may drink, use drugs, and even cut herself.

Teenagers, like many troubled adults, do not have good impulse control. The part of their brain that allows for higher reasoning and self-control is not fully developed. They act in the moment without truly understanding the consequences of their actions. They sometimes commit acts of violence against themselves or others because they are not mature enough to genuinely grasp what death means. Parents become understandably frightened by their teenager's poor judgment and will try to control their teenaged children through punishment and rules. They may become quick to judge and stop listening carefully to what their teens are communicating. Even if they want to hear what their child has to say, it can be challenging because teenagers can be insecure, intimidated, and inarticulate.

It's never too late to start teaching children how to identify their feelings and recognize that feelings aren't so powerful after all, and can be taken charge of. But if you are a parent who wants to teach this lesson, you must learn it for yourself first, otherwise you will have no credibility.

If you are an adult struggling with addiction or self-destructive behavior, it may be because you've never learned how to unconditionally love yourself. If you do not unconditionally love yourself, the pain of self-hatred can be so intense that you feel you must blot it out by drinking, gambling, or buying things you want but cannot afford. All of these behaviors will only worsen your situation and create more pain for you. You must begin healing yourself and your karma by loving yourself exactly as you are.

The Art of Loving Unconditionally

To experience unconditional love for ourselves and others, we have to refrain from focusing on ourselves and our problems. Pessimism and complaints take us away from feelings of love and repel those who love us. I'm not saying that you have no reason to be unhappy. Everyone has troubles, and some people face tremendous challenges in life. I have known people who have suffered from chronic pain for years, or who have been victims of violence or abuse, or who have experienced one loss after another. Life is very difficult for some, but the recipe for healing remains the same for everyone. Generating negative emotions always dims the light of love, while creating positive emotions makes it easier for us to love.

To get your mind off of your own woes, concentrate on others and their needs. Volunteer your time and help other people. There are opportunities everywhere. Every time you act kindly toward someone who is ill or under stress, you will connect with your loving feelings and feel empowered. It's easy to fall into the trap of thinking that if you cannot fix all the world's problems, you might as well do nothing at all. But any small step you take toward healing yourself or helping others heal can be significant, and will take you out of the habit of feeling sorry for yourself.

Love yourself unconditionally. By understanding that you, like everyone else, have to live by the Law of Karma, you will come to see why you behave in ways that cause you to feel guilty or ashamed afterward. You must forgive yourself, and love yourself unconditionally. Only then can you break your bad habits and act more lovingly.

By loving and accepting yourself, you open yourself up to even more love and find it much easier to be kind and compassionate toward others. People will want to be around you and do things for you to ease your burdens. Feelings of pessimism and isolation will disappear as you discover that self-love and self-acceptance draw to you people who are also loving and accepting.

Unconditional love for yourself and others erases negative karma and delivers health and balance to your life. It actually helps your body to heal and have a strong immune system. Allow your love to flow freely rather than blocking it with pride or dimming its clarity with the pollutants of hatred, anger, resentment, jealousy, and depression. As you begin to experience the feeling of well-being, it'll be easier for you to act in a loving way toward yourself and others, even when you are in a crisis. Nurture and kindness flow forth from unconditional love.

The way we love when we are allowing our ego to be in charge is a false kind of love. It causes us to be very controlling and creates suffering for everyone. Authentic love unites people by driving out fear. We connect to each other very powerfully at an energy level when we experience this divine form of love. In fact, if you are at the deathbed of someone you love very dearly, and you tell them you love them, they're very likely to linger on rather than passing into the other realm because you are extending them a lifeline. They will hold on to life for your sake. This is why so often people will say, "I cannot believe that I was at my mother's side every minute. Then as soon as I stepped out of her hospital room to get some coffee, she died." That happens because even when someone is comatose, their soul is aware of the love connection and will not find the courage to break it until you break it or you give them permission, saying, "I'm here, I love you, and it is okay for you to leave me now." Loving unconditionally means letting them go so that their suffering on earth can end.

Our connection to others, including strangers, becomes apparent to us when we love unconditionally. We start to care about how our actions affect others. It's not that we feel guilty all the time, but that we are conscious of what we are doing. The other day my friend and I were in a drugstore ready to check out, and she said, "Let's go to the register at the cosmetics counter. I bought some makeup, and I know that the clerk in cosmetics makes a small commission if she rings it up." Similar thoughtful acts of kindness and generosity will come easily and naturally when you make a point of connecting to love and loving more perfectly. You will see opportunities to be compassionate, and you will feel generous. You will stop seeing yourself as just another victim of circumstances in an uncaring world, and you will stop thinking, "I cannot be bothered to help anyone else. I have too many troubles of my own. Let someone else deal with the problem. It's too inconvenient for me to be nice or generous right now."

Loving unconditionally is easier when you have wisdom. Wisdom allows you to see clearly, to step back from a situation and from your feelings of hurt or anger and observe what's really happening. It allows you to depersonalize people's negative behavior. You will see that they are operating out of fear and have their own karmic issues to resolve that may have nothing to do with you. The person who is rude to you may be frightened that if he isn't in control of every situation, he will suffer. Love him and do not let his negativity dim your love. When He was crucified, Jesus said, "Forgive them Father, for they know not what they do." People act out of unconscious fear, anger, and self-hatred all the time. They truly may not be aware of how cruel they're being, and if you point it out to them, they may go into deep denial to avoid the pain of facing their issues.

Wisdom allows us to see that we cannot force people into being honest with themselves or with us. You may be brilliant at analyzing their problems, and able to explain to them what you think is causing their behavior, but it may not have any effect on their denial and lack of self-awareness. As someone who counsels people, I have to have the wisdom to accept that I cannot change anyone. I can only lead the horse to water; I cannot make him drink!

In fact, many people have deep-rooted psychological issues that the most well-trained and highly skilled psychologist in the world wouldn't be able to help them heal. Love others, accept them as they are, and pray for them, but do not let your ego get in the way and tell you, "I understand what's wrong with this person. I'll just explain what she's doing wrong and tell her she'd better fix her behavior, or else." That kind of attitude is not loving and will only cause you pain.

When I offer this advice to people who are agonizing over someone else's behavior, again and again I hear, "I cannot do that. I cannot accept the situation. I'm not Jesus Christ." None of us is, but loving in a Christ-like way should be our goal.

To make it easier to love unconditionally, start by acknowledging that you've fallen short of that goal. You will feel better right away. Catholics practice confession in order to cleanse themselves of denial, guilt, and self-loathing so that they can love more perfectly and begin acting in a more loving way toward themselves and others. Once you are in a more loving state, you will discover ways in which you can make a situation better. You will find the courage to call someone and say, "I'm sorry," and you will be able to learn the lesson your suffering has to teach you.

If the person you reach out to won't accept your apology or forgive you, accept that. Look at them with love and recognize that by not being able to forgive you and move past what happened, they are holding on to pain. Have compassion for them. Allow them to change in their own time.

Sometimes it seems people will never change, but there is always hope. I had a client once who was very unhappy in her marriage because her husband was cruel and callous, but she didn't want to leave him because she was financially dependent on him. She asked me about his future, and I told her that her husband would not live a very long life, but that something tragic would befall him and cause him to become a much more loving and kind person. My prediction made her angry and she stopped calling me, but a few years later she got back in touch and told me that her husband had been diagnosed with cancer and undergone a dramatic transformation. Facing death opened his heart and made him loving, caring, and generous. Before he died, he was able to resolve some of his karma and make his last years with her very happy ones.

Not everyone makes this leap, however, which is why we are so amazed when we see miraculous changes in people. Most of us have to work methodically, for many years, to heal our karma and stop behaving in ways that cause suffering. Healing ourselves takes patience, hard work, and time, which allow us to gain perspective and wisdom, and help our negative feelings to fade. Everyone heals at a different pace, and some people are stronger than others are. Unconditional love, wisdom, and an understanding of the Law of Karma make it easier to accept that you can only change yourself, not others, and even then, transformation isn't easy.

To love unconditionally, we have to start by accepting ourselves, other people, and situations exactly as they are right now. We have to recognize that each of us is on our own spiritual journey and will make mistakes. Giving in to anger, despair, hatred, judgment, or frustration prolongs everyone's suffering.

Our resistance to accepting things as they are lowers our vibration and takes us away from divine love. No matter how hard we try to force a situation, we cannot fix it until we heal ourselves.

My client Theresa has a son named Michael who is married to Sandy, a kind, hard-working young woman. I know Sandy is a good person because I have met her a few times, but Theresa has a long history of finding excuses for not liking her son's romantic partners. Theresa criticized Sandy so often and started so many battles with Michael that finally, he got fed up and he and Sandy stopped speaking to Theresa and her husband, who has sided with his wife. His absence causes Theresa great pain, but her ego will not allow her to admit that she created her suffering. She cannot see that it isn't her son that needs to change. If she is to have any hope of healing her relationship with her son, Theresa needs to heal herself first. She needs to look at why she feels such a need to control and judge other people to the point where she alienates them. Recently, Theresa began squabbling with her daughter, insisting that her new boyfriend is "no good." Until Theresa unconditionally loves and accepts herself, she will continue to suffer and act in the same old destructive way.

One of the ways to discover what it is you need to heal within yourself is to look at the people who most upset you. They are often mirrors for the issues you have not faced in yourself. If you cannot stand how stubborn your child is, take a look at your own stubbornness. Look, too, at how you've dealt with other stubborn people. If your father had to have things his way, and your romantic partners haven't considered your feelings or needs, and your bosses do not listen to your ideas, the problem may be that you need to be stronger and less willing to conform to what others want. You may be in the habit of overreacting to any small sign of stubbornness because you think, "Uh oh, this person is going to push me around and make me miserable." As long as you hold that belief, you won't bring yourself and the other person to common ground. You will get stuck in resistance and suffering, and stubbornness will remain a hot button issue for you.

It takes a lot of love to replace fear, anger, and resistance and create harmony with others. Unconditional love brings people together, even when just one person is willing to try to love authentically. When you are loving and accepting, you not only melt your own negative emotions, you also help others let go of their fear, anger, resentment, and despair. You heal yourself and others by changing the energy vibration, raising it to a much higher level.

When Jesus said, "Love your enemy," He understood just how difficult it is to do so. He didn't say, "Love your enemy, unless he's really awful and it's hard to love him, in which case you are off the hook." He also didn't say, "Love your enemy, and let him walk all over you, cross all your boundaries, and mistreat you." The way to love unconditionally without getting badly hurt is to be clear on what your boundaries are, be honest with yourself about your weaknesses and needs, and accept that you may not be able to influence the other person to change.

The same advice applies to international problems. People often say, "You cannot reason with a terrorist," which is true, but no one is saying that is the only way to love our enemies unconditionally. What we can do is to love terrorists enough to set firm boundaries and do our best to prevent them from creating negative karma. At the same time, we have to empathize with their frustration, fear, and desire to control others. If we can do that, we can understand why they became terrorists, and we can be effective in preventing others from turning to a life of violence and religious fanaticism. We can inspire people who interact with terrorists to see them as they really are—a force of evil—and influence them to stop supporting terrorism. We have to defuse terrorism the way we defuse a bomb, with care and precision, instead of confronting it with force and violence. It takes courage to face difficult problems. Great evil happens when good people look the other way and say, "It's not my problem and I don't want to risk speaking up." Terrorists have families and friends who might inspire them to stop creating negative karma. Even if we can do nothing to influence terrorists—or criminals, or anyone else who is cruel—we can influence those around them. By practicing unconditional love and acting in a loving way, we inspire others to do the same, to embrace love instead of hatred, and to stand up to evil. The darkness of evil disappears when we bring in the power of light and love.

Too often, we buy into the man-made idea that power lies in force instead of in love. Love and kindness are always more powerful than force. But we become so terrified of the pain we might feel if a situation does not unfold the way we'd like it to that we blind ourselves to the truth. We are so afraid of suffering that we hurriedly join in the battle, trying to outwit, outsmart, and outmaneuver whoever we think is our enemy. Our fear, anger, and vindictiveness weaken us, and we become cynical and depressed when we see how powerless we are to influence others through force.

You can work toward the goal of loving perfectly by aiming to be more loving every day, in every moment. Pray for everyone who is sick or suffering, and send them your love. Every time you hear about something terrible happening in the world, stop and create a feeling of love and wish for every person to feel love in his heart. When you are angry or hurt, stop yourself, forgive yourself and others, and create a feeling of love. Never go to bed angry. Create a feeling of peace as you drift off to sleep, and when you wake up, generate a feeling of love to start your day.

The Lesson of the Law of Love:

Nurturing and kindness are divine.
Stealing, killing, hatred, and betrayal are man-made.

Despite all the justifications people have for being cruel to others, God doesn't buy any of their arguments! The Law of Karma prevails regardless of our reasons for acting out of alignment with the Law of Love.

Free yourself from the suffering caused by operating according to man-made laws. The moment you recognize you are speaking negatively or treating someone disrespectfully, notice it and recognize that you are in a state of anger and ego, dimming the brilliant power of your love. Forgive yourself and change your thoughts immediately, so you can generate feelings of love and compassion for yourself and others.

Nourish your love through your everyday actions. Stop yourself every single time you feel angry and vindictive, and recognize that your feelings are out of alignment with divine law.

Always remember that other people, even children, have their own karma. You cannot control anyone, so do not frustrate yourself by trying to do so. You can attempt to guide people by lovingly expressing the truth to them and clearly setting boundaries to protect yourself, and you can prevent a lot of suffering for yourself by sticking to your boundaries. Do not compromise what is most important to you, but do not let your ego dictate your priorities, either. Unconditional love means allowing others to make their own decisions and find happiness in their own way. If your ego is in charge, when others do not follow your plan and have different ideas about how to live, your feelings of love and acceptance disappear. As soon as you stop unconditionally loving others, you start drifting toward the man-made laws that make excuses for harsh judgment and cruelty.

You cannot live anyone else's life for them and you cannot fix problems through force. When you live according to the Eternal Principle of Love, you recognize and accept that some people are born with more immature souls or more unresolved karma than others (this is why you will often see a family whose children grew up without any serious problems, except for one child who constantly struggles and is chronically in trouble). Living according to the Law of Karma makes it easier to accept that we all differ in our ability to handle life and make good decisions.

Do not let anyone convince you that we "have" to kill people who have harmed us or that we have to hurt others in order to get them to change their ways and do what we want them to do. Have faith that everyone will eventually learn from the karma they create and let go of your need to be their judge and jury. Trust that they will awaken to divine law more quickly, and will stop inflicting pain on themselves and others, if you let the light of your unconditional love shine brightly for the world to see.

THE FIFTH
ETERNAL PRINCIPLE:

The Law of Harmony

There is divine order in the universe,
and we are meant to be in harmony
with everyone and everything.

When I think of harmony, I often think of music—of notes working together to create beautiful sounds that are both soothing and energizing. Of course, much of the music recorded over the last few decades lacks harmony, but that's because it reflects the discord in our world.

Musical harmony has often been said to be reflective of God and to have the potential to connect us with the spiritual realm. In the Middle Ages, composers avoided certain musical intervals because these sounds were said to draw people away from God and toward sin. Instead they wrote music using intervals that were considered spiritual. That day when I was five years old and nearly drowned in the river near my home in Romania, I heard music that could only be described as heavenly, beautiful beyond anything I'd ever heard. It calmed my fears and made me feel completely at peace with this strange, unearthly experience. I now realize I was hearing the music of divine harmony.

In fact, music can be tremendously effective for creating feelings of peace and balance. It even has healing powers. Claudius Conrad, M.D., a classical pianist and surgeon, published research showing that by listening to Mozart's music we can lower our blood pressure and reduce the need for pain medication. He believes Mozart, who often suffered from illnesses, was drawn to creating certain combinations of notes that eased his discomfort. Singing or chanting, which creates the vibration of music in our bodies, has a similar healing effect. It connects us to the Divine and raises our own vibrations, freeing us from negative thoughts and feelings. According to Ayurvedic medicine, singing the sacred syllable AUM (the three letters in the word stand for the names of the gods of water, fire, and air) affects every cell in the body and our biofield of energy, healing any disharmony. Most religious traditions include some form of chanting or singing designed to help people feel connected to the Divine. These practices actually allow people to resonate with spiritual energy.

Harmony goes beyond music, however. It's an energetic state in which you are aligned with divinity and in balance. When you are in harmony, you are healthy, happy, and creative. When you are in disharmony, you are out of balance and experiencing disturbances in your mood, mind, and body.

Even if you are biologically healthy, the psychological disturbances caused by your disharmony and imbalance will manifest as physical illness.

Harmony is the opposite of chaos and confusion. Harmonious music and the harmonious placement of objects in a room reflect divine order. They are not only lovely, they are vitalizing. Most people have trouble feeling calm and energized in a cluttered room with clothes spilling out of dresser drawers and on the floor. We feel frustrated when we cannot find things and drained by the sight of all the unbalanced piles. The art of Feng Shui is based on the idea that by balancing the flow of energy in your living space, you can balance the flow of energy in your life and free any trapped energy that is blocking you from feeling healthy and happy. When everything is in order and balanced aesthetically, energy flows the way it is meant to and you experience peace, beauty, and joy.

The Divine order of the universe isn't easy to perceive and understand, but whenever you are in alignment with it, everything seems to be working just perfectly. Even problems do not seem to be problems, because you are able to recognize that they're likely to lead you in a good direction. God didn't create a plan and then sit back to watch it unfold. God is always involved in what is happening, intervening at times in order to correct our course. Not long ago, I sold my house in Romania, using a real estate agent who came very highly recommended by a friend. I had no reason to suspect this agent was dishonest, but she seemed to be stalling about sending some documents, and when she arrived in America with them, I thought it was very odd that she had them prepared in a small Romanian town far from where the house was located. She urged me to expedite the deal, so we found a notary and signed the papers. Later, I felt uneasy about our interaction, and I asked God for guidance. I sensed that I should send my copy of the papers to an attorney in Bucharest, so I did. Very soon, he called me up and said, "Carmen, I have some bad news. This woman is a charlatan. According to these papers, she sold your home for a quarter of its worth, and we do not know how much she was really paid by the buyers. . . . But there is some good news, too. The contracts aren't legal. The notary never signed them." The unexpected "mistake" of not having a notary signature saved me from having to go through with the deal, and I was able to get out of it and put the house back on the market for what it was worth. Divinity intervened with a "mistake" that turned out to be quite fortunate, and that set things right.

When you are living in sync with the divine plan, "mistakes" very often turn out to be lucky ones. You find out that you do not have to fix all your problems because many situations work themselves out on their own.

Harmony and the Other Eternal Principles

As energy beings, all of us are intertwined with each other and the universe, working together like an enormously complicated machine that is both organic and creative. The divine plan, which God set into motion, is constantly unfolding and changing, surprising us with its perfection. When we exercise our free will, we can choose to integrate with this plan or fight it. If we submit to it, our lives will be far more harmonious.

The Eternal Principles are intertwined as well, complementing each other and working together perfectly, just like the planets moving in their orbits, never straying. The planets keep each other in place with their gravity. If one were to break away, the entire solar system would become chaotic. This is true of the laws of the Divine as well. When we create harmony, we work with the Law of Totality and maintain balance with our environment and the people around us. We do not fall into an adversarial relationship to the planet, mistreating and dominating it, and it doesn't mistreat or dominate us. We stop competing with others, and we do not feel the need to force them to operate as we do. One of my clients is in constant conflict with her teenage son. She worries about him all the time, and she is always trying to control him or manipulate him into doing what she wants. She won't listen to him and then wonders why he won't listen to her. We cannot create balance by rejecting people or situations and then insist that they change to suit us. We have to recognize that all relationships involve a balance of give and take and that if we want peace and harmony we cannot behave as if we are the only ones with needs and desires that matter.

When you are in a state of harmony and balance, you do not perceive that there are problems all around you, and you do not feel overwhelmed and out of balance. You do not worry about spending too much time at work and neglecting your children, or spending too much time with your children and neglecting your marriage. You create balance because you go with the flow instead of agonizing over your troubles or fighting with people. Using the Law of Wisdom, you recognize which situations you can change and which are beyond your power to fix. You love unconditionally rather than trying to make others conform to your wishes, and trust that if a situation is unjust and imbalanced, the Law of Karma will realign it.

Aligning ourselves with all the Eternal Principles inevitably creates a state of harmony. Through understanding and accepting the Law of Karma and the Law of Love, I was able to let go of any anger or resentment toward the real estate agent who had tried to swindle me. I accepted the situation and the consequences of my choice not to investigate this woman, or real estate prices, before I agreed to work with her, because I am wise enough to recognize that I played a part in creating the situation. I have learned my lesson, and because I try to live according to the Law of Karma and the Law of Harmony, I am creating a state of peace and balance in my life rather than trying to seek revenge against this woman.

Harmonious Relationships

You can choose to live according to the Law of Harmony and create peace and balance in your life, but you have no control over what others choose. This is something you must accept, especially when you enter into a relationship. You can commit to obeying the Law of Harmony, but if your partner isn't willing to as well, you won't be able to create harmony together. Harmony within a relationship requires a commitment to putting the relationship ahead of one's personal fears and needs—you serve the partnership more than you serve yourself. If both partners do not agree to do this, there can be no balance.

All relationships have give and take. To align yourself with the Law of Harmony, you have to pay attention to how much you are giving so that neither you nor your partner has to carry most the weight of making your relationship work. You must have the courage to be honest with yourself and self-correct whenever you recognize that you are being unloving or selfish, and resolve conflicts quickly rather than dragging them out or escalating them.

Creating a harmonious relationship also requires that you not allow your partner to get his or her way all the time or mistreat you. This kind of behavior destroys balance and eventually, the relationship itself. It is also important not to avoid conflicts out of a misguided desire to keep the peace. Genuine harmony requires you to face your painful issues and those of the one you love. Although all partnerships have their high points and low points, overall, in a harmonious relationship there is consistency to how you treat each other, so that each partner feels loved and in a state of peace.

To achieve balance, you must work with the other Eternal Principles, including the Law of Wisdom and the Law of Love. You have to be honest with yourself about your role in any conflicts, and work through your own karma as best you can rather than creating negative karma by treating your partner, or yourself, badly. My clients complain to me about their husbands, looking to me to validate their stories of victimhood. The only way to alleviate their suffering is to be sympathetic and gently guide them into recognizing how they are participating in the drama of their marriage. If we avoid healing ourselves, we will never achieve harmony in our lives or our relationships.

Some marriages aren't meant to be, because one partner is not willing to do the work of serving the relationship and putting it first. I'm convinced that the reason half of marriages end in divorce is because too many people avoid dealing with their own karmic issues. They think that if they leave the marriage they will find a better partner and their lives will run smoothly. But if the problem in the marriage is the karmic baggage you've brought with you, you will carry it right into your next relationship. Then you will end up with the same problems you had before. Regardless of whether or not the relationship works out, trying to align yourself with the Eternal

Principles, including the Law of Harmony, will move you into a more balanced, happy, healthy situation.

And as I have said before, there are people who are psychologically disturbed and unable to participate in healthy relationships with others. Their psychological issues prevent them from creating harmony or consistency. Someone with a personality disorder can be kind, loving, and even charming, then turn around and act completely the opposite when things do not go their way, often blaming others and accusing them of not loving them enough. Someone who engages in compulsive, unbalanced behavior, such as drinking or gambling too much, or putting their addictions ahead of the relationships and their own well-being, is in a chaotic, unhealthy state. These disturbances have to be healed within to create a harmonious relationship with someone else. A very kind and smart young woman I counseled confided to me that she didn't fully trust her fiancé, and from what she had told me, I was certain the marriage was a bad idea. Her fiancé had an enormous amount of psychological baggage, and there were plenty of indications that after the wedding day he would be controlling, miserly, and unfaithful. She didn't want to take a hard look at his inconsistent behavior, preferring to believe that his disturbing characteristics would magically go away once they got married. This is never the case. Our desire to create harmony with others is so strong that we will try to ignore the harsh reality that some people are not ready to work with us. They cannot open up and trust that they will experience joy and love in a relationship. They will not let go of their need to be in control. Some people thrive on conflict. They feel invigorated by a fight and the prospect of intimidating someone else into seeing things their way. They are not yet capable of harmony.

A Harmonious Approach to Changes

The Divine plan is not static. The world is always changing and so are we. But if we align ourselves with the Eternal Principles and recognize how they affect our lives, we won't feel so frustrated by change we cannot control. By creating harmony within, accepting what is, we can raise our vibrations and attract better situations in due time. A man I know suffers from a terrible degenerative disease. As his disease progressed, he faced the difficult choice of dependence on heavy painkillers or being in such agony that he could not drive a car or walk for more than a few feet. He began meditating to try to ease his pain and chose not to resist the situation. By sharing the truth of the situation with his friends instead of hiding it, he learned of a researcher who had studied new medications and methods for alleviating pain, and he now has some new options. In addition, he recognized that working too hard and trying to deny his limitations was worsening his emotional and physical pain, and he took the pressure off of himself to contribute more to his family's household income. Answers and possibilities come to us when we choose to live by the Law of Harmony.

An important aspect of this story is that creativity and connections to others will help you in all sorts of situations. However, you must be open, loving, and trusting to access these resources. Aligning yourself with the Law of Harmony allows you to tap in to all the possibilities available to you, while anger, despair, and resistance to what is happening right now will push away divine help. The best way to deal with unexpected changes is to be accepting yet curious and open to the good that may already be on its way to you, instead of focusing on what you've lost.

Balance and the Male and Female Energies

Earlier, I explained that a circle represents totality and balance. To create harmony in our lives, we need to be in harmony with the divine plan, and we need to balance our energies. Giving and receiving must be balanced. Male and female energies, which everyone has regardless of their gender, must be balanced as well.

According to the Bible, God created Eve to complete Adam. Both male and female energies are needed for harmony and creation. These are opposite energies that complement each other. The male energy is active, and the female energy is receptive. People often mistakenly believe that "receptive" means "passive" or "inert," but receptivity is like a magnetic force. Think of how a paper clip will leap toward a powerful magnet: this is the power of female energy.

All of us have both male and female energy; in fact, in our previous lives, we've all been both men and women. People who are gay or bisexual have more of the opposite gender's energy. If someone is born into a male body but has more female energy, and is attracted to other men, it may be because his soul came here to work out some sexual issues from a previous lifetime. Remember, we can never know the source of our own karma, much less someone else's. The important thing is that we accept ourselves and each other as we are and focus on how we can heal our karma.

In any romantic relationship, heterosexual or homosexual, opposites attract. Someone who has more male energy will be attracted to someone who has more female energy because we are drawn toward achieving balance and harmony. A romantic soul mate is someone who complements you energetically. Very often, your soul mate will have more female energy while you have more male energy, or vice versa. (Of course, as I have said, we are also attracted to people whose karmic issues match up with our own, so your soul mate may feel irresistible to you for this reason as well.)

Two complementary energies fit together like halves of a wheel, allowing both of you to move forward in your growth. Your attraction to each other keeps you together even when you are suffering in the relationship. You may momentarily feel you cannot stand to be with your partner, but you will be irresistibly drawn back to the relationship because your energies complement each other. If you are willing to work together, you can both learn and grow, but if you are resisting the process of healing your karma, you will create disharmony. If the discord becomes too intense, you may break up with your partner, but your energy will remain the same and you will attract a similar partner next time, someone who may be a new soul mate. The attraction to someone who shares your issues is very efficient when you consider that we are here to resolve our karma. No one pushes our buttons and compels us to break out of our old, destructive habits like the person we are intensely attracted to!

Why We Don't Obey the Law of Harmony

We contradict God's plan and create imbalance in the divine order whenever we use our free will to disobey the Law of Harmony. We do this because we haven't been taught to trust in divine order, and we believe that politics, law, and religious edicts are the only way to keep humankind from descending into chaos. We rely on our own minds to solve our problems and organize the world. The man-made laws and rules we design are inadequate, inefficient, and often in direct contradiction to God's laws, so we constantly have to update and refine them. English poet Percy Shelley addressed these fabricated notions in his sonnet, England in 1918:

> *Religion Christless, Godless—a book sealed;*
> *A Senate, Time's worst statute, unrepealed."*
> *Are graves from which a glorious Phantom may*
> *Burst, to illumine our tempestuous day.*

In today's confused world, we must act collectively to destroy the phantom of negativity, the low-vibration energy field in which we've all become trapped as a result of man-made laws.

To discover the divine order, we have to set aside the messages in the man-made world and see through our own limitations. We cannot allow ourselves to be intimidated by left-brained mathematicians and intellectuals who scoff at the idea of synchronicity. There will always be people who insist that encountering an old friend in the most unexpected place is entirely due to statistics and probability, and we shouldn't believe there is any more significance to it. The right brain, which is able to receive messages from the Divine and tune in to divine order, knows better. We do not listen to its wisdom because we are embarrassed by the thought that someone might think we are foolish if we think that the Divine brought that person back into our lives for a reason. When we listen to the right brain, pay attention to coincidences, and notice how the problems in our lives are solved without our having to worry or work at fixing them, we start to believe in divine order. We recognize the subtle messages that God sends us instead of dismissing them or ignoring them altogether.

Another reason we turn our eyes away from divine order is religious dogma. When the great spiritual teachings are reduced to "My God is better than your God," or "My beliefs are right and yours are wrong, so you'd better change yours," religion becomes an excuse for dominating others and leads to conflicts instead of harmony. It's not up to us to figure out why some people are born into one culture and its religious traditions and others are born into another, or why some are raised to value spirituality over dogma and others are taught the opposite. Our job is to accept religious differences while striving to live according to divine law, even when it is difficult to do so and even when it contradicts our own religious training. Priests and religious leaders do not truly grasp the beauty and mystery in their own religion when they interpret their religion's teachings too literally. Any time we use religion to separate one person from other, or use it to punish others, we are creating discord and conflict, and at the same time we are denying the Law of Totality, the Law of Karma, and the Law of Harmony.

We also disobey the Law of Harmony whenever we become too attached to success and security in the physical world, forgetting our eternal nature. Let's say you are living a good life and have some financial security. But you decide it is not enough, because you are scared that something terrible might happen to you, or you are feeling unhappy and you think more money will make you feel better. You want to have a great deal of money for your retirement and yet be able to buy anything you desire today. In short, you are in a scarcity mentality, yearning for more and more. The discord inside of you may drive you to pressure your partner to make more money, regardless of what he wants or whether working more hours is good for his health. Or, you might push yourself to make more money and ignore the toll that working relentlessly is taking on your health and your relationships. Your inner discord creates disharmony outside of yourself.

The solution is to become aligned with harmony and not be so attached to material wealth. You have to recognize that you do not need more money than you already have, and that the cost of acquiring it is going to take you out of balance and cause you to suffer now, or later. If you make more money as a result of living in harmony, then you are meant to have it and you will enjoy it more, because you are not so dependent on it or fearful of losing it.

We also turn away from the Eternal Principle of Harmony because we lose faith in others. We start to believe "if it's meant to be, it's up to me." Alienation happens sometimes, but if you trust in the divine laws, your faith and courage will return to you. Help will arrive, and your circumstances will improve.

When people feel alone and powerless they may turn to deceit, manipulation, and materialism to make themselves feel better, but it never works. Their fear, anger, and depression can eventually lead to physical ailments. You cannot heal painful feelings by achieving power over others or becoming wealthier or more admired. I have counseled celebrities and extremely wealthy people, and believe me, fame and fortune do not create well-being. They are more often a curse, exacerbating the problems we already have. I have seen families use their fortunes to torment each other and embarrass each other in the newspapers, all because they believe they will feel better if they have more power than the people they are angry with. Instead of gaining power, they destroy their relationships, isolate themselves, and become deeply unhappy. The real power lies in living in harmony, in alignment with God's plan.

Globally, we are out of balance, especially with our male and female energies. In ancient times, human beings worshipped both male and female gods. They recognized the power of the sacred feminine, which is a receptive and creative force. Every culture throughout the world once believed in its own individual female gods: Women figures were deified as often as male figures and were esteemed just as highly. Isis, for example, was the mother goddess of Egypt, Ilmater was the creator goddess of the Finnish race, "Mother Earth" was the womb from whom Native Americans believed all humankind sprang forth, and Danaan was the bearer of the first Celts. In Babylonia, the goddess Astarte was regarded as the maker of man and woman. Similarly, Rhea of the Greeks mothered Zeus and the first Olympic gods, and the Romans believed Juno served as the queen of the gods. Indians revered Aditya as the architect of human life and wife of Vishnu, the Chinese saw Dou Mou as the goddess who birthed the first human rulers of the world, and South Americans prostrated in front of the creator goddess, Bachue. Ancient peoples in Southeast Asia looked up to Si Deak Parujar as the female author of humanity, and Yemanja became an important river goddess to the Africans.

But in time, male energy began to be overvalued, and female deities went out of favor or became relegated to minor gods. Men stopped respecting women and revering their ability to bring forth life. Eventually a man had ultimate say over the fate of his children, even though his female partner brought them into the world and cared for them as infants. Tribes began to believe that they needed more than they already had in order to survive. Instead of living in harmony with the divine plan and with other people, they waged war against each other. Men, who could become warriors, were respected more than women, who brought forth life. The consequences continue to be chaos, starvation, and war. Wherever women and female energy are least respected, we find the greatest suffering. We are meant to bring these two complementary energies back into balance. Only then can we stop creating so much pain in the world.

The Benefits of Living According to the Law of Harmony

Living in harmony gives us strength, because when we are in harmony, we don't feel the need to struggle endlessly to make our lives work. We accept what is, trust that things will get better as long as we live in alignment with the Eternal Principles, and find the courage to heal what needs to be healed. By remaining connected to the Divine instead of separating ourselves from God, we have access to all the sacred resources of creativity, strength, and love.

Many people today are caretaking for others and yet also trying to raise children, make the world a better place, and be good friends and spouses. They have very high expectations of themselves. If they are not careful, they will burn out emotionally and physically. You can't keep giving and giving without replenishing yourself. When there is no balance between giving and taking, dysfunction and disease occur. Aligning with harmony restores courage, strength, and trust in the divine plan. By asking for God's help and being open to whatever form that assistance takes, you can unburden yourself and bring yourself back into a state of harmony and balance.

Family and global karma affect our harmony as well. We can try to do everything right and live in accordance with divine law, but something bad still may happen to us because of karma we share with others. The Law of Totality keeps us connected with other people. We have no control over flash floods, earthquakes, or other natural disasters. More and more, such events are happening in unusual places—not long ago, tornadoes appeared in New York—and the disasters are becoming more intense. The global financial crisis, just like global warming, is meant to wake us up to how out of balance and harmony the human race has become.

When we are affected by great tragedies that are out of our personal control, we often feel victimized by these terrible events. Nobody deserves to suffer, but as human beings, we are all connected, so if just one person creates disharmony, it affects other people and even the entire planet.

The good news is that when you live according to the Law of Harmony, you can also affect others, and the world, in a positive way. Even if you cannot personally solve global warming, your decision to compost your table scraps and spoiled food contributes to the health of the planet and creates good karma. Picking up litter someone else dropped and spending a little extra money to buy products without excessive packaging or made locally rather than trucked over long distances all contribute to bringing the world back into balance and harmony. Extending trust and not panicking over money will help ease the financial crisis. And any time you make even the smallest attempt to create harmony with another person, within your community, or in the world, you are healing yourself and others at the same time.

By choosing to live in harmony and staying connected to others instead of isolating yourself, you also end up healing your feelings of powerlessness and alienation. You are able to recognize that you play an important, if small, part in helping other people. The Universe supports you whenever you choose to create harmony and nurture your connection to others and to God.

Living in balance allows you to perceive things differently. You stop thinking of life as a game you have to win by accumulating more power, possessions, and influential friends. You trust that you have enough to meet your needs and take responsibility for creating feelings of happiness no matter if your fortune is good or bad at the moment. You recognize that even when you have suffered a loss, something new and wonderful will come into your life, because that is the nature of the universe. Some things die but then other things are born. Not long ago, a woman I know named Lindsay lost her father, Sam, to cancer. While Lindsay was at her father's bedside, a woman who attended Lindsay's church gave birth to a baby. When Lindsay went to church for the first time after the funeral, she met the woman after the service, saw the baby boy, and learned that the woman had named him Sam. In that moment, she knew her father had sent her a message to remind her that for every death there is a birth, because balance is part of God's divine plan.

Life moves in cycles, from the cycle of the day to the cycle of the year, to the ten-year cycles of our lives. We forget this because we live in a materialistic world that tells us we are not affected by natural cycles, but only need to use our willpower to be in charge of our lives. We are encouraged to achieve more success and acquire more material possessions, never stopping to rest or reflect. Advertisements and the media direct our attention to whatever is new. We're told about the latest trends in everything from parenting to cooking, and urged to watch the hot new television shows on the latest flat-screen, plasma TV. Because we feel isolated and lonely, we go along with these shallow prescriptions. We long to feel connected to others, a part of something larger than ourselves. But taking part in the latest fad or trend is never as satisfying as connecting to others through the force of love.

If you talk to older people and learn about history, or talk to people from other cultures, you will find yourself feeling connected to all of humanity at the level of the heart, or soul. You will realize that people aren't so different after all, and you do not have to win people over to your opinion or your tastes to feel a sense of belonging.

It's also helpful to get out into nature regularly, because nature will remind you of the cycles of life. Notice which flowers bloom every March, and which ones follow a few weeks later. Nature restores our sense of well-being, because its cycles remind us that health and joy can return to us, and that losses are offset when something new comes into our life or when what we thought was gone forever returns to us.

Music is a wonderful tool for bringing yourself back into harmony. Listen to music that uplifts you, and to songs that remind you of happy times in the past. Discover new music so that you can make new, wonderful memories. One of my clients, Suzanne, is a single mother. She had a difficult Christmas season caring for her elderly mother, driving her to and from the hospital while her little girl patiently sat in the back seat. Instead of feeling sad about having to spend so much time in hospitals and watching her mother suffer, Suzanne played Christmas music. One song in particular made her, her mother, and her daughter all laugh. They sang along with it together and played it over and over again. The next Christmas, after her mother had died, Suzanne put on that CD and she and her daughter listened to the song remembering how happy they were singing it the year before. They were sad, as well, but they felt connected to Grandma through that music.

Singing is a wonderful way to create a sense of harmony, as is playing a musical instrument. Through music you can transport yourself out of anger, sorrow, jealousy, or frustration and even lose track of time as you raise your vibration and resonate with positivity. Whenever you create positive feelings, you attune yourself to the divine plan and create harmony.

If you are in conflict with someone, keep in mind that you cannot resolve anything until you create harmony within yourself. Otherwise, you cannot feel compassion and love for the other person, who may not be willing to apologize, make amends, or change their ways. The only way to ease your suffering is to obey the Eternal Principles, including the Law of Love: you have to love that person unconditionally. When you do, you won't feel overwhelmed by anger and resentment should they choose not to create peace with you. By putting yourself in a peaceful state, you strengthen yourself for a confrontation, and you know that you can confront the other person with love.

Never remain silent if you are in conflict with someone. This thoughtless response is a sign of excessive pride, or what the Greeks deemed as *hubris*. First, it is harder to bring yourself back into harmony and balance, and to experience compassion for yourself and the person you are in conflict with whenever you've left something unresolved. Second, your silence may prevent you from helping that person return to a state of harmony with you. As long as you accept that your words may make no difference to the other person, it is almost always a good idea to bring up the difficult issue. If the other person reacts badly, then focus on creating harmony for yourself. Be compassionate toward him, remembering that he is creating his own suffering by choosing to disobey the Law of Harmony.

Whenever you are in pain but do not know where to seek help, ask for divine guidance, and be patient. Divinity will always intervene in some way, though not necessarily how and when you expect it to. As I write this book, people all over the globe are suffering terribly because of the economic crisis. We should all be praying for the divine intervention that will inevitably come. We're starting to realize that we are in need of new leadership, and that we have to do our own part to make the world better. Even the best leaders cannot solve problems if we are not willing to help them. We have to stop putting ourselves and our desires ahead of anyone else, because that creates disharmony. The more we create harmony in our own lives and act in alignment with the Eternal Principles, the more quickly divine intervention will arrive. Like a singer holding a note, we have to work to stay in alignment so that we do not drift out of harmony with the Divine.

The Lesson of the Law of Harmony:

Harmony and peace are divine.
Conflict, competition, and war are man-made.

Harmony causes everything to flourish. Your family life improves, your abundance grows, and your need to be in control disappears. Instead of resisting life, you are able to surrender to the divine plan. You become like a perfectly tuned violin in a sublime orchestra.

But in the man-made world, we do not want to surrender or sacrifice. We believe it is a sign of weakness to compromise and find common ground with others. We see peace as something lovely but fragile and weak, so we try to solve our problems with war or by forcing situations and creating conflicts. We are certain we will win, but then we become angry, frustrated, or depressed because we cannot control other people or the world around us.

Harmony frightens us because we do not trust that we can live in peace. We're afraid of being taken advantage of if we let down our guard. There are many cruel and disturbed people in the world, but if we allow our fear of them to shift us out of balance into a state of suspicion, then we give up something very precious: our inner peace. But the truth is, we do not need to worry about someone else attacking us because we've already allowed our negative thoughts and emotions to inflict damage on us—destroying our own sense of harmony.

When we lose faith in the Law of Harmony, we resort to competition to get what we can in a world where we feel we cannot trust anyone. Competing with others in order to motivate yourself to do better, while maintaining positive feelings about them, is fine. But that is very different from acting through jealousy and envy, or insulting others in order to boost your own ego. If you compete in order to feel powerful and to dominate others, you create discord and suffering.

If you can find the courage to believe in harmony and a divine plan, you will raise your level of consciousness and begin to see it at work in your life. If you let go of your resistance to the Eternal Principles, you can move from merely saying you like harmony and peace to actually experiencing them in your life. You can stop trying to compete with or control others and begin to accept them as they are.

Harmony allows us to feel a sense of fellowship with others instead of a sense of competition and isolation. It prevents us from being judgmental. Judgmentalism is based on a sense of scarcity and disconnection: we see limited resources in the world, feel that we cannot attain them without competing with others, and try to gain power by harming someone else. When we judge others, we ignore our own flaws. We are hypocritical. It's funny how we never seem to notice that we are doing the very thing we are judging someone else for. Maybe our flaws look slightly different, or we exhibit them to a different degree, but our judgment is still hypocrisy. Separating ourselves out from others and saying, "I'm not like him, I'm a much better person" creates disharmony and disconnection instead of balance, harmony, and a beautiful symphony.

Learn to say, "Let go and let God" when things aren't working out as you would like. Learn to accept others as they are and put your trust in the divine order. If you do, you will pull yourself out of a state of disharmony and back into a state of peace and balance.

THE SIXTH
ETERNAL PRINCIPLE:

The Law of Abundance

Abundance is an energy state that manifests material wealth and other, more important forms of wealth.

"Both abundance and lack exist simultaneously in our lives, as parallel realities. It is always our conscious choice which secret garden we will tend . . . When we choose not to focus on what is missing from our lives but are grateful for the abundance that is present—love, health, family, friends, work, the joys of nature and personal pursuits that bring us pleasure—the wasteland of illusion falls away and we experience Heaven on earth."

—*Sarah Ban Breathnach*

The Universe was designed so that all of us would have everything we need. Jesus said we should consider the lilies of the field, which do not have to work, yet are arrayed in splendor. Luxury items and gold coins are not genuine riches, and true abundance isn't something you have to toil and sweat to achieve. Abundance isn't something you can lose or have taken away from you. It is an energy state, like joy or love. You have the power to create this state at any time by thinking of and feeling grateful for all the blessings you have, and by giving to others even when it calls for sacrifice.

Whenever you are thankful and generous, you align yourself with the Law of Abundance, and the Universe will respond by providing you with abundance. Your material wealth and opportunities for making or receiving money will begin to increase to match your state of abundance.

Limited, man-made ideas about wealth and abundance can make you feel angry and victimized if you do not have the financial situation you think you deserve. When you fear that you do not have enough money to protect yourself from harm, it is only natural to worry. I have had very wealthy clients who feel certain that they could lose their fortune any day, even though that is almost impossible given the number of investments and properties they own. In a sense, their wealth traps them, because it prevents them from experiencing a sense of joy and security without money. The thought of losing "everything" is devastating to them. They cannot imagine how they could exist without their sizeable fortune.

Having been poor, I know what it is like to not have food in the house or running water. Yet, like the lilies of the field, my family and our neighbors were abundant in love and a sense of community. Even the fear of the communist government couldn't dampen our sense of abundance. When someone was in need, others stepped in with food, comfort, and transportation. Our financial resources were few, but we were creative and resilient, and found ways to achieve our goals.

We are meant to have and enjoy all that we need. However, so many people are out of alignment with the Eternal Principle of Abundance that many have become fearful, greedy, and miserly. When we look around us at the harsh reality of the man-made world, we find it hard to believe we can get everything we desire without someone getting less than he deserves—and we do not want to be the person who doesn't have enough! Our sense of scarcity leads us to look out for number one at the expense of others, and to believe that there are limited opportunities and only a small amount of wealth to be had.

Creativity and Abundance

The energy state of abundance feels expansive, not constrictive. It opens you up to the deepest level of creativity—divine creativity—allowing you to perceive endless possibilities. God has an infinite number of ideas about how to create harmony, beauty, and boundless abundance to bestow upon us. God is the continually renewing resource for creativity!

Because we live in a state of scarcity, we forget that we can draw on the divine resource of creativity at any time. We blind ourselves to all the many ways in which we could make our lives better. Think about the abundance of sunlight that reaches our planet. It fuels all life on earth; why wouldn't we be able to use it to fuel our cars and homes? We may not have the technology to make this happen today, but why haven't we been focusing on the goal of solar power and investing money and time into converting to that form of energy? Because our fear and our scarcity mentality prevent us from envisioning a life after fossil fuels! Creating the energetic state of abundance opens our eyes and triggers our creativity.

Whatever the problem, you can find the answer inside yourself by communicating with God, but if you are pessimistic and negative you will block yourself off from the Divine Source and lose your constructive energy. Abundance allows you to feel your wondrous connection to God and recognize that there is plenty of happiness and joy available to you. All you need to do is to appreciate the abundance you've been given instead of focusing only on what is missing from your life.

Most people believe they do not have enough money. But money is just a form of energy we work with, moving it around and directing it here or there. You cannot depend on it to be there for you, but you can depend on the power of abundance to fuel your creativity and resilience. The Law of Abundance, combined with the Law of Attraction (which draws abundance to you) and the Law of Manifestation (which allows you to act in ways that generate wealth), helps you create a fulfilling, joyful, healthy life.

Being in a state of abundance changes our perceptions. We focus on what we have instead of obsessing about what we do not have. In America, we have plenty of money and resources. We also have a lot of loneliness, violence, and suffering, because our values are out of alignment with the Eternal Principles. We are blocking the proper flow of abundance.

When you have little money, you have a greater sense of the power of a loaf of bread, and it is easier to be aware of God and follow the Eternal Principles. Buddha renounced his wealth in order to become enlightened, while Jesus said it is easier for a camel to go through the eye of a needle than for a rich man to get into heaven. Both of these great teachers understood that it is difficult to be wealthy without being attached to that wealth and assigning it too much importance.

The people in my home country, the Romanians, who have suffered so much and had so little food, money, and freedom, have tremendous respect for the arts. Many of them have learned through experience that music and art connect us to the healing power of the Divine. Great art changes the body's frequency, raising its vibration, but here in America, where many of the most important artists in the world have honed their craft, we are cutting arts programs in the schools. Our priorities have become completely mixed up.

Learning how other people live and think helps us to view ourselves more clearly. When we deepen our understanding of the human experience, we nourish our sense of abundance because we foster our sense of connection to the divine and Divine Law. Art, poetry, literature, music, and mythology help us to look beyond our current problems to notice all that we have in common with other nations and cultures. It is not as important that we can identify a specific work by the painter Toulouse-Lautrec, the Sufi poet Rumi, or the musician Louis Armstrong as it is that we appreciate their rich artistry. As we learn to appreciate the beauty of our world, we see the potential of the human race and recognize our common humanity, which reminds us of the Law of Totality.

If you have children, expose them to the arts. You may be surprised by how open they are to appreciating everything from 1920s popular music to Auguste Rodin's sculptures. Children do not feel intimidated by their lack of knowledge, so they are willing to experience art and ask questions. In contrast, adults will often feel embarrassed that they do not know what the "must read" novel of the year is or the name of the latest "hot" new musical artist. Learn from children: Let go of your self-judgments and delve into great art, music, and literature. It will remind you of your connection to other people and to God, and will help you to align yourself with the Law of Abundance.

Abundance without Material Wealth

Abundance is about being joyful no matter what you possess, no matter what your circumstances. While in Romania recently, I decided to visit some of the monasteries in the gloriously beautiful countryside. There was such joy in the faces of the nuns I saw. One nun had graduated from my college at the same time I had. As I talked to her, I realized we'd had two very different destinies: I had been able to experience fame, fortune, and success in a career, while she had spent her entire adult life in a monastery, owning only the clothes on her back. She looked so healthy, happy, and vibrant—

she even jumped over a fence to pick some fresh fruit for me, leaping like a teenager, which I certainly cannot do!

This woman has never yearned for a bigger kitchen or a better retirement investment account. All she knows is that she loves God and is happy to spend her days praying for others, working in the vegetable and flower gardens, and supporting the work the church is doing on behalf of the poor. I was mesmerized by her. She has an abundance of vitality, health, and love, as well as a powerful relationship with God. She doesn't need anything more and is not striving to "fix" her life. If she has goals, they are probably quite simple: to feel even closer to God, to see her garden grow even more lush, to help others even more than she does now. She is truly contented and filled with a joy that overflows and touches those around her.

Of course, some Romanians are angry that communism's collapse didn't immediately lead to American-style prosperity, but that is not the common attitude in the country. Most Romanians just want a decent life, with food on the table and a roof over their heads. They value friendship and community. When I was in the countryside, some of the locals discovered that my family and I were visiting from America and insisted we come to their home for lunch. They put out every bit of food they had on their simple table and seemed proud and joyous to be able to share what little they had with complete strangers. In America, no matter what the amount in our bank accounts, we are quick to give in to fear and distrust, and that pulls us out of a state of abundance.

In my younger days, I was a celebrated pop singer in Romania. My band and I played to stadiums of ten thousand screaming fans, who threw wildflowers at us in appreciation. Those were wonderfully happy days for all of us. We were young and filled with energy, expressing ourselves musically, creating harmony and inspiring other people to believe in their dreams. We didn't have or need private jets or designer clothes. In fact, I used to sew my own clothes. My sequins looked beautiful on television, but up close, the stitches were clunky and you could see that I was not exactly a brilliant seamstress. I never felt a sense of entitlement to an easy life and pricey designer clothes, because I had never met anyone who had those things. In those homemade gowns, I felt rich.

In fact, when I left Romania to perform in America for the first time, I only had $80 in my pocket. I spent $60 on a bottle of perfume someone was selling at the airport, because I'd never before had the chance to own a luxury item and I wanted to know what that experience was like. When I got to America with my $20, I was shocked to learn that the promoter who was running the tour of European artists had lied about what was in my contract. I wasn't going to get nearly the amount of money I'd been promised. Though I didn't know how I was going to have enough to eat, after so many years of living in poverty, I had complete faith that I would have everything I needed. After all, I had always somehow managed to eat even though I grew up poor, and I had experienced the miracle of getting out of Romania. Why wouldn't I trust in the Universe? I vibrated abundance, opportunities, love, and support, and, eventually, wealth came to me in due time.

A Healthy Attitude about Wealth and Abundance

Many people exist in a state of scarcity. They focus on attaining whatever they think will create security, peace, and joy for them. Often, my clients will say to me, "If I only had more money!" They genuinely believe that a lack of money is the only thing standing between them and the life they want for themselves. It's true that money can buy some things that can be very important, such as food, clothing, and shelter, but almost every American has access to all of this. Yet we are still unhappy. Although there are many impoverished people in the United States, it is a rich country.

People may believe they are poor because they struggle with credit card debt and have a house with only one bathroom. But I have met people who live in almost inhuman conditions and possess an amazing spirit. In America, the poor are often better off than a lot of people in the world. I do not say that to diminish their suffering in any way, but to point out that no one in the United States is completely lacking in resources. Unfortunately, when we live in a state of scarcity, we are not able to recognize and use the abundance that is available to us.

The poverty of not knowing about the Eternal Principles is far worse than the poverty of having little food and no access to good health care—and I say that as someone who grew up poor and had to be hospitalized as a child for almost a year because common asthma medications weren't available in Romania. I still remember how frightening it was to try to draw breath and be unable to fill my lungs. And yet, I was surrounded by people who tried to live according to divine law. The poverty I experienced was merely financial poverty. I had a wealth of love.

If more people, including those who have plenty of material wealth, could live according to the Law of Abundance, we could end much of the suffering in the world. Our greed and "looking out for number one" mentality goes hand in hand with a fear that we will never have enough to feel truly safe. A frequent excuse for not investing more money in education and programs for poor children is, "We do not have enough money because our taxes are too high already." Yet, if we are afraid that a country might attack us, we will find and spend billions of dollars to wage war on them! We allow our fear to dictate our spending habits instead of allowing love to guide us.

There's certainly nothing wrong with wanting to have more money in order to be able to do things for those you love. We want to make their lives a little easier, and to give our children a better future by providing them with good schools and private lessons that will help them develop their talents. But in America, the focus on having more money and more possessions has become completely out of sync with our true needs and with the divine definition of abundance. Just see how shoppers will fight with each other at Christmas time to ensure they get the last flat-screen TV in the store; it's absurd! When together we choose to live according to the law of abundance, everyone has what he needs.

And while it's true that in America anyone has the potential to rise up from poverty, that doesn't mean someone is poor because he has character flaws. People fall into poverty because of mental or physical illness, psychological problems that overwhelm them, financial catastrophes, and a host of other problems that have to do with karma. Again, we cannot possibly know someone's complex combination of personal, family, and global karma. God doesn't want us to judge each other. He wants us to take care of each other. Jesus broke bread with prisoners, prostitutes, and the much-hated tax collectors. He told the crowd ready to stone the adulteress that he who was without sin should cast the first stone, meaning that none of us has the right to sit in judgment of someone else.

Money, Power, and Fame

When we do not understand the nature of abundance, or value what is most important in life, we lust after material wealth, sacrificing our integrity and compassion in order to achieve it. Wealth can be a force for helping others. But if we are afraid of losing our power, we will become greedy and hoard our riches. Then money corrupts us, or starts to flow away.

People commonly associate fame with money and power. Just as money is temporary, fame can be fleeting. The power of fame can make it easier for us to help others, but if we only use fame to achieve more glory and attention for ourselves, we will feel a sense of scarcity.

People will reach a certain point of wealth and still feel empty. They try to accumulate even more, and become even more detached from God. A wealthy client of mine just couldn't get enough money and sued her grandparents for cutting her out of their will. Although she was already one of the richest people in America, the more she had, the more she longed to have. Other wealthy people are called to go in another direction, because they come to recognize that materialism isn't working for them. Sometimes, it is illness or a horrific loss that wakes them up and compels them to discover their relationship to God and bring themselves into alignment with the Law of Abundance.

Why Some People Don't Have Enough Money and Some Have Too Much

Many people are enslaved by materialism. Some even believe that those with money are blessed by God and those without are out of favor with the

Divine. They don't recognize that by obeying man-made laws instead of the Eternal Principles, human beings have created an unfair distribution of material wealth. It's we, not God, who have created this imbalance.

Abundance is a very positive form of energy, available to everyone at all times. When we vibrate abundance, the Universe responds by bringing us circumstances that reflect our inner wealth. However, we get caught up believing that wealth is the same as money or financial security when it isn't. Another factor we forget to consider is that the Law of Karma and the other Eternal Principles have an effect on whether we attract or manifest wealth. It is not as simple as "Believe in God and yourself, be positive and do the right thing, and you will have all the money you desire."

If you try to maintain a high vibration, creating the emotion of gratitude and the feeling of abundance, then yes, you are more likely to attract and manifest money. However, not all of us need a lot of money to create a happy life and do what we came to this earth to do. Your soul did not choose to incarnate in order to enjoy fine wines, luxury homes and cars, and expensive jewelry! You may end up owning those things as a part of your journey, but you will not necessarily appreciate or enjoy them. Many of my wealthy clients are afraid that others will take their money away, so they become distrustful, isolated, lonely, and unhappy. They become too focused on themselves and their problems, and do not reach out to help those who are less fortunate. What good are millions of dollars if you have no friends, no sense of being able to do something to help the world, and no sense of purpose?

At the same time, some of the happiest people are almost penniless. They work hard and also generate positivity and joy. They feel proud they are doing their best each day on the job. They know that their work is important, and that how they interact with others makes the world a better place. They spend their time caring for their elderly parents, helping their children with their homework, or assisting others. They know that they are loved, needed, and appreciated, and that they are making a difference.

Every lifestyle has its pros and cons. Not all of us are meant to have lots of money, although we are all meant to experience abundance. Mother Teresa could not have done her rewarding and important work if she had been managing an investment portfolio, several homes, and a group of employees. Bill Gates could not do the type of work he's doing to address AIDS in Africa without spending a lot of money. We need to let go of our simplistic idea that the amount of money we have determines our happiness and whether or not we can make the world a better place.

Our karma has a huge influence on the flow of money in our lives (remember, all of us have individual karma as well as family and global karma we share with others). If we become greedy, our riches are likely to drain away. Not long ago, when I was in Romania, I was asked to predict who would win the World Cup. I do not follow sports, but in the past, I have correctly predicted the outcome of major sporting events. I had a very strong sense that the Soviet team would win this particular sports contest and had no reason to doubt that my intuitive abilities would fail me. To my great shock, the Soviets lost. Many people who had lost money betting on the game e-mailed me and the television show I'd appeared on to express their anger. I felt terrible, and put a lot of thought into how this could have happened. I came to realize that because people had used my talents as a metaphysical intuitive to profit, they created negative karma. They attracted the wrong information in response to their low vibration, and I was the conduit. (Although I trust in my predictions, I have never bet on sports or any other events—and I do not play the lottery or try to intuit the winning numbers.) Once I saw that people were using my predictions to foster their greed, I understood why God had, in a sense, tricked me. I have vowed never again to predict who will win a major sports event. I do not want to participate in the creation of negative karma.

Similarly, a caller on Fox News recently asked me to predict which stocks would do well in the future. I told him that if he were to give me a list of stocks, I could tune in to my intuition about each one of them and tell him whether I felt they would do well or not. But as I told him, we shouldn't focus on stocks because soon, we're not going to have a stock market anymore. Our ideas about money will change dramatically in the coming years. It's time we start thinking differently about what wealth is and how we can grow it.

When people unexpectedly receive a lot of money, such as when they win a lottery or inherit a large sum, they are meant to use that abundance to create good karma. But if they give in to greed and become miserly, using it for selfish purposes, they soon find themselves in the same or even worse financial situation than they were in before they received the money. It may be that what lottery winners are attracting isn't just money, but the opportunity to face their negative karma and work through it.

Unexpectedly receiving money we haven't earned can create a scarcity mentality. We feel guilty and start giving away the money to anyone and everyone without any thought to the power of the money. By not taking responsibility for using the money wisely, we create negative karma.

We can also inherit money that has negative karma attached to it—for example, a fortune that was created through exploiting and hurting others. This kind of "tainted" money brings negative energy along with it and can create more misfortune for the person who receives it than not having it at all. If you recognize that your newfound riches were created by someone who hurt or exploited someone else, use that money to right the wrong in some way. A proofreader I know was very upset when she was working on a book that she felt encouraged an attitude of hatred and even violence toward gay people. She wrote a note to the person at the publishing house who had given her the job, suggesting that the publisher might want to consider questioning the author about what he'd written. But as a proofreader, she didn't have the authority to take out the ugly passages. When she received her paycheck, she sent a generous contribution to a charity that helps victims of anti-gay violence.

Money is a powerful force that can make a bad situation worse or can turn it around in a dramatic way if the person makes the right choices and uses the money wisely. Even a small amount of money, given with great love and compassion and generosity, can make a difference in the world. When his disciples discovered that a woman left only a small coin in the charity box at the temple, Jesus pointed out that the woman was also very poor, so her gift and sacrifice were far greater than that of the wealthy people who had donated large sums.

Being cynical and distrustful, looking out for number one, and worrying that you might not have enough tomorrow if you give any money away today, do not create joy and security. There are people who live in chronic pain but find joy in life every day. They're much happier than the person who is constantly at the plastic surgeon's office.

Abundance Changes Forms

Another reason people do not have money despite their clear, conscious intention to generate wealth, and despite their gratitude for all they have, is that change is inevitable. Abundance changes its form, and we have to accept that it doesn't always show up in exactly the way we want it to. However, we can work with the abundance we have to fashion it into another type of wealth. For example, an abundance of talent and enthusiasm can lead to work that generates a lot of money.

Again, creativity plays an important role in the Law of Abundance. By remaining in a creative, open state, we plug in to an infinite reservoir of choices and opportunities. If what you are doing isn't working for you, let go of your fears and take a risk. After living in this country a few years, I discovered to my great sadness that there was not much of a chance for me to make it in the music business here. As a female pop singer no longer in my early twenties, I found door after door closed to me. I knew I had abundance in my life, but I had to be open to its other forms in order to find new opportunities for myself. I went on to make money as a metaphysical intuitive, a therapist and marital counselor, an author, and a jewelry designer. I loved my work and never allowed myself to get depressed or believe that because my musical career had come to an end, my time had passed. We can always reinvent our lives if we are willing to be positive, embrace abundance, and work hard. To align yourself with the Law of Abundance, you have to open your eyes to see what your gifts and blessings are, and then work with them.

It's hard to feel a sense of abundance when we have experienced a loss. We can wonder where we should go next and what we should do now.

Everything passes away and everything changes. Whatever the void in your life, you do not have to feel empty forever. If you can let go of your fears and remember that abundance changes form, you will discover your resources. Have faith that by connecting to God and aligning yourself with the Eternal Principle of Abundance, you can plug into an endless pool of resources and change your vibration.

Claiming Our Right to Abundance

Sometimes, people block themselves from abundance because they feel they do not deserve to have wealth and happiness. I come from the eastern block, where most people were poor. Communism was supposed to make us all equals. When I first arrived in America, I was shocked to see such wealth and such poverty in the same place—there weren't homeless people on the street corner where I was from. We were raised with the belief that we are all the same and deserve the same. Being a famous singer had brought me certain privileges: In 1979, refrigerators in Romania were extremely hard to come by. Fortunately, I had a singing gig at a refrigerator factory, and the man there allowed me to buy one for my family. I was thrilled! And yet, I felt guilty, too. I didn't feel entitled to have a refrigerator when so many had to do without.

Here in America, people often believe that if they have more than someone else does, it must be because they worked harder for it or are more deserving. But of course, that isn't always the case. People who do not feel good about themselves, or who are very sensitive to others' needs, can have difficulty being comfortable with material wealth. They feel guilty, thinking they haven't earned the riches available to them. God doesn't want us to feel guilty or uncomfortable. He wants us to enjoy the luxury of having wealth, whether it is an income that allows us to vacation at the finest resorts or to pay our basic bills and still have money left over to save for the future and eat at a restaurant once in a while.

You do not help anyone by feeling bad about yourself and ashamed of your wealth. Enjoy your abundance, but share it, do not hoard it. Don't create negative feelings by thinking to yourself, "I do not deserve this." God wants you to have that money for a reason; explore what it could be.

However, if you become greedy, and do not appreciate the wealth you have, you will create an imbalance. No amount of money can make up for the negative karma you generate. We're not supposed to take more than we need or be miserly. If we accumulate too much, refusing to share it, the Universe will bring something negative into our lives to restore balance. As they say, God gives with one hand and takes away with another.

Creating Abundance

An endless supply of abundance, health, security, joy, and creativity are available to us, but we have to do the work of living by the Eternal Principles so that we can maintain our access to the flow of riches God wants to pour into our lives.

Pray to God, ask for blessings, and see God in everything you do. Become inspired by inviting God in. Breathe deeply and allow your thoughts and feelings to shift. We become more positive as we let go of fears and our limited and distorted thinking patterns. We cannot create abundance without God's help, without plugging into the reservoir of the Universe and aligning ourselves with the Eternal Principles. We are like a battery that needs to be recharged with divine energy in order to maintain a state of abundance.

You can think you are feeling good and doing well, but if you are not also being generous and experiencing gratitude you will not be in a state of abundance, and soon your circumstances will change. What we do not appreciate slips away. What we do not give away depreciates in value.

Whatever you have, whether it is possessions, money in investments, a regular salary, or a close relationship with your child, it is important to feel and express thanks for it every single day. Make a ritual of spending a few moments each day being quiet, closing your eyes, and focusing on the feeling of wealth you experience when picturing your child's loving face, or seeing yourself signing your paycheck and depositing it with the bank teller.

If you have a nice view from a window in your home, sit and look out, saying a prayer of gratitude for the beautiful world you live in.

If you are struggling financially, work on your karmic issues about money so you will have an easier time aligning with abundance. Focus on working hard and smart. Stop giving to those who do not appreciate you or your efforts, and do not be fooled into thinking you need only to close your eyes and wish for money to have it show up in your life. Value what you have today. Acknowledge your riches and wealth, and you will stop feeling fearful or anxious about money. Only then you will attract wealth instead of repelling it. In the Romanian countryside, people who have very little money are able to breathe fresh, clean air, walk through tranquil forests, and smell the fragrance of hundreds of wildflowers that dot the hills and valleys. What greater riches can there be?

If your home has no natural beauty and you have no money to decorate, you can clean and straighten what you have. Arrange it nicely. It's inexpensive to paint, and you can find low-priced, quality furniture at rummage sales or even on the street on bulk pick-up day in a wealthy neighborhood. A friend of mine loves her 1950s Formica table and chairs, which remind her of her childhood and the simple pleasures her family enjoyed. She found the table on the street and bought the set of chairs for $20 at a church rummage sale. When she has people over for dinner, she loves to tell the story of how she came across her table on a street corner one rainy night when she was feeling sad. "It's as if God put it there as a special gift for me to cheer me up!" she says.

Whatever you have, no matter how much or how little, always take time out to feel grateful for it. Say prayers of thanks, say affirmations expressing your joy over your abundance, and keep a gratitude journal. Gratitude helps us to correct the distorted belief we all fall into at times: "I don't have enough!" We spend so much time and energy worrying about money but do not stop to appreciate all the food we have in the pantry and refrigerator, or the fact that we can go to the grocery store and purchase more food. We forget that whatever our mild ailments, most of us enjoy excellent health. If you have all your mental faculties, remember how many people suffer from dementia or brain damage. Be thankful that you are able to rely on your memory and cognitive abilities. If you have adequate clothing, efficient transportation, steady employment, friends who care about you, and family who loves you, you are very lucky. If you do not like what's happening in your town or in America, be grateful that you can complain to the government without being thrown in jail. Be thankful that if your representatives do not respond to your needs, you can vote for someone else to represent you, or you can run for the position yourself—and you won't have someone burst through your door in the middle of the night to take you away.

If you have difficulty feeling that you live in abundance, look at those who are not doing as well, and ask yourself, "Am I truly suffering?" Seneca, the Greek philosopher, said if you really want to be happy, look behind you not in front of you. So visit a poor country or neighborhood for a reality check. Don't compare yourself with those who have more money than you do. Look at those less fortunate and ask yourself, "What can I do to make their situation just a little better?" You may be surprised at how empowered and joyful you feel just by doing one small thing for someone else.

Giving and Generosity

When you feel genuine abundance, you have the urge to share it with others. If you have wealth but are afraid to give some of it away, you need to let go of your fear of scarcity. If you receive money unexpectedly, give at least some to those less fortunate than yourself. As soon as you decide how big of a check to write, increase the amount to the point where it makes you a little uncomfortable. Give without thinking about whether you will receive recognition. In this way, you will learn to stop equating abundance with money and start to experience true abundance: the secure and wonderful feeling of having more than enough to give, and the joy of sharing what you have with others. Some people believe in tithing, but I think it is better to ask yourself how much you can really afford instead of automatically thinking you have to give away only a certain amount.

Whenever you see someone suffering, help him if you can. Sacrifice your time and money for his benefit. Ask God to bless this person, and say a prayer of thanks for your own good fortune. If you are walking down the street and see someone who is in a wheelchair or homeless, say a prayer for him. Look him in the eye, and smile or say hello, even if you can do nothing else. Sending anyone love is a marvelous gift on its own, and if you can help a person out in some way, that is even better. In your own community, go to work for a food bank or community organization, help in a soup kitchen, or volunteer to tutor children after school. Help out at a nursing home—you can teach a class, entertain, or replenish their bookshelves with good books. Do a fundraiser to generate money and bring attention to a problem in your community. You will meet people and share joy with each other as you work together to make the world a better place in some small way.

Each morning, ask yourself, "What good can I do today that will make me feel like I can influence the world for the better and help even just one person?" Don't become attached to receiving praise or credit. Now, someone in need may take advantage of you if you do not listen to your intuition about them or you try to meddle in their karma. Let go of the image of yourself as a grand rescuer, and you will see more clearly how you can help people without creating more negative karma for yourself or them. Be careful not to get stuck in old behavior patterns that do not serve your spiritual growth.

When we accept that the Universe rights itself through the Law of Karma, we can accept that sometimes our trust will be betrayed. We do not allow the actions of others to prevent us from reaching out to help the world. Living in abundance requires that we trust in the totality, in humanity itself. This can be hard to do considering there are a lot of untrustworthy people acting out of insecurity and a fear of not having enough. As an individual, and as part of the larger whole, we have to be cognizant that there are people whose souls are new to this world and are therefore at a very low level of evolution. We can protect ourselves from them, without blaming or judging them. If we are willing to be generous, we can help them regain their own ability to trust.

In the book *Les Misérables* by Victor Hugo, a priest catches a thief who has just escaped from prison. The priest tells the thief to take all his silver but to use it to live a life of honesty and care for his fellow man. This extraordinary act of generosity teaches the thief that there is goodness in the world. He regains his ability to trust other people, turns away from crime and desperation, and prospers. This is how we are meant to live—to stop being so afraid of sacrifice and to claim our power to do good.

It can be hard to see how we are making a difference when we turn on the news and hear the latest horror story of suffering. Try not to watch the news! Read the newspaper instead, and even then, avoid reading the overly negative stories. Do what you can do to help the world and trust that you will inspire others to give of themselves as well. The more of us who act generously, the closer humanity comes to making a quantum leap into a more loving way of interacting with each other.

Allow divinity to flow through you, and be in a state of receiving God's grace. If you are not grateful and open to what the Universe brings, believing instead that what you have isn't good enough, you will push away anything that can lift you up, including people who care about you.

Spirituality and Sacrifice

The element of sacrifice is missing in many spiritual quests today. Too often, people focus on feeling good about themselves in the name of being "spiritual." You can climb to Machu Picchu, visit sacred temples in India, or go to an ashram and meditate for days on end, and it may help you awaken to your spirituality. But, you can do the same thing by being grateful and experiencing the abundance that you already have in your life. I have known people who have made expensive spiritual treks and not changed a bit, and others who have developed a much deeper relationship with God without spending a penny.

Spirituality gives us a sense of balance and contentment that has often been referred to as grace. When we are truly in touch with our spirituality, it seems that all is right with the world. We accept what we cannot change and have the courage to change what we can. We do whatever needs to be done and give of ourselves without calculation or complaint.

In contrast, if our charitable work is about going to fancy parties and getting our photographs in the society pages, or about competing to be the most admired and powerful person in our volunteer groups, then we are not giving and sacrificing. We are bartering. We trade our sacrifice for a specific payoff and block the flow of abundance into our lives.

You do not have to wait for a traumatic event to bring you closer to God and put you in touch with your spiritual side. Focus on abundance now, generously giving of yourself so that you can erase your negative karma.

The Power of Abundance

When we experience abundance, our feelings of lack disappear. Our problems do not seem overwhelming, and we do not feel an urge to have more in our lives. We find it easier to create good karma. We become even healthier, wiser, and more patient with ourselves and others as we accept the ebbs and flows of material wealth. We become more giving and more willing to sacrifice for the greater good.

Americans worked very hard and sacrificed a lot to achieve the prosperity they enjoyed after World War II. That wealth was lost when we gave in to fear and became obsessed with personal success over the welfare of others. Companies became nearsighted, looking only at the bottom line. Our country became myopic as well, focusing on "What's in it for us?" when dealing with other countries.

We've reached the point where it seems we have to be at least somewhat dishonest in order to win and get ahead in business or politics. It doesn't have to be this way. Divinity will put us back on track. Although there have been times since the 1950s when we began to move toward the Eternal Principle of Abundance, now more than ever, we are in need of focusing on what is good for everyone. There's karmic payback for greediness, but we don't like to take responsibility for our mistakes that came out of greed. You do not have to take personal responsibility for events you had no role in, but you can express love, compassion, and generosity toward those who suffered because of actions that your neighbors took—actions that may have benefited you in a roundabout way. Jesus didn't say, "Take care of the poor, the sick, and the imprisoned unless you aren't personally responsible for their circumstances." He just said *do it*!

Remember the Law of Totality and the Law of Karma. If you have to sacrifice a little bit for someone who is suffering through no fault of your own, you create good karma that benefits everyone, including yourself. Affirmative action is a good example of what is required of us: sacrifice for the greater good. You may lose a job opportunity or a place on the college freshman list due to affirmative action, but when you support its intention of creating equal opportunity for all, an even better opportunity will come to you as a result.

There is no way to say what the right amount of wealth is for any particular person. To live in balance means that whatever amount of money you have, you use it for the greater good. You do not have to think about your money a lot or give it a lot of attention. Don't concern yourself with how others spend their money, because we all have different values. I have a client in New York City who bought a horse that is boarded in North Carolina. She can only visit the animal every three months. Some might think she made a foolish purchase, but owning a horse was this woman's lifelong dream, and she truly values her horse. It gives her tremendous joy and helps her maintain a vibration of abundance.

We all want different things, but we have to allow everyone to have abundance. We have to avoid greediness and taking more than our share. Even in little ways, we can get rid of our hoarding, greedy mentality. One of my neighbors held on to some very beautiful and expensive baby clothes her daughter had worn because they had great sentimental value. Then she heard from a friend about a young, single mother who was struggling to earn a living while caring for her newborn, colicky baby girl. My neighbor realized that this young mother would truly appreciate the clothes and gave them to her friend to pass along. When she heard that the young mother was elated by this unexpected gift, it lifted her own spirits and made her feel far more abundant than she'd felt by hanging on to the clothes or selling them. She just wanted someone to appreciate the baby clothes as much as she had.

The Lesson of the Law of Abundance:

Giving and sacrificing are divine.
Greed and selfishness are man-made.

The real power of abundance is the ability to give things away *and* to give of ourselves. If we want to live abundantly, we must learn to give and sacrifice.

We live in a materialistic culture where we are encouraged to value money over genuine abundance and to believe that wealth and influence will protect us from unhappiness. Too many people only care about amassing a fortune and gaining power over others so that they can feel they have nothing to fear. They become greedy and selfish and turn away from the ultimate source of power and security: the Divine. Sadly, they do not realize that abundance is such an energizing state that it eradicates fear. Abundance gives us the strength and stamina to continue giving, loving, and being compassionate even when our circumstances are extremely challenging. It eliminates that inner void that too many people try to fill by achieving and accomplishing more.

Caring about our personal success above all else has led to a mentality of entitlement and cutting corners. There is no escape from karma. If you take more than is rightfully yours, you literally won't get away with it. One of my clients used to brag to me about how he paid hardly any money in taxes because he had such a smart accountant. He enjoyed a very wealthy lifestyle, and while his cousin had lent him a great deal of money to start a business that eventually failed, he felt no need to pay him back. When this man got audited by the IRS and had to pay fines for taking writeoffs he couldn't justify, he was in shock, but I wasn't surprised. It was a karmic payback. Selfishness and cheating never pay off.

How much do you need, really? The Law of Love and the Law of Abundance are intertwined. If you live in scarcity, your relationships will be conditional, because you will attract people who are only interested in what they can get from you. But if you live in abundance, you will be amazed at how many loving, caring, generous people will show up in your life.

If your life isn't working for you, if you have money but no joy and little love, then you are not aligned with abundance. You're living in a state of scarcity and in danger of believing that your only responsibility in life is to yourself. If you've adopted this attitude, you are blocking the genuine abundance you deserve.

In a state of abundance, we recognize that we are fine and our resources are always adequate. We know there is always plenty for everyone when we are aligned with Divinity. We do not feel the need to scramble for power or money, or put up with abusive people in order to try to hold on to a job, a relationship, or a situation. We can close the door on them knowing that a new one will open.

Open yourself to the divine source of abundance and creativity, and your entire energy will change. You will want to give to others, and even sacrifice, regardless of whether they give you attention or praise in return. You will discover the many gifts you have to offer the world, and find opportunities to hone and use them for the benefit of yourself and others, even strangers. Then you will begin the sacred, holy work of healing.

THE SEVENTH ETERNAL PRINCIPLE:

The Law of Attraction

The Universe works with us to
bring us what we desire.

One of the most talked about Eternal Principles is the Law of Attraction. I cannot tell you how many of my clients have said to me, "The Law of Attraction doesn't work for me, and I do not understand why!" There are two core key aspects to understanding how this Principle works. First, this divine law interacts with all the others. Second, there is often a big gap between what our conscious mind desires and what our subconscious mind wants to attract. It's the subconscious mind that most influences our vibration and what we bring into our lives.

The Law of Attraction and Other Eternal Principles

Just as you cannot write a symphony with only one note, you cannot create a happy, fulfilling life using only one of the Eternal, Divine Principles. They all act together, influencing each other.

I had a client who was gorgeous, brilliant, Ivy League educated, and financially stable. She often said she wanted a powerful man to be her husband, and she attracted many billionaires, but she had so many unresolved psychological issues about men that every partner she had ended up betraying her. She wasn't able to control her own fear and jealousy when it came to men. So, while her conscious mind insisted that she wanted a loyal lover, her subconscious mind had very different ideas. It knew that what she really needed to resolve her karma about men and power were opportunities to experience betrayal and learn her lessons. The Universe responded to the strong intent created by her subconscious mind. God wanted her to be happy in a relationship and knew she could not be as long as she held on to her distrust of men and her need to be in control in a partnership. The Law of Karma, working with her subconscious desires, dictated what she would attract. The Universe responded by bringing her exactly what she needed— the kind of men who would cause her to suffer enough to want to change. This is what brought her to my office, where she began to face her issues and resolve her karma.

If you are now thinking, "But I don't deserve to suffer!" don't assume that the Divine wants you to be unhappy. It's not a matter of what you *deserve*, but of what you are subconsciously attracting. It's as if you've unknowingly placed a personal ad that says, "Looking for a man who is unfaithful, manipulative, dishonest, and charming, to help me work through my issues of unworthiness and trust" or a classified ad that says, "Wanted: An opportunity to learn how to feel good about myself even if I have no money." God responds to the ad placed by your subconscious.

The only way to end any pattern of attracting negative situations into your life is to become conscious of it and change your karma so that you change your subconscious intention. Remember, your subconscious holds all the memories of your past experiences in this lifetime and in previous lifetimes. Your right brain, the seat of your subconscious, is aware of all your unresolved karma that needs addressing. Although you cannot completely resolve all of your psychological issues and heal all your karma in this lifetime, the more you are aware of them and actively working to resolve them, the better your chances of changing your vibration and attracting what you consciously desire.

Keep in mind that karma has different layers to it. There is money karma, health karma, and emotional karma. Maybe you do not have any karmic issues about money, so your financial situation is fine, but you may have issues about your body, health, and emotions that cause you to attract illness. All of us are exposed to toxins in the environment, but not everyone's immune system responds by going into overdrive, creating disease or breaking down and allowing pathogens to take over. Two people with similar genetics and lifestyles can have very different states of health if one has unresolved health karma (perhaps even left over from another lifetime) but the other does not.

The moment you work on your own unresolved karma, you change your vibration at a cellular level, emptying your energy field of some of the toxic residue that slows it down. However, if you haven't completely cleansed yourself of that residue, it will start to grow again, like a cancer. You will think you are over your anger about how your parents neglected you in your childhood, and then your boss will be too preoccupied to assist you on an important project and you will overreact because neglect is still an issue for you. It takes constant work to clear your karma. It's like keeping up with the dust in a large house! But little by little, you change what your subconscious attracts, bringing it more in line with what your conscious mind desires.

Attraction and Totality

Because of the Law of Totality, we are connected to each other through our subconscious. Groups of people share karma that attracts situations to the group. Right now, America is dealing with unresolved karma about money. Too many greedy people have attracted and manifested financial problems. Even people who have good personal karma with money are caught up in the economic problems caused by the larger group. Each of us has to work to heal this karma, even if, as individuals, we didn't contribute to its creation. Instead of being angry or resentful, we should see this as an opportunity to create good karma for ourselves as we help other people to resolve our group's karma.

The Law of Totality, working in conjunction with the Law of Attraction, causes us to attract into our lives people who share the same karmic, psychological issues. These issues can play out in many different ways. We do not always recognize why we are drawn to certain people until we get to know them better. A client of mine discovered that the romantic partner she'd just broken up with was an alcoholic. He told her that she should start thinking about alcoholism in her own family, because he'd learned in AA that many times, women who are attracted to alcoholics have an alcoholic parent. The more we talked about it, the more she felt that one of her parents had been a quiet alcoholic. She mentioned this to a very close friend of hers from their high school days, and the friend said, "Well, that would make sense. Every one of our close friends has an alcoholic parent or sibling."

My client thought this was highly unusual, but I explained it is actually very common. These six friends were all very different in personality, but were drawn to each other through a shared karmic issue. They were so supportive of each other that they were able to help each other address their collective karma.

Attraction and Abundance

The Law of Abundance also works with the Law of Attraction. We bring into our lives whatever our subconscious needs, but if we learn to recognize what genuine abundance is, then we can begin to consciously attract it.

Over the years, I have found that no matter where I go, people around the world want basically the same things: love, stable relationships, a good life, and enough money so that they don't have to struggle. Everyone has different ideas about how much money they need.

What is it that you really want? Could you be happy with less "stuff"? Think about all of the possessions you have in your garage, basement, and closets. Do you even know what you own? How many toys are in your child's room? When you go to a fast food restaurant and get a "happy" meal, does that toy really make your child happy, or does it end up under the car seat with a half dozen other cheap toys that amused him for two minutes? How many times have you bought something in order to push aside a negative emotion, rather than because you really needed or valued it?

When we look more closely at what we long for, we realize that our feelings of want or lack prevent us from attracting material wealth, or we attract it in a way that makes us suffer somehow. We may have so much wealth that we feel trapped, or we find that our friends or family members become jealous because they cannot keep up with our new lifestyle.

Lack and insecurity lead to desire and the feeling that we cannot be happy or solve our problems unless we have more wealth. I'm not saying that it is possible to go through life with no desires whatsoever, or that it is easy to let go of fear or hopelessness when we are struggling every day to make ends meet. But we do not have to let our desires cause us to feel a painful sense of lack. The moment we start to embrace genuine abundance is the moment we begin to change our states of financial abundance.

Money can make life comfortable and give you a false sense of security, but there is no real security in the material world. In fact, when you feel your connection to the divine, feelings of hope and abundance will be there for you no matter what is happening around you. What you want to attract begins to change. You realize you do not really need a bigger house, and though a nicer, more reliable car would be helpful, you recognize that you already have what you most need. If you use the Law of Attraction to gain more power and more symbols of wealth, just to give yourself a false of security, you are misusing this Divine Principle. God wants us to attract abundance. Be open to when and how He answers our prayers.

Attraction and Harmony

Even when we get what we wish for, it may not be as fulfilling and wonderful as we imagined it to be. People become disillusioned when infatuation fades and they see their romantic partner more realistically. I've had clients who attracted a lot of money, then realized it wasn't the magic key to their happiness after all, and even brought them new problems.

Whenever we are given a lot of money without having to work for it, an imbalance is created and the Law of Harmony comes into play. Just as there is give and take in our personal relationships, there is give and take in our relationship to abundance. If we receive too much, we are supposed to give more, or the Universe will correct the imbalance for us. This is why it is so important to see money as a form of energy that we should share with others. It will make you focus your energy on things you do not need and that will overwhelm you. You will not have time for what's important.

Attraction and Wisdom

When we are aligned with the Law of Wisdom, we feel grateful for what we have in this moment instead of angry, resentful, or sad about what we do not have. The higher vibration of gratitude attracts abundance to us, while the lower vibrations of fear and scarcity attract situations that force us to work through the unresolved karma that is creating those feelings. Wisdom means knowing what to appreciate, what has lasting value. It prevents us from listening to the false values of the man-made world that tempt us to create negative karma, lower our vibration, and attract situations that will make us self-correct.

Attraction and Love

People naturally long for romantic partnership. We are hardwired to want love and experience sexual communion with another. However, unresolved karma will always affect the types of partner we will attract.

When you align yourself with the Law of Love, you have the wisdom to accept that you are never going to attract a flawless partner who will be endlessly giving and treat you with the utmost kindness every moment of the day. Such a person doesn't exist! You have to love people unconditionally, even when you do not like their behavior.

Too often, people treat relationships as if they were disposable. If they find themselves not getting along with their partner, they become angry and defensive, even cruel or callous, and start to think, "Maybe I just need to attract a better partner." Over time, couples can erode the love they have for each other because they do not have the courage to look at their own behavior and expectations, and adjust them in order to strengthen the partnership they already have.

Advice on how to communicate lovingly to your partner even when you are hurt or angry, and how to build intimacy and trust, can be found everywhere: in bookstores, in the office of a therapist or marital counselor, in magazines and newspapers, and on television programs. Yet with all this advice available, people often ignore it or do not make use of it. They allow their unresolved karma to keep them stuck at the same level of emotional and spiritual development. Then, when the initial attraction or infatuation with their partner wears off, they let the relationship fall apart instead of nurturing it. All relationships require you to set aside the ego's desires and nourish the needs of the partnership.

Years ago, when people had fewer expectations of their spouse, marriages lasted longer. The challenge today is to value your partnerships for what they can teach you and provide you. At the same time, you have to recognize that no partner can fix your unhappiness. You have to love unconditionally and have realistic expectations. I'm not saying you have to stay in a bad relationship, but you have to be careful not to quickly judge your partner as the bad guy and you as the one who is giving more, loving more, and doing more. Otherwise, your relationship will turn sour, and you will end up attracting a new partner who has all the same unresolved issues the old one had. The only way to attract a better partner is to work on yourself and raise your vibration.

Attraction and Manifestation

According to the Law of Manifestation, we must take action if we want to manifest what we desire. You can spend hours reciting affirmations with great feeling, but it isn't going to produce the results you are looking for if you do not follow through with action. Attraction is different from manifestation in that attraction brings things to you while manifestation allows you to make things happen in the physical world.

The Real Secret of the Law of Attraction

People have said the Law of Attraction is a secret kept from us by people in power for centuries. I do not believe that for a moment. I believe that the real secret is that once you change your karma, what you consciously desire also changes! For instance, many people long to be rich. If someone recites affirmations about being financially wealthy, closes his eyes, and visualizes being rich, focusing his intent on drawing in millions of dollars, that is fine—there is no reason to be ashamed of that desire. However, the question is why would anyone want or need so much money?

People flock to workshops about the Law of Attraction often to learn how to attract material wealth. Some of them may want large amounts of money because they have a dream they'd like to fund. They see money as the ticket to helping them in their pursuit of saving abandoned animals or inspiring others to make their own dreams come true. If they have a pure intent, to use the money for the good of the world, they will get the resources and wealth they need. But if they have some other karmic issues going on, one of two things will happen: either they won't attract what they desire, or they will but also attract problems that will cause them to face their issues. They might attract a wealthy investor who is domineering and abusive. They will have the funds for their projects, but also have to work through their issues about cruel authority figures.

Recently, I read a book by an author who gives workshops on the Law of Attraction. I couldn't help noticing that she didn't mention giving to others, loving them unconditionally, and serving the world with our talents as crucial to attracting abundance. She said that Jesus was wrong when He said, "Blessed are the meek, for they shall inherit the earth." In my view, this woman doesn't really understand the Law of Abundance and the Law of Attraction and how they work with the other Eternal Principles.

I think that most people who consciously desire wealth, desire it for all the wrong reasons. They don't realize that with a lot of money comes a lot of responsibility. Everything comes with a price tag. Some wealthy celebrities have an entourage of people they employ. They are afraid to slow down and rest because they worry about the people who depend on them for income. That's a lot of pressure, and some of them do not handle it well. People may dream of owning a mansion but do not realize how much work and money it takes to maintain one. I have many wealthy clients, and believe me, they spend a lot of time with their accountants and financial advisors. There is nothing wrong with having all these responsibilities, but no one consciously asks the Universe to bring them meetings with lawyers and accountants! Money seems the easy solution to every problem, but the real solution is to solve your karma and attract genuine abundance.

If you have unresolved karma about wealth and abundance, you will either not attract material wealth or it will come to you with strings attached in order to get you to resolve that karma. If you do not have unresolved karma about money, you will probably be very happy with whatever abundance you do attract, whether it is a million dollars and a wealthy mate, or a winning $10 lottery ticket and a romantic partner who is loving and kind but currently unemployed. Don't misuse the Law of Attraction to align yourself with greed!

How to Work with the Law of Attraction

Everyone can benefit from discovering their unresolved karma and addressing it. We all have to work to discover our hidden patterns of negative behavior, especially when life seems to be going well. We are here on earth to resolve our karma, no matter how little or great. We are not here to "coast along," enjoying ourselves but not evolving. If we fool ourselves into believing we have nothing to work on in this lifetime, or that it isn't important to address our unresolved karma, karma will make itself known by attracting problems to us!

Use Affirmations, Visualizations, and Prayer

One of the most powerful ways to work with the Law of Attraction is through visualization. Affirmations and visualizations work hand in hand with prayer.

Words, both spoken and unspoken, have tremendous power, converting our thoughts and feelings into reaction and reality. What we think about, and what we say, affects the world around us. That does not mean there are certain words that will prevent you from attracting what you want. "I want to get out of debt" is not as powerful an affirmation as "I am making more money every day," but the word "debt" does not attract debt. Nor does the word "want." When you continually say to yourself, "I want to get out of debt, but it is just so hard to do," you create feelings of worry, fear, and scarcity that lower your vibration. Use words to generate positive emotions. This is the idea behind affirmations.

Visualization is an even stronger tool for working with the Law of Attraction. While words are powerful, they are generated and processed in our left brain, which is limited by our own cognitions and established patterns of thoughts. Images, on the other hand, are the language of the right brain, where all our subconscious awareness lies and where we can find the door to the great wisdom of the collective unconscious and find guidance and answers to our problems. In fact, if you meditate deeply, you may find visual images coming into your mind that actually come from somewhere else— the collective mind, which is able to break the rules of time and space.

Neuro-linguistic programming, or NLP, uses words, imagery, and emotions to reprogram the subconscious, creating neural pathways in the brain that become new roadmaps for thinking and feeling. Each time you imagine yourself sitting down at the kitchen table across from your spouse and feeling loved and loving, you reprogram your subconscious to know what it is like to be in a good relationship with a romantic partner. Then, even though you are not currently in a relationship, and all your past relationships were unhealthy, you can create a new memory. Yes, it is a memory of something imagined, not real, but that does not matter to your subconscious! Your subconscious adds this experience to your collection of memories, reprogramming your brain to be familiar with what it is like to feel loved by a partner. You can change your karma about relationships just by sitting alone, creating a fantasy! You can use images and words to imagine yourself attracting whatever it is you'd like to attract. In doing so, you will begin to change your karma.

Prayer also helps us to attract what we want. Praying empowers us and makes us feel connected to God. When we pray, the doorway to the Divine, which is hidden in our subconscious, opens wide and the feeling of love and acceptance comes pouring into us as God's light shines into our body's energy field. We invite God in to help us create physical, emotional, and mental well-being. God's healing light has tremendous power to help us heal our karma, giving us courage and hope. Whenever we feel lost, scared, or needy we can pray, and God will come in and begin healing those low vibration emotions.

Some people think that accessing the subconscious, which we do when we activate our right brain, opens us up to attracting evil spirits. In all my years of communicating with the Divine and allowing in other energies, including those of people who have died, I have never, ever experienced a dark, ugly, intruding force. It's not that negative, low-level energy entities aren't out there. They are, but they only come around when you generate negative energy for them to feed off of. They cannot do much harm. It is living people, not the dead and not evil spirits, who have the power to truly hurt others. If you are very negative and attract a negative energy field that includes some low vibration entities, they will drop away as soon as you begin raising your vibration. And then you will start attracting more positive energies.

Develop Wisdom and Unconditional Love for Yourself

If you love yourself despite your flaws, you will find the courage to be honest with yourself about the karma you need to resolve. It can be painful to admit that you attract people who take advantage of you, even though you are doing so subconsciously. There is no reason to be ashamed of what is hidden in your subconscious because everyone has failings and weaknesses. If you avoid looking at this darker side of yourself and choose instead to cling to the belief that you are a victim, with no influence over the situations in your life, you will only perpetuate your suffering. Remember, the Law of Love requires that you be compassionate and forgiving of yourself.

Allow Yourself to Receive

It's often hard for people who are naturally "givers" to receive help and abundance from others. If you are uncomfortable with receiving, work on resolving the karma that is preventing you from taking in and retaining what you are attracting. Let's say you consciously want money: You focus your intent on increasing your income, and you work very hard. But then you find yourself uncomfortable with your improving financial situation. You start giving too much money away, not managing it well, and letting it slip through your fingers. This is what happens when you are meant to learn the lesson of receiving.

It may be that you are meant to have a lot of money so that you can focus on other issues you need to resolve rather than struggling with finances. Or you may be meant to come into contact with wealthy people so you can help them resolve their own karma. I came to America with almost no money, just the promise of some income. After I accepted that I wouldn't be a wealthy and popular musical artist here, I took a job in a doctor's office doing clerical work. As luck would have it, I made a prediction for one of his patients, who told actress Candace Bergen about my intuitive abilities. I did a reading for her and she was so impressed, she spread the word. Before I knew it, celebrities and socialites were calling me for readings, and I was earning a lot of money. I was able to further my education, earning two doctoral degrees, in order to help my clients even more. I could have been devastated that I didn't have the singing career I wanted, but I came to accept that I had a different destiny. My goal wasn't to attract money, power, or fame. I received what I needed in order to do what I was meant to do.

I also understood that the Universe hadn't blessed me with my gifts of insight, or with a great deal of money, just so that I could enjoy shopping and eating fine meals and live an easy life. At the same time, I trusted that there was a reason I started out poor and a reason I had money now. I can only guess at the Divine's reasoning, but I do know that by gratefully receiving whatever abundance flows into my life, I am aligning myself with the Eternal Principles. You may feel uncomfortable with what you attract, but God wants you to accept it and work through your karmic issues.

Open your channels to whatever God wants you to receive, in whatever form and timing the Divine decides upon. What you get may not be what you expected. It might be far more rewarding. Then again, you might get exactly what you want, if that's really what's best for your soul. The Universe recognizes no limits to what you can attract.

Material goods can provide earthly comfort, and there is nothing wrong with that. We should appreciate them, but we shouldn't become attached to them or value them too much. Enjoying wealth by spending it on things you don't need but find pleasurable can be like a rest stop on the road. It's helpful to get some respite from constantly moving forward in your growth. Eventually, you have to get back on the highway, so that you can travel toward your destination: the resolution of all your personal karma.

Question Your Ideas about Happiness and Abundance

Open yourself up to different ways of thinking about happiness. Why do you want what you want? We are programmed by our belief systems, and much of the time we do not stop to question them. The truth is, what seems very important in one culture isn't much valued in another.

Look at marriage, royalty, the presidency, and churches. These are all man-made institutions we have created because we think they are terribly important to our well-being. But they do not necessarily help us align with

The Eleven Eternal Principles

divine law. We assume these institutions will last forever, but history has shown that we shouldn't count on it. If we put the Eternal Principles first, we can transform all of these institutions to become better tools at helping us live according to divine law. Then again, we may even end up getting rid of them completely. I believe there will come a time when we won't need governments, royalty, or money, because we will be able to organize ourselves to create peace and stability without them.

To align ourselves with the Eternal Principles, we need to become more worldly. We need to examine the breadth of human experience instead of assume that everyone else's perspective and experiences are just like ours. In America, we are told that teenage daughters naturally rebel against their mothers, that this is "normal." But that isn't the norm in Europe, where daughters tend to become even closer with their mothers in their teen years. When you have the expectation that your child's teenage years will be filled with strife and poor communication, you attract and manifest that reality. Your children pick up on the suspiciousness and defensiveness in your body language and tone of voice. They may become secretive, manipulative, and distrustful in response, making everyone feel miserable. You will attract the situation of conflict between parent and child because you've created the negative thought "My teenager and I are not supposed to get along."

Becoming more aware of other experiences opens you up to better possibilities for yourself. You can consciously choose to reject ideas such as "Teenagers and their parents always fight," or "I have to have a lot of money in order to be happy," and discover ideas that attract much better situations into your life.

The Lesson of the Law of Attraction:

Well-being and contentment are divine.
Suffering and longing are man-made.

God wants us to be happy, healthy, and contented. He wants to meet our every need and free us from the pain of yearning for what we do not have. All God asks of us is that we follow the divine laws so that we can have clarity about what we truly need.

When we distance ourselves from God, we create a sense of fear. We are afraid of being alone and vulnerable in the world, so we grasp at whatever we think might make us feel a little stronger. But as soon as we satisfy one desire, another comes along. The four-bedroom house isn't good enough; we need a five-bedroom one. We decide we have to have something bigger and better. Our constant longing for something outside ourselves makes us suffer. Even when we get what we want, it doesn't make us happy for very long. Our feelings of scarcity return, and we begin pining all over again.

Well-being and contentment are states of satisfaction we can only achieve when we live according to the Eternal Principles. With clarity about what is most important in life, you can see that there is always love, hope, and peace in your life if you are willing to open your eyes. If you can appreciate what you have, your perspective will change. You will stop seeing what you do not have and be amazed at all that God provides to you. Then, you will feel confident that the Universe is working to bring about even better circumstances for you in the future. Your confidence and appreciation will raise your vibration, allowing you to attract what you most need and what will lead you to the greatest happiness. Experience a sense of well-being today, and let the Law of Attraction begin to do its work.

THE EIGHTH
ETERNAL PRINCIPLE:

The Law of Evolution

God intends for us to continually evolve
to a higher state of consciousness.

Recently, there has been a surge of interest in psychics, mediums, 2012 prophecies, energy medicine, and the answer to the question "Where are we going as human beings?" We have more curiosity about the invisible world and sense that we are on the brink of a great transition. We see the pace of change has increased dramatically, and global problems have become dire. We say we want change, but we are afraid of what change may bring. We are fearful of suffering and afraid of the unknown. The work of evolution can be hard and sometimes painful, but we need to raise ourselves to a higher level of awareness before it is too late.

The ancient prophecies of many civilizations point to this era as the time when humanity will evolve or perish as we undergo tremendous shifts in our experience as beings on this planet. Ever since we chose to manifest physical bodies and create humanity, it has been God's intention that we survive. God has always directed our evolution. He intends to help us evolve to a higher state of consciousness, as individuals and collectively. We will do this by resolving our karma and awakening the parts of our brain that normally lie dormant or barely used. We will change the way we think, feel, live, and age, leaving behind our identification with the man-made world as we remember our eternal nature. We will remain conscious of the fact that we are immortal souls who have temporarily taken on a physical form in order to cleanse ourselves of karma.

We once evolved to survive the Ice Age, and now we will evolve to survive the changes that will happen on this planet as cosmic forces assert themselves. To start, we have to stop resisting our evolutionary process and making our problems worse. We need to stop pushing back against the forces of change and growth.

Spiritual evolution means rising above our emotions and egos, helping our souls to become wiser as we shed our karma. Usually, we do this through many failures and mistakes and by creating much suffering for ourselves. We also have the choice to consciously, deliberately devote our attention to aligning ourselves with the Eternal Principles and resolving our karma. If we take this proactive approach, instead of waiting until our suffering compels us to act, we will feel some discomfort, but it will not be nearly as bad as the suffering we would cause ourselves by refusing to go along with the natural evolution of the soul and our species.

As beings whose nature is light energy, we need to purify ourselves and heal our corner of the divine energy matrix. As human beings trying to save ourselves and our planet, we need to "step it up."

The Human Brain, Consciousness, and Evolution

The brain plays a huge role in our evolution of consciousness. Our bodies evolved to have two hemispheres of the brain, which create our perception of duality, right and wrong, up and down, black and white. The world of our senses exists because we are able to perceive it as real and separate from the invisible realm of the Divine.

The left brain understands mathematics, logic, and the rules of traditional physics (such as cause and effect). The right brain allows us to experience tremendous creativity and reality beyond time and space. It understands the rules of quantum physics, which defy the laws of traditional physics.

As long as we live in this world, we must use both sides of our brain. Jesus said we must render unto Caesar what is due Caesar and unto God what is due God. He was telling us that while we are in human form, we are dealing with two realities, the man-made and the Divine. As both sides of our brain work together, we understand our nature as eternal light beings and as creatures with physical form.

Over the course of human evolution, the left brain has come to dominate our thinking and perceptions. We've become unbalanced in the use of our brains, and we have forgotten the potential of the right hemisphere, which the ancient mystics and medicine men recognized and worked with. We haven't begun to imagine what we can create as we become more right-brained, more balanced in our use of our brains, and more aligned with the Divine. Even as we work with both sides of the brain, allowing the right brain to have more influence on us than it has in the past, we are also meant to make use of the pineal gland, which sits between the two hemispheres, and the pituitary gland, which is located near the hypothalamus in the base of the brain. These glands are believed to be the seat of intuition, the portal into the akashic plane where we can know what happened in the distant past and what will happen in the future. We are meant to further evolve and begin making use of this intuitive capacity. Unfortunately, many people are still mostly operating from the far more primitive, emotional area of the brain, the limbic brain, which includes the hypothalamus and amygdala.

When we see something, the information goes through our eyes and activates our hypothalamus, causing an emotional reaction. The information then travels to the pituitary and pineal glands, and we have an intuitive reaction; we get a glimpse of what is happening beneath the surface of the situation and of an immediate intuition about what we should do and what will transpire next. We may get a feeling or sensation that we are in danger, or that someone is lying to us, or that what we are seeing is deceptive. This information, along with our emotional response, then travels to the rational mind, located in the cerebral cortex, which interprets all of the information, using logic.

More often than not, the cortex will overrule the intuitive mind and begin to look for evidence that supports our initial emotional reaction. There's a saying that goes, "When you are angry, count to 100 before reacting." It's good advice, because we need time to counteract our usual habit of letting the emotional center of the brain be in charge. The goal is to allow the cortex to override the hypothalamus and to develop our intuitive abilities so that eventually, they can play as big a role in our thought processes as our cortex does.

Your emotions, created in a less-evolved area of our brain, can lower your level of consciousness and your vibration. Anger, jealousy, sadness, and hatred must be filtered and processed so they do not lead to acting destructively or to attracting situations that mirror these dark feelings. Whether you lash out physically at someone you think has offended you, or you feel bad about yourself because you are intimidated by someone else's success, you are responding to raw, negative emotions in a damaging way. You are not allowing the more evolved parts of the brain to dominate your thinking and reactions. Understanding how the brain processes information from the physical world can give us insight into our emotional responses.

Let's say you are on the freeway and a car cuts right in front of you, forcing you to slow down quickly. Your eyes take in what happens, and the information is processed in your brain. First your hypothalamus is activated, contributing to physiological changes that create feelings of fear and anger, and then your intuitive center gives you a message about what's happening. It's likely that you won't get this intuitive message, either because you are in the habit of ignoring your intuition or because you allow your strong emotions to override it, or both. In a case of road rage, a driver may become so angry that he will drive dangerously in order to pull up next to the other driver and scream at him. Fortunately, most of us are more evolved then this. We hear the strong message from our emotional center, may not hear the quiet message from our intuitive center, but we will listen to the message from our cortex, the rational mind that keeps us safe.

The cortex responds with thoughts about what's happened. If an emotional response is very powerful or you are not evolved enough, your cortex will immediately begin manufacturing negative thoughts that support your emotional response: "He must have done that because he's a jerk! He has *no* respect for me! He could've killed me!" If you are more highly evolved, your cortex will be in the habit of constructing thoughts that are more creative and positive, such as, "Wow, he's driving recklessly. I do not know what's going on that he's driving that way, but I'd better get away from him in order to be safe."

After you brake or steer into a safer position, your conscious mind tells you that you're out of danger. Your sympathetic nervous system now becomes activated, slowing your heart rate and breathing, and stopping the release of the stress hormones so that your body can return to a relaxed state.

A more highly evolved mind would allow the intuitive area of the brain to send its message to you loudly and clearly, possibly even overriding the rational cortex. An even more highly evolved mind would have an active intuitive center that would take in information and begin to work with it before the event actually happened in the world of the senses. You'd be able to know that there is a car driving erratically before you even saw it come up behind you or appear in the road ahead of you. You could respond defensively long before he swerved into your lane. It may sound strange, but this can happen when your intuitive mind is awake and your mind is evolved enough to let its messages dominate.

The Evolution of Human Consciousness and Wisdom

Our brains have enormous capacity, two hundred times that of the most powerful computer, but we are not making full use of them. In fact, we are only working with a small amount of our brain's abilities.

To evolve your brain, your first step is to develop the habit of overcoming primitive, emotional responses and allowing the cortex to override them. You can do this by regularly examining your thought processes.

We create thoughts around our negative emotions so often that it becomes a habit. Cognitive therapy, and regularly examining your thought patterns, allows you to create new mental patterns so that you can develop a new habit of allowing your cortex to overrule your emotions so that you can more accurately assess any situation. Then you can stop automatically reacting to conflicts with others as if you were in actual danger and in need of the energy-providing stress response. You can listen to someone's words and rather than getting angry and thinking, "How dare she say that to me, and attack me like that!" you can say to yourself, "What she just said was rude; something must be upsetting her." You won't instantly feel the need to attack that person or yourself with harsh words. Rather, you can consciously decide what to do next, based on your more positive thought. You might even develop enough compassion that your response will be, "She's being very rude. I wonder why? Maybe she's really upset about something bad that happened to her." You will choose to be loving and kind in response, and you will find the courage to say, "I'm sorry, I do not understand why you are upset," and ask "Did I do something wrong?" It takes strength to listen to someone else express anger, but the wiser you are, the easier it is not to take her rage personally.

As we develop a higher level of consciousness, we bring into our physical reality the compassion and love that exist when we are freed of the weight of our bodies: the same level of consciousness we have after we've died and our souls are once again in the invisible realm. Our negative emotions disappear. Hatred, resentment, and desire for vengeance dissipate. Sadness and suffering evaporate. We remember our traumas, but have no emotional response to them. If we evolve our brains, reprogramming them to be more aligned with divine law, we can lessen the intensity of our negative emotions while we are here in this life. We're meant to do this as individuals and collectively.

Thousands of years ago we may have had very little primitive technology, and science and medicine had yet to be discovered. But I believe we had advanced wisdom and a higher level of consciousness than we have today because we regularly tapped in to divine wisdom and creativity.

As we became more left-brained in our thinking, and more convinced that the material world is the only realm of existence, we lost this wisdom. The ancient Greek physician, Hippocrates, born about 460 B.C.E., said, "Let food be your medicine." Today, we are rediscovering the healing powers of our food. How could we have forgotten this great wisdom? For years, we have tried to improve on God's food, processing it and even genetically altering it. In the 1920s, advertisements in American magazines claimed that canned soup was far superior to homemade versions. In the 1950s, physicians began telling women not to breastfeed their babies but instead to use commercially prepared formulas that they claimed were superior to the food nature made. It is amazing how we have convinced ourselves that we know more than the Divine! And now we are dealing with illnesses and diseases that were rare before we began changing our food supply. It was because of our human arrogance that we discarded Hippocrates' smart advice!

I believe there is lot of ancient wisdom that has become lost over the centuries, as we've replaced the knowledge we've received from the Divine with our own ideas. People killed the ancient priests who were the caretakers for a culture's wisdom traditions and burned all written records so that they could be replaced with the wisdom of the invading peoples. It's interesting that many of these lost writings are beginning to be discovered. The "heretical" texts of the early Christians that flesh out what is written in the Bible were lost to history until after World War II when forgotten scrolls were found near the Dead Sea in Israel and a place called Nag Hammadi in Egypt. (In fact, it's interesting to note that these texts were discovered very shortly after the detonation of the first atom bomb, when human beings developed the technology that would give them the potential to destroy the planet. Perhaps we discovered them because we're meant to remember their lost wisdom!)

Even Nostradamus burned many of his texts and his collection of ancient books one night when he became angry. Out of fear or anger, we've incinerated records of wisdom again and again, forcing ourselves to spend many years recovering the knowledge that was lost. We need to stop allowing our negative emotions to control us and rediscover divine wisdom.

Over the centuries, we've developed many technologies. Sanitation, running water, the cultivation of crops, and the domestication of animals are all very important technologies that improved the quality of life for humankind, giving us more control over our environment. The printing press as well as the telegraph, telephone, radio, television, and Internet increased our ability to communicate ideas and spread knowledge to all the corners of the world. But now we are realizing that for all our technology, we are on the brink of destroying our environment and ourselves along with it. In fact, our technologies have become not just positive developments but threats to our survival as well. Fossil-fuel-burning engines create global warming, while nuclear devices, technologies for waging germ warfare, the Internet, laptop computers, and cell phones make it easier for those who wish to harm others to do so.

Despite all our technological advancement, we have only recently begun to develop our wisdom. The breakthrough of psychology and Freud's identification of the subconscious mind led to explorations of consciousness. At the same time, we were making discoveries in quantum physics that caused us to rethink our ideas about what constitutes reality. We began moving in the direction of divine wisdom once again.

In 1856 Sigmund Freud was born. The father of psychology, and the first modern man to recognize the existence of the subconscious and understand its effect on us, began publishing his findings at the beginning of the twentieth century. A few years later, Carl Jung expanded upon Freud's ideas. Unlike the atheistic Freud, Jung believed in mysticism and insisted that there was a connection between individual awareness and a larger, collective unconscious that was related somehow to divinity. In fact, he was a big believer in the psychic mind and the ability to break linear time.

At the same time that Freud's and Jung's ideas were being formed, published, and discussed in the western world, new spiritual movements were taking place in America. Spiritism, New Thought, and Theosophy, all metaphysical philosophies based in the idea of individuals being connected through consciousness to each other and to the Divine, began to be embraced by westerners. We were starting to rediscover the wisdom of our ancestors, experiencing Divinity firsthand instead of merely believing in the teachings of priests and scriptures. Einstein and others began making discoveries about the nature of reality, which led them to the realization that the old rules of physics no longer applied at the largest level of reality (quantum physics) or the smallest (quantum mechanics).

Where We Are Now

At this stage in human history, we are reclaiming the ancient wisdom and beginning to be less fearful of God and the divine order. We are questioning religious dogma and becoming curious about Divinity. We are educating ourselves on matters of spirituality. However, we are not yet applying what we are learning, at least, not on a large scale. Long ago, the New Testament enhanced our collective wisdom, adding to the ideas about God presented in the Old Testament. Today, we are just beginning to develop a deeper understanding of our relationship to God. We are writing the stories of a new bible.

In the process, we are reexamining our long-held beliefs and institutions. This frightens many people and causes them to cling to old ideas. Even as some human beings are becoming more evolved, others are resisting this growth by embracing the very literal, rigid interpretations of the ancient wisdom teachings of all the religions. Around the world, people are subscribing to religious fundamentalism because they recognize that something vital from the past has been lost. What they do not recognize is that we did not just recently get off track from God's plan for us. We did not begin to lose our way in the 1960s, when feminism, the counterculture, drugs, and eastern religion began to take hold in America and spread to other cultures, or in the modern era, when societies became more secular. We got off track in ancient times, when we turned away from the divine laws, perverting them into religious dogma and into laws designed to help certain groups of people thrive at the expense of others. This misuse of divine law continued into the dark ages as the Catholic Church made rules designed to keep the wealth in the hands of a few. The 1960s were not the beginning of the end of our connection to God; they were the beginning of our asking questions and raising our awareness.

Fundamentalists of all religions are not returning to the fundamentals of spirituality and deeper consciousness. They are returning to the dogma set forth by those whose intention was to create security for their specific group, whether it is a group of light-skinned people, land owners, or people loyal to a particular religious hierarchy. The genuine fundamentals we all need to return to are the Eternal Principles. Those who want to raise their consciousness and move human awareness forward are meant to prevail over those who want to move us backward.

Why We Must Evolve to an Even Higher Level of Awareness *Now*

The coming era of change, including the shifting of the earth's magnetic poles, is likely to cause great upheaval and perhaps even tremendous loss of human life. Previous pole shifts, and earthquakes, tsunamis, and atmospheric shifts, may have been the cause of the sudden extinction of dinosaurs and later, of certain mammals. A new pole change may disrupt electronic communications and create changes in the atmosphere and the earth's geography. We do not have enough data to know exactly what will happen, but it will be dramatic.

It's unlikely that we will be able to do anything to stop these events, but we can maximize our ability to take care of ourselves and each other by raising our consciousness and aligning ourselves with divine law. The more we are able to trust each other and work with each other, the easier it will be to minimize the damage done to humankind by the natural disasters that are

Mother Earth's response to our treatment of her. We'll open ourselves up to new ideas and greater creativity once we let go of our fear, our materialism, and our old ways of operating.

Although we face a difficult era ahead, with the most cataclysmic changes beginning in 2012, we will have transitioned into a one thousand-year era of peace as of November 2033. Humanity will be at a much higher level of enlightenment.

What We Can Do to Begin Our Evolution

Our first job is to slow down, take a deep breath, and ask ourselves, "What am I learning?" "How can I more closely align myself with the Eternal Principles and with God?"

People are at different levels of evolution and perceive the world with different eyes. Those who are more spiritually advanced cope very well with difficult situations. They overcome tragedies through wisdom. Those who haven't evolved very much become trapped in their own difficulties, blocking themselves because they just cannot move on from the past. Unlike evolved people, they do not find solutions to their problems, so they become self-destructive and angry. Evolved people can suffer the same difficult circumstances as others do, but they are open to possibility and learning. This allows them to be creative, and to risk trusting others to help them. They move forward, addressing their issues, attracting better circumstances as they keep their fear at bay. They will help humanity collectively survive the coming upheaval.

Right now, many people are in denial of the changes that we are experiencing. They're trying to make more money and create more security for themselves, and are so caught up in the present that they lack vision and imagination. They're scrambling to figure out how to maintain their old ways of operating, holding on to man-made institutions instead of opening themselves up to better possibilities. We are meant to let go of denial and begin the process of transformation now, working with the Universe to co-create better lives and a better world.

Everything that happens on earth is for the purpose of our evolution and the evolution of all. We have to reexamine what we've always taken for granted, whether it's our lifestyles, our religious or secular beliefs, or our ideas about health. We are stunned by how mixed up our world is. The idea that our banking system in America is so much more precarious than we thought frightens us. We're feeling anxious because September 11 taught us that we can have the greatest military force on earth and yet a handful of people on a suicide mission have the power to paralyze us with fright. We wonder, "Why are all these terrible things happening?"

The answer is that God always sends situations that will push us toward evolution. The saying "what you resist persists" is a karmic truism. And everything we resist also creates and increases our suffering. For a long time we have avoided the transformation we are meant to undergo. The more we try to control our lives by living according to man-made laws, the more we are blind to our karma. The more influence our karma has on us, the more pain we cause ourselves. Whether we like it or not, we have to transform. We cannot avoid it. We have to let go of denial and resistance and open ourselves to Divine assistance.

How We Will Evolve, with Divine Help

Those who are aware that we are in dire straits often look to technology to save our planet and ourselves. Technology will play a role in our evolution, but more importantly, our divinity, our connection with God, will evolve our brains and our minds. Creating a higher state of awareness will bring us closer into alignment with the Eternal Principles and awaken us to divine wisdom. This is what will allow us to survive the crises and threats we are facing.

We long for a savior who can transform our dangerous situation. Many believe Jesus will return to help us, or that the Divine will intervene in some other way. God will definitely help us, but it won't be Jesus or an angelic being who saves us. It will be humans working in conjunction with God by raising our awareness. We have to stop looking outside of ourselves for rescue. When we start raising our own consciousness, Mother Earth will stop creating so many natural disasters, and our barbarism will heal. Together, we will affect the energy matrix and bring us, collectively, to a higher vibration.

In the past, we thought we could use violence, or words and ideas alone, to lift up those who commit violence against others. Now, we are becoming pessimistic, cynical, or disheartened when we see how difficult it is to influence those who are operating at a very low level of awareness. Some people are too limited by their belief systems to be affected by our urging them to recognize that what they are doing is wrong. The way they see it, they are simply trying to survive, and if other people do not understand that, so be it. Some of them are so misguided as to think that what they are doing is beneficial for everyone. People justify everything, from being materialistic, greedy consumers who will betray their own friends in order to make money, to imposing their harsh, fundamentalist religious beliefs on other people in order to force us to live according to their narrow interpretations of God's laws. The Taliban certainly thinks they are helping the world. But, of course, they are harming it. If we are going to awaken these people who are deeply misguided, we have to do it by influencing their energy field, not by talking to them or dropping bombs on them.

We have Divinity to help us. It's God who brings planets into our awareness, infuses them with certain types of energy, and keeps them in orbit. It's God who created the cosmic forces that affect us here on earth.

While we gaze at our changing world in shock and confusion, we begin to experience a great, collective moment of introspection. The ancient calendars end at this point in human history because the prophets and seers knew that this would be the time when we stop and assess our progress. It's as if high school has ended and we need to ask if we earned our diploma. Did we learn our lessons, or do we have to learn something more before we can go to the next stage?

Our awareness of global warming is the result of the Divine getting through to us. We're recognizing the symptoms of an ill earth and an ailing society. We are starting to wonder what's going on. We're becoming more aware of our own mortality and our connection to the fate of the planet and to all of humanity. If the banks and mortgage lenders foreclose on a large number of houses, that affects us, even if we are not homeowners. The cost of fuel is rising and that affects the cost of our food. We're seeing connections we never saw before, and realizing that none of us functions alone. God is awakening us to the Law of Totality, tapping us on the shoulder, but we have to be willing to align ourselves with this Law and make changes in the way we perceive, think, and act. It is time for us to evolve.

How Our World Will Change As We Evolve

As we evolve, we will come to recognize we do not need all of our man-made rules and institutions. They won't be necessary if we change ourselves. In the future, children will learn about the laws of today and say, "I do not understand. Why did people have to be told not to steal from each other, or take advantage of each other?" They will be as baffled by our current institutions as children today are baffled by the idea that many years ago in America, people owned slaves, and cannot understand why adults are stunned by the election of an African-American president. In the future, hurting others through greed and selfishness will be such a rarity that young people will have difficulty understanding why we had any need of prisons and police. If this sounds preposterous, think of how strange it is to imagine people employed to hunt down witches in the Middle Ages and burn them at the stake—but it happened.

We created our laws and institutions in order to solve our problems, but they haven't eradicated killing, stealing, betrayal, or anything else that has plagued humanity since the first human beings walked the earth. Our one hope for fixing the problem is to re-access the ancient wisdom of the Divine.

We do not have to be extremely intelligent to be able to do this. Divine law is so much simpler than the complicated rules we invent in order to prevent civilization from descending into barbarism. We do not need more rules or harsher punishments if we change within, altering our energy field as we align with Divinity. Jesus said, "Love the Lord your God with all your heart and with all your soul and with all your mind." This is the first and greatest commandment. And the second is very similar: "Love your neighbor as yourself." When Jesus told us, "All the Laws and the Prophets hang on these two commandments," He was talking about an evolution of consciousness that allows us to unconditionally love ourselves and others despite our suffering. When we align ourselves with the Eternal Principle of Love, we do not need laws to tell us how to treat other people. It goes without saying that we won't harm them, or ourselves. We do not even need the Ten Commandments to tell us how to live if we truly experience unconditional love for ourselves and others. We know what to do without having to be told.

There will always be people of lower level consciousness, but someday soon, we will not be so dependent on man-made institutions to keep people from harming each other. We'll be able to get rid of some and simplify others, sort of like organizing our files on the computer and deleting the ones that are duplicates or that we aren't using.

Today, however, all our complicated and contradictory man-made laws are choking us. Take our ideas about money: Originally, we came up with a simple symbol to represent value that could easily be exchanged. Now, you could go in a rage trying to figure out your taxes or how the credit card company figures out your finance charges, or understand what a "derivative" is. People who have a Ph.D. in Economics from MIT cannot explain the complicated financial packages that led to the mortgage crisis! We spend a lot of time worrying about money, trying to invest it properly and make sure we have enough of it, only to find that we had so much less control than we thought we had.

When we look around at the deterioration of empty, foreclosed houses, we can see the physical evidence that our man-made laws, based in greed and lack, result in decay and destruction. We need to simplify our lives and the way we interact with each other, letting the Eternal Principles be our guide. Then we can grow past these unnecessarily complex ways of creating a sense of order and security in our lives.

The ancient people of many different lands had holy men and women who knew that real security lies in living according to the Eternal Principles.

They knew the secrets to tapping the potential of the human brain and communicated with the great matrix of Divinity and collective unconsciousness. Sadly, we've forgotten this wisdom, but we can choose to learn it again. Better yet, we can share with others our understanding of how to awaken our brain to its greatest potential so that all of humanity can break free of its man-made limitations and save us from destruction.

Current global thinking is chaotic and negative. We share many emotional wounds that we need to heal so that humankind can experience more love and joy and raise the level of our collective thinking. We can, and do, each play a part in this evolution.

How We Can Evolve As Individuals

One way to evolve your consciousness as an individual is to alter the way your brain processes information. Your goal should be to stop giving your strong, negative emotions so much weight, thereby allowing your feelings and thoughts to create an unnecessary panic response of fight-or-flight. By gaining insights into your thought processes, either through cognitive therapy or introspection, you can consciously choose to think differently about your experiences. You can decide to stop personalizing everything that happens to you. You have the power to stop seeing yourself as a hapless victim of circumstance. You do this by being mindful of the tendency to allow your emotions to rule your thoughts, and then making a better, more positive choice about how to interpret events.

There are several tools that can help you in this process. Breathing exercises can help ward off a panic attack in the moment. When performed regularly, these exercises will slow down the fight-or-flight response. Meditation allows you to become aware of any uncomfortable feelings, thoughts, and physical sensations you've been ignoring. Once you are aware of what you've been running away from, you have to deal with it by looking at the choices you are making, and choosing instead to think and act in alignment with divine law.

Remembering your dreams and analyzing them afterward can also help you to discover what is hidden in your unconscious and then process it. Just as you clean up your computer and delete files you no longer need, you have to find the polluting debris in your mind and get rid of it.

Many times, my clients will say, "But I cannot let go of my anger," or "I just cannot move on." The reason they cannot release these destructive emotions is that they're holding on to the thoughts that create them. You have to let go of your justifications for your negative emotions, not because you are wrong for being depressed after a loss or angry after a betrayal, but because they'll cause you to suffer and remain at a lower vibration.

If you are working on an issue, release your negative thoughts and the feelings they create; then you should see results. You should notice that a situation that previously would have made you furious now is merely irritating. You should feel more balanced, less blown about by the winds of fortunate. Overall, your life should be working better.

I have seen people transform and change their energy field, sometimes dramatically. If you are still in therapy after many years, you've made little progress with your issues, and your life is on the brink of disaster—your finances are precarious, your relationships are unsteady, your self-esteem is shaky—then you are not doing the work you need to do. Be gentle with yourself. Bravely commit to facing and working through your problems. Change your therapist or go into therapy for the first time. Be more honest with yourself as you look at your life. Question the stories you've told yourself about your victimhood and powerlessness.

You also need to resolve your karma. What is not understood by the mind stays there, like something in the stomach that cannot be digested. Karma clogs your system, lowering your vibration. It's like a heavy cloud, thick with dirt and impurities. Process it and you will cleanse yourself, and raise your vibration.

How you communicate matters. People communicate differently, even in our own language. We mean to say one thing and say something else because we are not speaking out of love but out of fear, anger, and frustration. Educate yourself about better ways of communicating, and about basic human psychology, and you will probably find it easier to be compassionate and loving toward those who have a lot of psychological issues—including yourself!

Learn more about spiritual matters through workshops, lectures, and books. Take the time to cultivate your spirituality through introspection, whether that means you meditate or go on retreats. This is the idea behind the Sabbath: it's meant to be a timeout from our everyday lives. However, we are not supposed to be rigid in how we treat our spiritual time-out. Jesus broke the laws of the Jewish Sabbath when He harvested grain to feed his hungry disciples. He healed a man on the Sabbath, because He knew it is not the man-made laws that matter but the spiritual ones. Jesus pointed out that if a sheep were to fall into a pit on the Sabbath, of course the shepherd would rescue it. We should not relegate our spirituality to one specific day and think that once we leave church or the retreat grounds on Sunday our spirituality gets turned off. We need to take time out to nurture our spiritual nature every day so that it is easier for us to access it at any given moment.

Sometimes we evolve as the result of circumstances outside of our control, such as when experiencing a moment of grace—a person can be changed the first time he sees something miraculous, whether it is a vision of the Virgin Mary or the birth of a child. We can also awaken to a higher consciousness and begin our evolution as a result of experiencing significant losses or traumas. Being open to the miracles and mystery of life can result in huge leaps in consciousness.

Learn from what others before you have learned. Former Muslim extremists and terrorists have said that their mind-set was forever altered after spending time in introspection while in jail and being exposed to different ideas through reading the Bible or talking to American interrogators who encouraged them to exercise critical thinking. Too often, we do not take the time to examine our thought processes. We operate the way we always have, without stopping to question our ways.

One former terrorist claimed that the unselfishness of a volunteer working with Amnesty International helped him when he was imprisoned to reject his belief system and hatred for the West. He was influenced by the higher consciousness of the volunteer. Another had a change of perception after seeing an individual surrounded on a street and beaten to death simply because he was Jewish. Those who say "You cannot talk to a terrorist" (meaning you cannot influence them at all) are not evolved enough to look at the roots of terrorists, or to listen to the lessons former terrorists have to tell us. As long as we remain in a lower level of evolution, we cannot help those who are in danger of falling into the trap of violent extremism or who are caught in it. And as long as we hold on to the false belief that people never change, we hold humanity back from its evolution. If a terrorist can change, any of us can.

We have so much to learn from the insights and experiences of those who have made a leap forward in their own awareness. Evolution begins with pushing aside the ego that says, "I'm not as bad as that person over there, so why should I change?" We have to admit there is work to do, we do not know everything, and we do not have a full picture of life. A limited view of life is like looking at a sculpture from just one side. When we can only see the part of the sculpture directly in front us, we argue with the people standing on the other side of that sculpture, insisting that our view is the correct one and always has been. We broaden our perspective by walking around it, seeing all sides, and synthesizing what we take in.

What Will Happen As We Evolve

Spiritual evolution takes us to the next plane of awareness. Our thoughts change, then our feelings follow suit. Even our body transforms as a result of our new, higher vibration. I have had several clients who were surprised when a physical ailment of theirs suddenly healed after they left a bad relationship or stressful job situation. They didn't realize their negative thoughts and feelings were manifesting the headaches, backaches, and stomach problems. They didn't know they held the key to returning to a better state of health.

All of humanity is experiencing illness. Our brain waves are creating a reality that is no longer working for us, one that is out of balance and out of alignment with divinity. We need to purify ourselves so that we can create a better world.

As each of us evolves to a higher vibration, we start perceiving differently. We recognize that other people, just like us, are operating from fear and frustration, and that just like us, they have the same basic desires. Because we see them differently, we are able to love them more perfectly and communicate with greater compassion. We can listen with love and attention.

Globally, people are beginning to recognize that the old ways of trying to maintain peace are not working. We need to do something dramatic to turn things around. We can make this evolutionary leap together if even just a small minority of people lead the way.

Evolution and the Other Eternal Principles

While we are in a low state of consciousness, we face the depletion of the earth's resources, including water and food. All around the world, we are seeing more food riots and disagreements over the use of precious water supplies. We're meant to recognize the Law of Totality and open ourselves up to discovering ways to share the earth's bounty.

If we obey the Law of Wisdom and the Law of Harmony, we will make good judgments about how to live in harmony with the earth.

To evolve to a higher level of awareness, we need to love unconditionally, as the Law of Love requires. We are now realizing we make more progress by talking to our enemies instead of isolating them (although we have to be very careful about our communication with them).

Very evolved souls who have shed their karma are able to create a high state of consciousness when they return to human form. They are able to activate parts of the human brain that allow them to perceive differently. From this higher state it is easier for them to set aside the distractions created by the world of the senses and interact with the invisible world of the Divine. These evolved beings are able to align themselves with the Eternal Principles more easily than younger souls can. They recognize that unconditional love has more power than domination, violence, and manipulation. They will help us evolve.

One of my clients is a very young soul, and is very dysfunctional. She told me she'd fallen in love with a man, but she experienced such extreme emotions whenever she talked about him that I knew she wasn't actually in love. She hardly knew this person and never spoke of why she loved him or what aspects of his she found attractive, other than his money and reputation. She'd become so obsessive about him that shortly after she began working with me, this man took out a restraining order against her. In some corner of her awareness, she knew that her behavior was unhealthy and unloving, even though she couldn't consciously admit to it. This small level of awareness is what brought her to me. Her family had engaged in so many power struggles over so many years that she grew up having no idea what a healthy relationship with another person looks or feels like. She'd had no guidance whatsoever on how to be loving or giving. I became like a mother figure to her because she was so desperate and needy. She knew I wouldn't judge her, and that I would listen to her stories about this man and her behavior, and I would say, "It's okay that you are obsessive, but let's help you heal."

As a counselor, I can do my best to help my clients, but as with any helping profession, there are times when someone has such deeply rooted issues that they are too terrified to explore them fully. This particular client couldn't bear the emotional pain of looking at why she was so frightened of creating a healthy relationship, so while she was willing to go into counseling and admit she had a problem, she strongly resisted any attempts to explore her deepest issues, no matter how gentle I was. She would change the subject or insist that it wasn't worthwhile to have conversations about certain topics. She longed to evolve but wasn't ready to take more than a baby step in that direction. Many people in the world are at this low level of awareness.

However, I have also seen people suddenly find the courage to deal with the most painful traumas that they had refused to think about for years, sobbing in my office and crying out in anger so fierce that it scared them.

They were then able to evolve to a higher level of consciousness and leave therapy knowing that they had done significant healing work. Evolution is not easy, but most of us have the potential to make a great leap forward as long as we are willing to begin the process.

Those who want to believe there are no ugly, painful issues to work through will strongly resist evolution. They do not want to face the darkness within them that has to be addressed, and they will pressure others to deny the problems as well. We must resist this temptation, as well as the temptation to elevate one particular person or group. We cannot predict who will awaken to a higher state of consciousness and who will not.

Evolution means clearing our karma and being compassionate, caring, and loving toward everyone. It means recognizing that war, hateful speech, and anger are draining and destructive and need to be replaced by positive interactions and creative ways of solving problems. We cannot change the outer world until we change inside. True evolution occurs from the inside out.

We haven't seen a major spiritual evolution in two thousand years, but now we are on the verge of a major change. We see the evidence everywhere, including on the bestseller list. We're fascinated by the Law of Attraction and by the stories of Harry Potter and his friends, which illustrate the transcendent power of love and working together with other people to overcome darkness. Those books became huge phenomena because we all sense that we do not have to continue our current suffering, that there is a different way to live that will bring us joy, abundance, and a sense of harmony. Each one of us can start evolving today and bringing about the world we long for and deserve.

The Lesson of the Law of Evolution:

Evolution, growth, and improvement are divine.
Stagnation and deterioration are man-made.

Crisis leads to evolution. Resisting evolution leads to crisis. One way or another, we are forced to evolve.

Our divine nature dictates that we move forward, constantly improving ourselves, and always striving to reach a more perfect state. That which is stagnant inevitably dies and becomes fuel for something else to grow. The dead body of a mouse decays and becomes food for bacteria, which break it down into nutrients that enrich the soil and nourish the seedling that busts out of its hull and stretches up through the earth toward the sky. This cycle allows the physical world to continually replenish itself. Yet in our limited state of awareness, we see death and destruction as end points. We mourn what is lost and what breaks down or decays.

As you raise your level of awareness, you start to remember that everything that seems lost isn't really gone forever. It just takes on a different form. You recognize that in the same way that Creation is constantly reinventing itself, your soul is constantly shedding old beliefs and thought patterns, using them as nourishment to help it grow. The lessons of your karma allow you to become wiser. Even the worst actions you have taken can be used as food for the soul if you stop denying what you've done. When we learn from our mistakes, we become better, more loving, and wiser people.

Decay or deterioration occurs not just in nature, but also in our minds, especially when we choose to cling to what we have, right now, out of a false sense of security. We decide we do not want to try something new and risk not liking it, or upsetting the people we care about, or losing something we value. We convince ourselves that we do not have to change. We tell ourselves that we have reached the point of success and happiness we deserve so we can rest and enjoy ourselves until very suddenly, death comes. Inevitably, if we live this way, in denial of the fact that everything is always changing, a crisis occurs. It will shake us out of our complacency and force us to return from our lifelong vacation so that we can get back to the work of evolution. God is like the teacher who takes us aside to ask, "Mid-terms are next week. Have you been studying?", or who gives us snap quizzes to remind us of how important it is to keep learning.

Even those with a very high level of vibration, who are at a high level of consciousness, have work to do. Usually, people in this state of being feel a passion or drive to serve the world and create good karma. But sometimes, even they become distracted by the pleasures in life and stop paying attention to all that has to be done for the good of humanity. Every one of us will get a chance to rest in peace after we die; while we are here, we have work to do. We have to evolve.

To maintain a higher vibration and not slip back into a lower vibration, we must remain vigilant. Regular spiritual practices reconnect us with the Divine and our purpose here on earth. Staying aware of what is going on in the world and outside our door is important as well. Many people choose not to watch the news, because it can be very depressing, but to completely detach from what is going on in the world isn't good either.

Wealthy people may write checks to their favorite charity or become involved in high-level fundraising activities, but they will stop feeling an emotional and spiritual connection to the people they're helping if that is all they do. When that happens, they begin to focus on petty disagreements between people involved in the charity and expend their energy engaging in power struggles, forgetting what they are supposed to be doing even as their vibration slips lower. Those who aren't wealthy but engage in positive activities such as parenting, serving the community, working for a company that provides quality goods, or whatever they spend their time doing, face the same danger. When parenting becomes a competition with the other parents, serving the community becomes more about serving the ego, or quality standards slip because cutting corners leads to a slightly higher profit, people's vibration will slow down. Their light will dim, and the Universe will respond with a crisis that will remind them to get back to work!

The other day, I read in the newspaper that the owner of several businesses in my community was found guilty of selling stolen goods. The amount of money involved was small in comparison to the profits he made honestly from his highly successful businesses. He must have been fearful that his wealth wouldn't be enough to keep him secure, happy, or successful. It was sad to read that this man, whose businesses were much respected and who was known for giving back to the community, had stained his reputation and risked losing everything he valued, from his businesses to his freedom, for just for a few more dollars. Unfortunately, this type of self-destruction happens when we turn away from divine law. We allow ourselves to become engulfed by the reality of the material world, where we have to fight to hold on to happiness and security, and where all that we work for will eventually slip away or decay anyway.

I have beautiful homes and I appreciate them, but every year, I spend money on their upkeep because in the physical world, things fall apart. Our things can fall apart, but we do not have to. We can identify with our divine, eternal soul, and align our thoughts, feelings, and actions with all of Divinity. When we do, we change our vibration to one of healing, growth, and improvement. Then the physical world, including our bodies, our homes, and our communities, will start to reflect our energy state.

Have you ever woken up after having been ill with the flu or a cold for a few days, looked around your home, and thought, "I have to clean up around here!" As soon as you are feeling good, you want your environment to reflect how you feel. The Universe works the same way. It immediately starts cleaning up once there is a shift into positive energy.

We do not have to worry about how to make our lives better. It will happen naturally when we align ourselves with the Divine Principles. The physical world hurries to fall into alignment with our new, higher, collective state of consciousness.

THE NINTH
ETERNAL PRINCIPLE:

The Law of Manifestation

The power to manifest what we desire
is our birthright, and we are constantly
co-creating reality with the help
of the Divine.

Our brain waves, the force of our consciousness, create physical reality. It's said that whatever we think about we bring about, but that is an oversimplification of the Law of Attraction and the Law of Manifestation. After all, we aren't the only ones projecting our thoughts outward and interacting with the material world. Billions of people on this planet are also affecting reality.

We act based upon our emotions, and, if we are more evolved, we act on our thoughts as well. In addition to influencing the world through our actions, which we can easily observe, we influence it through the force and quality of our brain waves. We do not simply attract circumstances that match up with our vibration, as the Law of Attraction suggests; we also *manifest* circumstances, bringing them about through our thoughts, feelings, and actions. Remember that attraction is different from manifestation in that attraction brings things to you while manifestation allows you to make things happen in the physical world. If our brain waves have a low vibration, we will manifest low-vibration situations. If we generate positive thoughts and emotions, and act in productive and creative ways, we will change our lives for the better.

It is important to understand that it can take an enormous amount of energy for one individual to influence physical reality. If you look at a rock, which has a very low vibrational level, and is an extremely dense form of matter, then focus your intent on making it float in the air in front of you, you are not going to see it jump up from the ground. If you have a dream to become a performer, write a book, or go back to college and change careers, your positive attitude and your vision of yourself achieving your goal will be helpful to you, but you will still need to work hard to get to where you want to be.

Our brainwaves really do manifest physical reality. Many people working together and using the power of prayer and positive thought can heal a person many miles away. Their collective prayers can cause a tumor to dissolve or skin tissue to grow more cells and quickly close up an open wound. This is the power of the Law of Manifestation. And often, our energy affects physical reality in ways we do not recognize.

Einstein discovered that energy never disappears; it only converts into another form. Light energy becomes chlorophyll, which is food for plants, which feed animals, which feed humans, who have thoughts and feelings that are forms of energy. Manifestation refers to ideas and thoughts and emotions—all of which are information in the form of light energy—that transform into solid form.

We think of energy and matter as two separate things because of our level of perception, but remember, at the quantum level, the very smallest bit of matter (a particle) flips back and forth between being matter and being light energy (a wave). Our interaction with and expectation of that particle or wave influences its nature. To understand the power of manifestation, we need to understand the nature of reality at the quantum level: everything that appears to be solid is actually an expression of energy that changes but never can be destroyed, and our observation of physical reality (the particle or wave) influences it. In other words, if we expect to see a wave, the particle will appear to be a wave. These rules of quantum physics help us grasp the Eternal Principle of Manifestation.

Every thought, feeling, and action is a form of energy, but it also has a physical reality. Because our minds are very active, creating new beliefs, ideas, and emotions, we are constantly changing our physical reality. Our challenge is to stop trying to affect the world only through action, and recognize that manifestation begins in the mind. Actions follow from there.

Manifestation from the Inside Out

Whenever your mind creates a thought, biochemical actions and reactions take place in your brain, which releases waves of energy that travel like sound waves or light waves outside of you. Most people aren't sensitive enough to pick up on these waves of energy consciously, but some can sense them subconsciously. These people are thought to have "psychic abilities" or "a sixth sense." In fact, there are people whose senses are so acute they can smell snow or hear someone breathing in the next room. For me, being able to access energy information that others cannot perceive is like being able to hear a very quiet sound or smell a subtle chemical change in the air. My ability to pick up on extremely subtle transmissions of energy is a gift, but I believe everyone's brain has the potential to do the same. We know how to develop those skills a little, but we do not yet understand how we can deliberately bring those parts of the brain fully online. The ancients knew how to fully awaken the parts of the brain that are dormant in modern man, but unfortunately, we have lost their wisdom.

Nevertheless, we do have the power to consciously choose better thoughts and beliefs in order to help us manifest a better reality. The energy of our thoughts affects the energy matrix and therefore the reality of our world.

Our thoughts also translate into words, feelings, and actions. In the brain, what starts as a biochemical reaction, an expression of energy, turns into a different expression of energy as the body responds to our conscious or unconscious thoughts. We move our lips, tongue, lungs, and throat to create spoken words, which produce sound waves. Our emotions create biochemical reactions (for example, fear causes the adrenal glands to release the hormones cortisol and adrenaline into the body while joy produces healing endorphins). These biochemicals affect our body's movements and our actions. Our emotions and thoughts lead to actions that influence other people and objects, whether we glower at them or smile, storm out of a room and slam the door, or touch someone's arm lovingly. In this way, the energy of a single thought manifests in physical form.

If you are not in control of your patterns of thinking and you let your subconscious choose your thoughts instead of putting your conscious mind in charge, you are unleashing energy that will manifest thoughts, feelings, and actions you do not want to experience. You will end up shaping your circumstances so that they match up with your low-vibration, negative feelings and beliefs.

What Happens When You Don't Acknowledge Your Role in Manifesting Reality

It's difficult to fashion the physical world in a positive way because we are usually unaware of how our negative thoughts and beliefs influence what we manifest. Our anger and frustration also drain us of the energy we could be using to achieve our goals. Consequently, we can feel as if we have no influence over the world. We feel abandoned by God, overwhelmed, and paralyzed. To escape this deeply uncomfortable feeling of powerlessness, we either withdraw or lash out. We give up and stop trying to make our lives or our world better, or we go on a furious rampage, blaming others for all the problems we see, taking a cynical attitude and again, giving up hope of changing matters. Either way, we manifest more suffering and more problems.

Self-righteous anger can create something positive if it wakes you up and then you turn your anger into passion and connect with divine strength. Anger that doesn't serve to awaken your wisdom will only consume you. You will be angry with the person or group you feel is harming the world, whom you are trying to stop. You will even become angry with the people who might help you in your cause. Eventually, you will have so much rage that it spills over onto everyone and you will sabotage yourself.

To make your actions effective, you must let go of your anger. When you do, you will experience higher-vibration emotions that lead you to discover your wisdom, creativity, love, patience, and compassion, all of which are the most powerful tools for influencing others. Anger is meant only to awaken you. Once you are awake, let go of it immediately; or it will block you from the important next step of opening to wisdom and creativity. You will still feel impassioned and driven to make changes. The difference is that instead of being driven by blind anger and getting stuck in a battle to fix the problems you see, you will be driven by passion that allows you to manifest a better situation.

Too often, we forget that we have Divine power to draw upon. We usually pray only when we are in trouble. When my husband became very sick recently, I prayed to every saint, morning to night. In times of crisis, we invite Divinity in, hoping to feel our connection because we realize we need help. But we should regularly pray for help. If your life is going along beautifully, pray for others so that they may experience joy and abundance as well.

Don't wait for something awful to happen before you reconnect with the Divine. Nurture your relationship with Divinity every day. Make spirituality a core part of your experience, as you see the beauty in your life and in the world around you and as you align yourself with the Eternal Principles. The strength you tap into will carry you through the most challenging of times, allowing you to manifest something new and more positive.

Another thing that happens when we do not understand, acknowledge, and direct our power to manifest physical reality is that we end up acting in ways that create suffering. We can try very hard to fix our problems, but if we do not change our inner, negative, unconscious beliefs, our work will be in vain. Our unconscious mind's power to attract and manifest is stronger than the power of our conscious mind. We need to become aware of our unconscious thoughts and resolve our karma, as well as take action to bring about the life we desire. Otherwise, we will be confused by why we want one thing but manifest something completely different.

So many people I meet are operating out of the fear and belief that they are unloveable, unworthy of happiness, and not special. It's amazing how many negative thoughts people create about themselves and then allow them to run through their minds all day long. It's rare to meet someone who is constantly creating thoughts such as "I can do whatever I set out to do!" or "Now, this is an interesting and unexpected challenge, but I'm up for it!" Instead, we play an endless tape loop of negative beliefs that disempower us. All our extraordinary skills remain unawakened because we do not trust ourselves and we have low self-esteem. We can do what we want, but we must believe in ourselves.

When we feel bad about ourselves, we can't find the impetus to take action. We think, "That won't work. I can't do it. I'm not going to bother trying." While there are challenges and obstacles in life, we must look at what we can do instead of focusing on our limitations. We have to stop believing in our powerlessness and work with the Law of Manifestation. The greater the number of people who do this, the sooner we will be able to solve problems that have plagued humanity for ages.

How Negative Emotions and Beliefs
Affect What You Manifest

The biggest block to positive manifestation is our emotions. We create a lot of negative feelings and assign them far too much importance. Emotions become like blocks of stone when we convince ourselves that feelings are unchangeable or permanent. If we sit with our emotions, quietly observing them and accepting that they are a part of being human, we will stop seeing them as all-powerful and overwhelming. Then, we will experience our feelings shift, and we will realize that emotions come and go. Children are much wiser than we are. They will feel intense frustration or sadness, sob and wail, and then suddenly run off into another room to play. They do not create involved stories about why they are so upset, how an emotion reminds them of how they felt six years ago when something else happened, how bad things always seem to happen to them, and so on. They feel their feelings and move on, which is what we are meant to do as adults. When we relearn this resilience, we will manifest better circumstances.

Too many people buy the belief that life is supposed to be suffering and the only release is death. The idea that "life is suffering" is different from "there is going to be some suffering in life." We're all going to experience unhappiness at times, but if you perceive that life is misery, you will constantly create a feeling of suffering and continually manifest it in the world. You must alter your beliefs and perceptions so that you can change your brain waves. Then you can stop being so afraid of what's to come and instead start manifesting what you hope for.

Many of our leaders today lack vision, and many people lack a vision for their own lives. How can we manifest a peaceful, harmonious, abundant world if we cannot even imagine it? We could not have freedom of speech, personal computers and the Internet, or support groups if some person or group of people hadn't turned away from negativity and toward creativity and envisioned these things. Once you know where you are going, and you take a positive attitude, the road to your destination begins to appear.

Habits, Brain Patterns, and Manifestation

To align yourself with the Law of Manifestation, you must understand how difficult it is to change your habits. All of us have habits. They are encoded in our brains as patterns of thought, feeling, and behavior. Your brain contains billions of neural pathways that determine how you think, feel, and act. All over the world, there are paved roads that hundreds and hundreds of years ago were rutted dirt pathways carved out by horses and carriages. Before that, they were probably footpaths. Each time a person or a carriage traveled over that path, the path was reestablished. Eventually, these well-worn paths were covered with cement and became modern roadways. The neural pathways of the brain work in a similar way. Every time you think the same thought or respond in the same way to a situation, you reinforce and solidify the roads in your brain. Each time you respond to criticism by becoming defensive and angry, you reinforce neural pathways that associate criticism with being attacked. Eventually, your neural pathway will operate so efficiently that you will react angrily to perceived criticism just as quickly and easily as if you were flipping a light switch.

To reprogram your brain takes time, effort, and practice. You actually have to lay down a new neural pathway so that instead of instantaneously responding with defensiveness, you can respond in a different way. To do this, you have to be aware of what your patterns are. Spend time in reflection and align yourself with the Law of Evolution, exploring and healing your unresolved karma so that you can manifest a better life and work with others to manifest a better world.

Manifesting Well-Being

What we need to manifest first is well-being. Mental, emotional, and physical health are equally important. Health and vitality give us the energy to act, to become courageous and creative. When you experience well-being, you are better able to be creative and envision a way to improve your life and the world. You are also able to follow through with positive actions, even in a challenging situation.

Mental and emotional health leads to physical health. Just as you do not have complete control over your karma (because you share karma with others) or your manifestations (because others are manifesting circumstances at the same time that you are), you do not have complete control over your physical health. You cannot control all the amount of toxins in the environment or make certain that every gene you have that predisposes you to illness remains dormant. Illness occurs, sometimes even despite a strong sense of well-being and contentment. If you get sick, it is not productive to dwell on why it happened and then feel guilty about your part in its manifestation. Instead, look at what lessons your illness can teach you. If you learn these lessons, you have a much better chance of manifesting health and curing or alleviating your illness.

Your thoughts and emotions become tangible, measurable biochemicals in the body. You can think yourself sick or boost your immune system by generating positive thoughts and feelings. Endorphins, biochemicals you can create through positive emotions, have enormous healing benefits. Endorphins are the body's natural morphine. They are the polypeptides you produce whenever you smile, laugh, or exercise. Endorphins are known to alleviate pain and to regulate growth, sexual hormones, and insulin levels, as well as protect the heart from cardiac disease and enhance memory and brain health.

While your positive emotions and thoughts can produce healing biochemicals, your negative ones can cause destruction within the body. Anger is an emotion that has physical reality. Like all emotions, anger is associated with biochemicals that can be identified in the body as they flow through the bloodstream. A thought such as "That person just lied to me to take advantage of me!" creates the emotion of anger as well as its biochemical response. Anger is a particularly powerful form of energy because it sets off a body response called the fight-or-flight syndrome. When we are overly angry, the sympathetic nervous system increases our blood pressure, heart rate, and the amount of sugar in our blood; makes our breathing become fast and shallow; and causes the release of the hormones cortisol and adrenaline into the bloodstream. This biological response gives us extra energy so that we can react to perceived danger by fighting fiercely or quickly fleeing. However, the body is only meant to use the fight-or-flight response when we are in true danger. If you are under stress or angry because someone has hurt your feelings, you are unnecessarily experiencing the fight-or-flight response and putting great strain on your body. Cortisol and adrenaline are very destructive to brain chemistry. In fact, people who are under severe stress have difficulties with memory and thinking clearly because of the oversupply of these stress hormones.

As individuals, we can manifest illness or disease. Collectively, we can do the same. Right now, we are creating a lot of illness in the world. For years, we have ignored the amount of toxins we put into the environment, and are consequently manifesting new diseases no one ever heard of before. As a group, we need to learn the lessons of these diseases so that we can change our karma. We do not have to suffer from epidemics anymore.

We accept that we are going to age and die. We do not fight our mortality, though many of us would like to prolong our lives. If we understood that as souls, we can change the very nature of our physical reality, we could begin to manifest healthier bodies and then we could truly live longer. We have the potential to use our minds to repair our cells and bones. If we want to live healthier, longer lives, we need to start embracing that potential.

We also need to embrace the fact that our disharmony with others causes disharmony at a physical level. A client of mine who was not a smoker developed lung cancer as her third marriage was failing. Illness is not simply a matter of external toxins affecting us or genes whose potential must be realized. We do not have to develop cancer just because many people in our family did if we choose to manifest well-being on the inside. When we are angry or in conflict with others, inflammation is created in our bodies. But we do not have to create inflammatory-based illnesses, such as heart disease and arthritis, if we are willing to give up living in a continual state of anger. As our well-being and feelings of peacefulness affect those around us, we affect the larger matrix. Then, humanity will not have to suffer from the terrible diseases we've collectively manifested.

Choosing to Manifest a Better
Life and a Better World

What do you want to manifest? What matters most to you?

I remember as a child, living in a tiny house with no running water, sharing with my family our great excitement when the only tree in our backyard went into bloom each spring. It was such a glorious miracle, and one we could appreciate because we had so little.

My family and our neighbors somehow always managed to find food and shelter, but we didn't long for material wealth. Of course, we looked forward to the day when Ceausescu would be ousted from power, and to obtaining more freedom and opportunities. But, we felt we had very little power to make these events come about. Over many years, Romanians began to change their minds about the inevitability of their government so that when a few brave souls began to protest, it took only about ten days before Ceausescu was removed from power. Romanians first had to believe freedom and a more open government were possible before they were able to bring about new circumstances. (Unfortunately, rather than arresting, trying, and imprisoning their dictator, the Romanians assassinated him, creating negative karma that they will have to resolve.)

Often, we work very hard for a long time to make something happen and then suddenly take a quantum leap, as we did in Romania. We see this with technology as well. If we believe it will be a long time before the world can rely solely on renewable, nonpolluting energy resources, then that becomes our reality. Fortunately, there are optimistic, creative people who do not believe the limiting predictions about how long it will take to invent new technologies. They are living according to the Law of Manifestation and inventing those technologies! If we could join them in their optimism, we would progress toward this goal even faster.

When you think about what you want to manifest, ask yourself about your true motivation. Be honest with yourself. Are you attached to getting something in return for your efforts, whether it is fame, admiration, power, or money? The Universe will support big projects that are honest, sincere, and unconditionally serving humanity and the planet. If someone's ego is driving a project that is supposedly for the benefit of others, it may succeed for a while, but soon that person will pay the karmic price for being greedy and the project will suffer. It's okay to dream big, to want to manifest a much better life and world, but whatever your dream, you need to make sure it isn't rooted in a desire for power and personal glory. If you are aligning yourself with the Eternal Principles, you will be happy about any progress you make even if it is taking more time and effort than you thought it would take.

Try not to be rigid about what you want to create. Be open to how your plan will manifest, and keep a pure heart. That way, you won't give up on your dreams when obstacles come along. One way to keep a healthy perspective is to look back on what your problems and roadblocks were five or ten years ago. What seemed hugely important then probably seems trivial now, or your problems most likely resolved themselves without your having to fix them.

When you broaden your perspective instead of being hyperfocused on your current problems, you will feel hopeful, enthusiastic, and patient. If you are on the right track and doing your best to learn your lessons, you will probably be shocked one day when all that you've hoped to manifest suddenly appears in your life.

How to Work with the Law of Manifestation

Whatever it is that you wish to manifest, you must visualize it and work for it. Relentlessly concentrate on your dream, and put all your effort into making it come true. If your dream is to have a sense of community so that you do not feel lonely, then do not let one day go by without envisioning yourself surrounded by loving, supportive people, and reaching out to someone to foster your relationship with him or her. If your dream is to have a home, a happy marriage, and a family, visualize that and take action toward it daily. You will never meet your mate if you only daydream and never meet anyone, go anywhere new, or take any risks. Every day move a little closer to your goal by acting in alignment with the Law of Manifestation.

If you find yourself feeling shy, scared, or hopeless, examine your beliefs and emotions and replace those negative feelings with ones that are more positive. Every day, work on resolving your karma and your issues so that you can become clearer on what you most want, have a pure intent, and engage in actions that will bring about the life you envision.

You may not have the freedom to put a great deal of effort into your goal every single day. Life intervenes: you have to deal with financial challenges, your children and elderly parents need you, and unexpected problems crop up. But if you go too long without connecting to your dream and doing something, however small, to achieve it, you may give up on it. Manifestation takes perseverance.

Avoid Negativity

Negative energy will lower your vibration, making it hard to manifest what you desire. Avoid being around people who gossip, judge, or blame, and do not indulge in any of these activities yourself. Don't follow the lead of someone who encourages you to have a cynical attitude or to be judgmental of others. If such a leader has skills or resources to share, you might be able to learn something from him, but be very careful about allowing your admiration for his talents and successes to blind you to his destructive beliefs and behaviors. Emulating such people and adopting their low-vibration beliefs will hold you back from manifesting positive circumstances and bringing your dreams into reality. Look to healthier people for examples of how to create what you desire. You do not have to succumb to snobbery or self-righteousness.

Sadly, we have too few leaders today who can put aside their own fears and their ego's desire for attention, admiration, and power in order to lead people into a higher level of awareness. Many of them start out with a dream of serving humanity but end up compromising their integrity and slipping into narcissism. They fear that otherwise, they won't be able to manifest their goals. We see this change occur in politicians, religious leaders, and community activists. We won't see unselfish, courageous leaders begin to emerge in large numbers until we begin to heal our collective fears and insecurities, and resolve our group karma. There isn't going to be a transcendent leader who will fix our problems for us. But we can follow Mahatma Gandhi's advice to "be the change you want to see in the world."

Always remain aware of how damaging anger, jealousy, gossip, and depression are. Commit to not letting them be a part of your vision of the world. Work at ridding yourself of destructive thoughts and feelings. Every time you feel a dark emotion, stop yourself, recognize that this will prevent you from manifesting joy, and make a conscious decision to take yourself into a higher state of consciousness. If you are angry, walk out of the room. If you are upset, take the time to go somewhere and cry until the feeling passes. Whatever you do, stop yourself from creating a train of thought that prolongs negativity. Say to yourself, "I'm furious right now and that is okay, because the intensity of my anger is passing away even now. I'm going to bring love and curiosity into this situation so that I can learn from it and start making it better." With practice, you will be able to create a positive intention very quickly.

In this way, you will develop the habit of recognizing when you are about to engage in a battle. Instead of charging into it, you will be able to defuse the anger and fear, bringing in a positive, healing energy. You do not have to feel discomfort in your stomach, throbbing in your head, or tension in your muscles caused by rage. Manifest peace and creativity in your mind and your body, express it, and transform the emotional energy in your small corner of the world.

Rather than avoid someone who is upset, or take on their negative emotional state, it feels wonderful to be able to approach them and gently validate their frustration while offering a possible solution or a little joke to lighten the mood. Whenever you do this, you recognize your power to bring yourself and the world closer into alignment with the Eternal Principles.

Be Patient and Work Hard Each Day

Be patient with yourself, because change takes time. If you find yourself losing hope and feeling powerless, break down your plan of action into small steps. A desire to meet a good partner, build a great relationship, and get married is a very large goal. It can be difficult to see what you can do today toward meeting it. The small step you take toward this goal may be to go on a date. Tomorrow you can exercise to boost your mood. The next day you may take some time to ponder a problematic behavior you want to change. Every day, you can take at least one small step toward manifesting the life you say you want.

Give up the desire for a quick fix to your greatest challenge. If you received such a gift, you'd be likely to squander it because you hadn't learned the lessons you needed to learn along the way to your achieving your goal. People who become rich and famous very quickly or who move in immediately after they begin a relationship with someone often discover this painful truth. Align yourself with the Divine and your goal will manifest exactly as it is meant to, in perfect timing, thanks to your hard work and attitude and a positive response from the Universe.

Be Open to How and When Your Dream Manifests

As a pop singer I just wanted to sing, to express myself and to lift other people up in joy. I didn't have specific goals about performing in a prestigious concert hall or making a certain amount of money. Before my career took off, I went to college and learned several languages, then took a job in an office to ensure that I would be able to have food on my table if I couldn't make enough money singing. Too many people think they should be making good money at their chosen career a year or two after they've begun. People are very impatient to create material wealth and the illusion of security. They have no idea how much hard work it takes to reach a goal, and they do not want to "pay their dues" to manifest their dream. If it takes longer than they expect to get to where they want to be, they start losing faith in themselves and give up. Or, they cut corners and cheat in order to get ahead. In which case, when they do reach their goal, they have to be extra vigilant to hide what they haven't learned and watch their back for enemies they may have made along the way. I have a client named Julie, who experienced a lot of stress at work after a younger woman was hired to help Julie with her workload. This younger woman was extremely competitive, and the boss encouraged her to battle with Julie to win new clients because she mistakenly thought this would be the best way to grow the business. Julie was not up for a hostile competition and was traumatized by the younger woman's scheming and gossiping. As it turned out, the younger woman never mastered certain skills that Julie had and would call her in the middle of the night, begging for help on a project—then denied the next day that Julie had helped her at all. I encouraged Julie to find a new job because I knew she was in a very unhealthy situation. Her boss and her coworker had so much fear and negativity that they manifested all sorts of problems, from long-time clients defecting, to employees being so upset by the new, competitive atmosphere, that they left abruptly. Julie maintained her values, left without creating a drama, and went on to a much better job where her talents were appreciated.

Afterward, Julie realized that as much as she had loved her previous job, the workplace had changed so much that the wonderful situation she once had no longer existed. It can be hard to accept that circumstances have changed and you have to find a new way of manifesting your dreams. It was very painful for me to give up my singing career after moving to America, but I had to accept that the music business here in that era had no use for a female singer of my age. I could continue singing, but I opened myself up to all of my talents and skills and envisioned a new path for myself. I still sing, but I have accepted that it is not my livelihood anymore. I'm okay with that because I have manifested a life that I truly enjoy, in which singing still plays an important part.

Go with the Flow

The universe has a natural flow, and we all have a destiny that steers us in particular directions. In my book *Decoding Your Destiny*, I discussed how to discover your personal destiny code, which tells you what your challenges will be and what areas of your life will be easier to navigate. If your destiny code indicates you are going to have difficulty with financial issues, you will struggle greatly to make money and keep it. If it indicates you won't have mother issues, it means you are not meant to have a difficult relationship with your mother or your own children.

However, whatever the natural flow of our destiny, you can interrupt it or redirect it, manifesting something different. When you work with its flow, your life will be easy. When you work against it, it can feel like swimming upstream: It's enormously hard work. It's like being in a relationship that you work and work at for years, and then you marry the person, and you realize it was a mistake after all. Then you meet someone else, and it feels so easy and natural. You may even know instantly "this is the one." You work at deepening the relationship, but you do not have to wear yourself out to avoid conflicts or create intimacy and trust.

When you find yourself struggling terribly, you may be on the wrong path, fighting the flow of your destiny. Hard work for the right cause, working with the Divine, can get tiring at times too, but overall, you do not mind it. You can work long hours, day in and day out, and you still feel it is the right thing to do. You're productive, not distracted, and you see results. Everyone has moments when they feel exhausted or lose faith, but that is different from rarely if ever feeling that the situation is right. "Going with the flow" means accepting your destiny and working *with* it instead of against it.

Accept When Something Isn't Meant to Be

Recently when I returned to Romania, television stations clamored to have me as a guest on their programs because I'd been such a famous singer there years before, and everyone was eager to find out what was happening with me. When I appeared on their top talk show, "Happy Hour," the ratings were the highest they'd ever experienced, and they begged me to do several more shows with them. The attention was humbling and thrilling, and I started to think about what might have happened if I'd stayed in Romania. After Ceausescu was overthrown, Romania started to do better economically, and the country is continuing to thrive today. If I'd stayed there, I'd be rich, and I'd probably still be singing. I could've made myself crazy thinking, "What if?" but I accepted that it wasn't meant to be.

Of course, it is easier to say, "I guess it wasn't meant to be" when life is going well for us. I have a very happy life here in America: I'm prosperous, I love what I do, I feel a sense of purpose, I'm close to my three, wonderful daughters, and my dear husband is still with me. I wouldn't have any of this if I hadn't left my homeland. The secret to acceptance is to look to the present and see what your gifts and opportunities are. Your life may not be all you want it to be, but if you appreciate what prosperity, joy, and love that you have, you can attract and manifest more of it. I had to accept that my life was what it was before I could start creating a plan for manifesting even better circumstances. I wouldn't have written my books or designed my jewelry line if I hadn't let go of the past.

When you look back at your life as if it were a movie with a plot that someone carefully constructed, you may start to understand why certain things happened. When you are angry with God for not bringing you what you desire, or not allowing you to hold on to what you had, remember that something even better can be created in the future if you are willing to align with the Law of Manifestation. You cannot stop something from happening if it is supposed to happen. You can certainly try, but God will find another way to bring it about. If a door closes, it is because it wasn't the right door for you. There's always some bigger reason why something about our life doesn't work the way we want it to work. Forcing a situation is going against divine law. If you align with the Eternal Principles, you will be able to look back at your life without regrets, and see that you wouldn't be where you are, in a happy place, if it weren't for the path you took and the experiences you've had along the way.

Be Creative

When you align with the Eternal Principle of Manifestation, you become creative and open to new ideas and taking risks. You stop being afraid of doing something different or untried. When you understand that creativity isn't necessarily about painting a picture or writing a song, you will find it easier to let go of any foolish notion that you are not creative. If you do not believe you are creative, remember back to your childhood and how you could spend hours in imaginative play. We're all creative. It's just that most of us forget how to embrace this aspect of ourselves.

In challenging times, it is more important than ever to be creative. People who have lost their homes or jobs have to be very creative to come up with a new vision for themselves and to find ways to manifest it. People who are caring for their children, earning a living, and taking care of elderly parents have to be extremely creative in order to juggle it all. My grandmother in Romania could make a meal out of any food we had available. Creativity is empowering and enriching, and it allows us to manifest something better. It starts with letting go of any negative beliefs about your creative powers and opening yourself up to possibilities.

How the Law of Manifestation Works with the Other Divine Laws

Manifestation and Wisdom

Sometimes we need to accept our circumstances, sometimes we need the courage to take a risk, and sometimes we require both. When you are touched by the Divine, you find your courage and can manifest what you desire—and find the strength to keep working at it, day after day, without losing your faith.

You can only manifest what is truly inside you. The Universe is never fooled by a pretense of courage; it has to be genuine. Be honest about who you are and have the wisdom to know the difference between what you can change and what you cannot—and remember, you can always change your attitude more easily than you can transform something in the physical world.

Manifestation, Harmony, and Totality

It's important to strike a balance between letting God fix your life, and trying to do it all yourself. Neither extreme is healthy or in alignment with the Law of Manifestation. You have to co-create along with God, being in harmony with the Divine, and also open to the timing and form of what you will manifest.

When you do the work on the inside, the outside work will go smoothly—that is, when you align your thoughts and feelings with the Eternal Principles, you will have a much easier time working with others and affecting the physical world.

On the other hand, if your life is not going well, it is a reflection of the disharmony within you. You are creating a conflict inside yourself. If you think someone else is holding you back from manifesting what you desire, stop looking outside of yourself. Look inside to see what is really going on. Ask yourself why you are trying to force matters, and what do you need to adjust in your own thinking?

Physical reality is a reflection of thoughts and beliefs. Remember that you are not the only one projecting your needs and intentions out into the Universe. Your desires are mingling with the desires of others. When you obey the Law of Manifestation, you are co-creating with the Divine. You are not working all by yourself; you are working with all of totality. It's not just you making things happen.

Manifestation and Karma

If you create good karma, you invite others to help you manifest your dream, and they will help you create even more good karma. Every time you make the choice to discover how you can change instead of insisting that the world change, you are on the road to resolving your karma. Be honest with yourself, be gentle and accepting, and then do the work of manifesting better thoughts, feelings, and actions. Your karma will change, and so will your life.

The Lesson of the Law of Manifestation:

Healing and well-being are divine.
Illness and disease are man-made.

Reality reflects what the mind projects. Physical health, mental clarity, and emotional well-being all begin in the mind. Collectively, our global problems are the result of too many people remaining in a low level of consciousness and manifesting a reality of illness, war, disease, poverty, and suffering. We can make a different choice, individually and together.

We choose differently when we heal on the inside. I had a patient once who had abandoned a child in her younger years and consequently carried around enormous amount of guilt. She developed ovarian cancer, which woke her up to her issues concerning motherhood. I worked with her on resolving her karma and letting go of her shame. With the help of chemotherapy to affect her tumor at a physical level, she was able to manifest health—and her cancer disappeared.

In working with people who have cancer, I find that often they have a disagreement with themselves. They do not experience inner harmony. There is a part of themselves they cannot integrate into the whole. This is reflected in the manifestation of cancer, which attacks the body from within. It's as if they are attacking themselves for being inadequate or making a mistake in the past. By letting go of destructive beliefs about themselves, they change their energy and begin manifesting health.

Often people will create illness and disease and unhealthy lifestyle decisions. Some people indulge in junk food and ignore their body's needs because they're temporarily distracted. If the only obstacle underlying our poor habits is an unawareness of what we are doing, we can make changes quickly when we start to manifest illness. When we observe that we have gained weight, or developed fatigue or a digestive problem, we are able to adjust our behavior on a physical level.

More often, unhealthy habits are based in an unhealthy mind-set. People will use food, drugs, and hard living as a way to avoid the pain of facing their karma. These distractions ultimately manifest illness.

When we align with man-made law, we do not recognize that our own consciousness and disharmony cause many of our ailments. We think they are physically based and so use medicines to treat the symptoms instead of asking ourselves why we are living the way we are. A friend of mine was in the hospital recently, and when she complained that she wasn't able to sleep well, she was immediately prescribed a powerful drug. No one thought about reducing the number of times she was woken up at night so that a nurse could take her temperature and blood pressure, or considered having a masseuse come in to help her relax, or gave her equipment to play relaxing music before bed. No one considered giving her a natural sleep enhancer such as melatonin or having her talk to a minister or psychologist about her stressful thoughts. Our medical mind-set is "if there's a problem, find a pill for it."

We need to be more in touch with our thoughts, feelings, and body's experiences. Too many people eat mindlessly, gobbling down food without reading labels or paying attention to how they feel after eating it. We can be more concerned with the quality of gasoline we put in our cars than the quality of food we put in our bodies. This distracted way of living is in contradiction to the Eternal Principles.

There are many healthy ways to address your physical ailments. You can take regular baths with Epsom salts, fast, or have massages to cleanse your body of toxins. You can meditate, focusing on the body and paying attention to any painful or uncomfortable sensations. You can use foods and supplements as natural medicines and exercise as a natural mood stabilizer and hormone balancer. Most important, you can use the lesson of the Law of Manifestation to change your consciousness, raising it to a higher vibration, to treat just about any ailment and bring back a sense of well-being to yourself and to the planet.

THE TENTH
ETERNAL PRINCIPLE:

The Law of Dharma

We each have a unique mission here on earth.

"It concerns us to know the purposes we seek in life, for then, like archers aiming at a definite mark, we shall be more likely to attain what we want."
—*Aristotle*

All of us reach a point in life when we wonder why we are here. Are we simply meant to reproduce, work, and die? The thought "there has to be more than this" is what propels us into discovering our dharma.

As you've learned, all of us are light beings who have taken physical form in order to resolve our karma and evolve. Dharma is the vehicle for this process. *Dharma,* derived from the Sanskrit word *dhr* meaning "uphold or support," is a concept from Hinduism and Buddhism that refers to both duty and destiny. When we perform our duty, we support the well-being and the evolution of the totality by resolving our own karma. Everyone benefits as a result.

Like karma, dharma has different levels. We each have an individual duty or dharma, but groups of people can share a particular dharma, and all of humanity is subject to the rule of dharma. We're all here not only to resolve our personal karma but also to help resolve the karma of the world as well.

We each have dharma that is reflective of our karma and our talents, state of evolution, and temperament. As we resolve negative karma and create good karma, our dharma transforms, but we will always have dharma. It will follow us after death into the next lifetime, just as our karma will, until all our karma is finally healed.

What Happens When You Align Yourself with the Law of Dharma?

If you love yourself unconditionally and are working on clearing your karma and aligning yourself with the Eternal Principles, including the Law of Totality, you will be able to recognize your gifts and your opportunities to serve humanity. You will stop focusing on fixing your personal suffering.

We may think happiness is the automatic outcome of doing everything right, like some sort of gold cup we win at the end of a race. Happiness is never a permanent state, something we can achieve and then hold on to. You can think you've resolved all your problems and arranged your life just perfectly, then suffer a devastating blow. Unexpected tragedies wake us up and remind us that we are not supposed to be aiming for security and lasting happiness in the physical world, which is unattainable anyway. We are supposed to live in accordance with dharma to resolve our karma. When we do that, we feel happy much of the time. We have a sense of purpose that carries us through difficult challenges and helps us maintain faith that our lives will get better. Our concern about the small problems in life starts to go away.

The other thing that happens when you live according to your dharma is that you stop feeling disconnected and lonely. You no longer want to cut yourself off from other people (or only interact with a small number of people you know). Isolation prevents you from fulfilling your purpose. You are meant to feel your connection to the Universe. Somewhere, someone needs your help, and you may very well have to leave your comfort zone to do your duty and assist them.

Dharma and Destiny

Many people confuse duty, or dharma, with destiny. Destiny refers to everything you will ever do, positive or negative. Because we have free will, and are influenced by the choices of other people, much of our destiny is not fixed. The moment of your birth and death are predetermined, however, and your birth date indicates the karmic issues you will struggle with in this life. Your destiny might be to struggle with health, but as you resolve your karmic issues about health you live out your dharma, which might be to educate and inspire others. You might develop a particular disease and become an advocate or spokesperson for people with the same condition, or a health activist who tries to influence the government, insurance companies, and voters to do more to eradicate this disease. You might work on a hotline offering information and support to fellow sufferers. Or, your disease may serve as a challenge that awakens you to a different dharma. You might learn the lessons of your illness and use them to resolve your karma and better serve humankind.

Whatever cards the Universe deals you, you can perceive them as challenges or blessings. Someone who led a purposeless life before developing a life-threatening illness or losing their child can turn that tragedy into an opportunity for personal evolution as well as for living out their dharma. One of my clients was a very wealthy man who did very little for the world. He didn't use his money or talents to help others. Instead, he put all his time, effort, and attention into making more money, building his reputation as a successful businessman, and enjoying his considerable fortune. Then, one day, his young son was diagnosed with a fatal, untreatable disease. All his money could do nothing to save the boy he loved. He went through a horrific time watching his beloved son die, but then something in him changed. He realized that all of his exceptional skills for organizing projects could be used to organize a charity that would help other children like his son, and fund research into the terrible disease that had taken him. It was wonderful to see how his heart opened as he threw himself into this new work. I attended a gala that he and his wife put on for the benefit of this charity, and sat in a corner of the room giving free readings for all the guests because I wanted to help out, too. As I looked at my client's face that night, it seemed to glow in a way that it hadn't before. He had found his dharma.

When you are going through a difficult time, having experienced a serious loss or had your dream shattered, it is hard not to feel victimized or powerless, and angry with God or fate. It is only in hindsight, looking through the eyes of your soul, that you can see the worst tragedies allowed you to discover aspects of yourself that were completely hidden. These gifts may well be the keys to living your life with a sense of purpose.

You do not have to suffer in order to discover your dharma if you consciously choose to take advantage of every opportunity to serve others. Adopt the attitude that you are here to help, and you will know what to do. Not a day will go by without your being able to help someone. You can stop and ask someone who looks lost if you can direct them, or joke with a harried waitress in order to lighten her load a little if only for a few moments. If there is a specific duty you are meant to take on, it will become clear to you without your having to think, "But what can *I* do? I'm only one person and I'm nothing special." Living this way aligns you with the Law of Dharma.

Personal Dharma and Ego

Although we are light beings who are interwoven with the great matrix of life, we are also individuals, each with our own temperament, talents, passions, and aspirations. Each of us has our own role to play in healing this world and serving humanity. Even if thousands or millions of others have a similar destiny, your role in uplifting humanity is unique, just as you are unique.

Much has been said lately about how destructive and problematic the ego can be. Having an "ego" in the Freudian sense, that is, having self-awareness and a personal identity, is part of being human. The ego is only a problem when we give it too much power, and when we mistake it for the sum of who we are and put all our focus on serving its desires. When we serve our ego, we forget that we are immortal souls as well as mortal beings with a personal identity. We need to remember that it is our eternal self that is genuine and lasting, and choose to identify with that self, serving it, instead of identifying with the ego and making it the center of our attention.

Don't make the mistake of thinking that if you explore who you are and what you have to offer you are being self-centered and egotistical. The Divine wants you to value your individuality and discover what your personal dharma is. You are meant to put your light on a hilltop, where it can shine outwardly. You are not supposed to hide it under a bushel.

If you were sheltered as a child, or weren't exposed to a variety of situations, you may not be aware of what your unique talents are. If you've repressed your natural inclinations in order to please others, you need to reconnect with that lost part of yourself so you can discover your personal dharma.

Some people think they haven't anything to offer others until circumstances appear that give them clarity. We think too small, and ask ourselves, "Who am I to do that?" If we convince ourselves that only certain important and influential people have a purpose, our dharma will remain a mystery to us.

Dharma Actions

To live in alignment with the Law of Dharma, you must act in a positive way to enhance your own evolution and healing as well as that of everyone else. Dharma is not something you work with once in a while when you feel like doing something positive. It's a way of life.

Your dharma may be focused on any of the following actions, or a combination of them:

- *Educating.* You might teach, work, or volunteer as a community educator, be a journalist or writer, or simply share your wisdom and knowledge with others.
- *Healing.* You might be a doctor, therapist, energy healer, chiropractor, or life coach. You might also be a medical researcher, a pharmacist, or a nutritionist.
- *Helping.* You might be the person everyone can count on to pitch in whenever there's a challenge, whether it's handing out food and clothing after a natural disaster or watching your neighbor's children when she has an emergency come up.
- *Inspiring.* You can use your own story, speaking bravely about your vulnerabilities and mistakes to inspire others to believe that they, too, can overcome obstacles.
- *Nurturing.* You can perform loving acts for other people, such as tend a garden, volunteer to help eradicate invasive plant species in

your area, or care for the earth in other ways, or rescue abandoned animals.

- *Giving.* You can send money or volunteer time, or go out of your way to help other people.
- *Mentoring.* You can coach someone who is new to your industry, teaching them what you've learned and encouraging them, or you can mentor a young person who needs a role model.
- *Facilitating.* You can be the person who makes things happen, bringing into reality great ideas, connecting people and resources.
- *Supporting.* You can sponsor an impoverished child in another country, lend emotional support to someone, or send love and prayers to those who are suffering.
- *Listening.* You can quietly take in what others are saying, feeling empathy without rushing to fix their problems. You can be a good listener to a friend, to a lonely neighbor or elderly person, or to a stranger as you work on a support hotline.

Every person's dharma has at least one of these elements, regardless of what they do for a living. Your dharma isn't necessarily tied to what you do to make money, or to your social position or your title on your business card. Anyone can listen, support, facilitate, and mentor, whether at work, at home, at school, or walking down the street. Let's say you are a customer service representative. Every time an angry, frustrated customer comes to your desk, you can *educate* her about your company's services, products, and policies, you can *listen* patiently, and *help* her solve her problem, *facilitating* a solution. Then, after work when you get together with friends, you can *listen* to them and *support* them when they talk about what a hard day they had, and *entertain* them by joking about the difficulties in life. You might serve as a role model, *inspiring* someone who is struggling very hard with his own karmic issues and is learning more about how to live according to the Eternal Principles by watching you. Every one of these actions is part of living in alignment with your dharma.

If the Universe has granted you power, talents, or blessings of any type, use them to live out your dharma. They are the Divine's investment in you.

Work toward growing that investment for the benefit of everyone and you will experience pure joy. I know several authors who write books designed to guide people in living better lives. They tell me that as much as they enjoy the benefits of writing—fame and admiration, control over their schedule because they work for themselves, selling lots of copies of their books, and making money—what really excites them most is using their talents to help others. Every time they hear from just one person how their book has helped that individual, their spirits soar. Whenever the rights to one of my books is sold to a foreign publisher, what excites me is not the prestige or the amount of money I'm paid, but knowing that my writing can touch the life of someone I have never met who lives in Sweden or Italy or Germany.

Years ago, I helped a homeless woman by giving her readings for free. She'd been an orphan as a child and suffered some horrific experiences. When I met her, she was facing many challenges, but she had a very good heart and aspired to not only take care of herself but also to help others who had a similar background. What she learned and the compassion she developed as a result of her suffering were a gift that would determine her destiny. In several readings, I saw that she would someday come into a lot of money, although I did not know how this would transpire. One day, she read in the newspaper about a class-action settlement against the orphanage where she lived as a small child years ago, and discovered she was entitled to a great deal of money. As soon as she received it, she insisted that she wanted to pay me for all those free readings I'd given her, but I turned her down. I knew she would "pay it forward," and I didn't really need the money. The last I heard, she was living in her own house and working to help other homeless people who have suffered like she has. At that moment, knowing that I'd played a small part in helping one other person find their destiny was enough for me.

What Happens When You Don't Live According to the Law of Dharma?

When you do not align yourself with the Law of Dharma, you mistakenly believe that purpose or meaning is something that you can create through the accumulation of material wealth, power, and reputation or fame. More than ever, people are convincing themselves that if they could just become famous, they'd be happy and feel important, but not every celebrity discovers his dharma. Yes, celebrities can have a lot of power to influence people for the better, and using their fame for good is part of their dharma, but simply being famous does not fulfill your duty or make you feel that your life has meaning. Many celebrities are obsessed with how famous they are and whether or not anyone thinks of them as has-beens, just as many wealthy people are terrified of losing their money.

Your eternal soul, who you really are, doesn't die just because you lose your fame and fortune. Your dharma—the vehicle for ending your suffering, resolving your karma, and fulfilling your purpose—will be with you no matter how your fortunes change.

Some people mistakenly believe that meaning and purpose can only be found in grand gestures. They know that *some* people are destined to cure AIDS or cancer, or end hunger in Africa, but when they cannot see a way that they can personally impact the world on a large scale, they do nothing whatsoever, and only dream about finding meaning and purpose.

The flow of divinity, combined with how hard we work, determines how much impact we have on the world. If you are kind to a few close friends, and occasionally write a check to charity, you are not going to feel a powerful sense of purpose and affect humanity in any major way. However, if you work at being unconditionally loving toward all, and serving the world in your quiet, small way, you may influence many people, inspiring them and showing them how they can find their own purpose. My father's father had been the prime minister of Romania, while my father was a simple man who had a job at the bank. Yet he never felt powerless to affect the world. Every day, he tried to help other people in some way. When he died, hundreds of people attended his funeral.

If you do not fulfill your dharma, it will be imprinted on your soul just as your karma is. Your soul will choose to reincarnate into a particular body and become part of a particular family, in a particular situation, in order to give you the best opportunity to heal your karma and fulfill your dharma. There's no way of avoiding this obligation.

How to Discover Your Dharma

Be Introspective

The key to discovering your dharma is to know yourself. Many people rarely engage in introspection. They go along in life without ever stopping to wonder why they act as they do, why they have the problems they have, or why they are here on earth. They wait until they have a brush with mortality, or feel a sense of meaningless so painful they can hardly bear it, before they slow down and begin looking inward.

If you are feeling overwhelmed by your life and do not know what road to take, begin to discover who you are. Ask yourself how you got to this point in life. What can you learn from your past? What are your secret dreams? What would you like to achieve before you leave this earth? What relationships matter most to you? What has been your role in the losses in your life—friendships, relationships, and jobs that ended? Are you sure you made the right decisions out of love for yourself and others, or did you act out of fear, anger, or another low-vibration emotion? Many people do not consider therapy until something terrible happens to them, but if you feel a lack of purpose and you are not introspective, I encourage you to consider entering therapy in order to find out what your dharma is and to better know yourself and what you have to offer the world.

Help Others, Even in Small Ways

If you are feeling sorry for yourself, turn your focus outward. Find someone who is worse off than you, and help that person. I once met a gentleman living in a nursing home, and at every mealtime he would go to the rooms of the patients confined to wheelchairs and offer to push them into the dining room. This man knew the secret to avoiding self-pity and depression is to do something for someone else. He was fulfilling his dharma.

Don't sit around waiting for some big opportunity to make a difference. Do something today, no matter how small. Mother Teresa said, "In this life we cannot do great things. We can only do small things with great love." Although we think of her as someone who helped thousands of people and inspired millions more, she fulfilled her dharma in small moments when she looked with love into the eyes of one dying person and smiled.

One of the reasons I always tell people I know "I love you" is because I know that we rarely receive thanks or appreciation for the hard work we do every day. It's not easy to live according to the Law and Dharma when you are exhausted by all that you have to do and feel that no one cares about the sacrifices you make. But I promise you, people do care! They are just so wearied by their own burdens that they forget to express their appreciation. Expressing our love and appreciation is a habit we must all work to develop. Every day, tell your children, your spouse, your friends, and your coworkers "thank you," and "I so appreciate how hard you are working at this." You can change their vibration. After you leave the office for the day, your coworker may feel so much lighter and happier that he drives more patiently and politely on his way home, and is more compassionate and loving toward his teenage daughter who's in a bad mood. Your love and kindness will reverberate in ways you won't even see. Never underestimate the power of love, compassion, and generosity to change the world!

Break Out of Isolation
To align with the law of dharma and perform your duty to the world, you have to integrate with others. It's becoming increasingly easier to be isolated and avoid people who aren't like us. Some people live in gated communities, ordering deliveries instead of mingling with others in stores, and socializing only with those who are in their own economic class. Some people spend a great deal of time at work and at the computer or playing videogames at home. They have limited personal contact with other people, and even then only interact with others who share their interests.

For someone who is an invalid, or lives in an isolated area, socialization through the Internet or the phone is certainly better than no contact at all. Anyone can affect other people positively by interacting with them in a loving way through online support groups, and staying in touch with people by e-mailing, text messaging, or calling them. However, if it is at all possible, try to interact positively with others face-to-face. Reading another person's facial expressions and body language, hearing their tone of voice, and picking up on their energy in person gives you much more information about what's really going on with them than reading their text messages, e-mails with emoticons, or Facebook postings. When we can physically be in the same room with someone we better understand what we can do for them and know when they are in need. Touching someone's arm, giving them a hug, or smiling at them transfers positive, healing energy to their light-energy body, affecting their emotions and physical health. Because of the Law of Totality, the good energy we send through prayer, the positive words we speak or write, and our kind gestures have an effect on others, but it is often easier for the person to feel the full force of the positive energy you are sending when he is physically with you.

It's easier to feel connected, and to align yourself with the Law of Totality, when you interact with others face-to-face. You also develop your skills for dealing with difficult emotions instead of running away from them. I have heard that some people today will break up with a romantic partner by sending a text message! How disconnected is that? Face-to-face conversations can be uncomfortable, but when we hurt other people in order to avoid our own discomfort, we create negative karma.

Be aware, too, of the way technology can separate people. I know too many families who share a big, beautiful home, but instead of gathering together in one room and inviting in friends and neighbors, each person goes to his own space, puts on his headphones to listen to music, turns on the television, or becomes involved in a videogame or on the computer. Make media-free time in your home.

Many people are shy or uncomfortable in groups or around strangers, so they prefer to be loners. If you are an introvert who needs time alone to energize yourself, that is fine, but you also need social connections.

Researchers have found that elderly people who have few friends and rarely socialize deteriorate into poor health and dementia much faster than their peers who have a social circle. When I first came to America I was amazed when people would say to me, "I cannot stand my mother, I haven't talked to her for years," or "My brother and I have nothing in common. I haven't seen him since my dad died." To me, family and friends are everything. At the hospital, when my husband was very ill, there was a steady stream of visitors every day. Yes, in my family, we have our disagreements and drive each other crazy or bore each other with the same old stories, but we support each other. Too many people are missing that.

When we remain isolated, we become depressed and lonely, and begin focusing on our problems in a negative way, making them larger than they are. As soon as you begin connecting with others, you start seeing ways in which you can live according to your dharma. You are able to lift yourself out of an obsession with all that seems to be wrong in your life.

It's not always easy to break out of your comfort zone and reach out to others. Take small steps at first. Travel, strike up a conversation with strangers, introduce yourself to other parents at a school event, and get to know your neighbors. Join a group that has a common interest. Approach people and ask them questions, or make a comment on what they're doing. I have had many conversations with dog owners who are walking their dogs— I'll ask them "Is that a King Charles spaniel?" even if I know the answer is yes, just to give them a chance to share their enthusiasm about their dog!

When you ask questions, slow down and listen attentively to the answers. People can tell when you are waiting for them to stop talking so that you can make your point! Pay attention to people's expressions and body language, and read between the lines of what they're saying. Ask them with genuine feeling, "How is everything?" and give them a chance to tell you what's really going on, but do not pressure them to reveal all the details.

All of this advice may seem obvious, but if you really think about it, you might realize that, like a lot of people, you've become more isolated over the years. It's easy to fall into the habit of relying on the same old friends or social outlets and to "stick to your own kind." All of us need to open up more. We need to look for opportunities to help others achieve a higher level of vibration. We can only do this if we are interacting with others, not if we stay home, alone, plugged into some piece of technology and focused on our own little world.

What Happens When We Align with the Law of Dharma?

When you work at fulfilling your dharma, your life changes. Abundance flows in. You attract and manifest wealth in a variety of ways. It may come slowly, because you are meant to more deeply develop your sense of purpose and resolve your karma, but it will come.

If you feel you have been suffering for a very long time and you are losing faith that your situation will change for the better, work on discovering your purpose. You will see your circumstances begin to shift. A healing energy will flow toward you, and your negative emotions will begin to slip away. You will no longer yearn for someone else to tell you that you are wonderful or to express his gratitude, because you won't feel needy and unappreciated. You will feel love and appreciation because you will feel closer to God. Living according to your purpose, doing what you were meant to do is enormously energizing. You can work long hours without tiring, and you can let go of criticism more easily and get around obstacles without feeling overwhelmed or negative. You can maintain a sense of enthusiasm.

I'm not saying that you won't have bad days or patches where you feel that you are stretched too thin, or your load is too heavy. None of us can sustain a sense of boundless joy and enthusiasm all the time. It's just that it is much easier to be happy and motivated, and do what you need to do, when you are aligned with the Eternal Principles and feeling the presence of God, and fulfilling your destiny by working with your dharma.

Even when your life is going well, take time to pray to God. Get out into nature and experience the wonder of the divine creation. If you do not, you may feel yourself being drawn away from Divinity and toward the man-made perceptions that cause suffering. Then, you will be in danger of feeling isolated and alone, which often leads to materialism, greed, and a lust for power.

To remain in alignment with the divine laws, you must keep nurturing your connection to the totality and all of divinity. Many times, I've seen people who had no sense of spirituality suddenly devastated by a loss. Often, they're able to reconnect to God and find strength, but until they do, they suffer terribly. In contrast, when we are living according to the Eternal Principles, using our dharma to resolve our karma, and constantly reconnecting with God, we are better equipped to deal with tragedy.

Living according to the Law of Dharma gives you a sense of peace. Conflict and negativity fall away because you are no longer thinking, "How can I win this battle?" You do not see life as an endless struggle but as a miracle to be appreciated every day. Because you are experiencing joy, you will feel the desire to help others raise their vibrations and be joyous as well. There will be fewer conflicts in your life. When one does arise, your instinct will be to try to help the other person shift into a state of tranquility, happiness, and understanding. The sense that you are being battered by life will go away, and you will discover your wisdom, find the courage to change negative situations, and serenely accept the limitations of your power.

The Law of Dharma and the Other Eternal Principles

The Law of Dharma works with the Law of Totality and Karma because, as I have said, by working to help others, you heal your karma and raise the vibration in your corner of the divine matrix. By using the Law of Wisdom, you will be better able to let go of your ideas of grandiosity, accepting that you do not have the power to change some things at the physical level, or to influence specific people to do what you think is best for them. Wisdom also allows you to find the courage to change what can be influenced. By loving unconditionally, you can stop judging others and instead find ways to enlighten and uplift them to a higher vibration. This is your dharma.

Dharma allows us to bring about harmony in the world instead of feeling we are in a constant battle with others to get our share of power and wealth. It helps us to recognize what is true abundance and create good karma, which will allow us to attract and manifest better circumstances. Finally, it allows us to participate in the evolution of all humankind, which is a humbling and empowering experience at the same time.

People can change their states of mind when they become involved in a movement that matters to them. They become enthusiastic and creative, and develop a glow because they know they are doing something important, even if the part they play is very small. Every one of us matters, and every one of us has the power to influence the whole through our individual actions. We'll know what to do once we start aligning with the Eternal Principles and opening up to the guidance of the Divine.

The Lesson of the Law of Dharma:

Purpose, expressing our gifts, and connecting with others are divine. Aimlessness, hedonism, and isolation are man-made.

Whenever we lose sight of the Eternal Principles and become mired in the man-made world of suffering, we start down a very dark path. First, we become aimless and lost. Then, to relieve our suffering, we grasp at the pleasures of the material world. But no matter how much money, wealth, or power we can grab for ourselves, we just feel more miserable, lonely, and afraid. Finally, we lose our ability to trust in the world, and we isolate ourselves. We feel alone in the world, lost, and frightened, and we just continue on this destructive path.

To get out of these dark woods, you have to follow divine light. The Divine will guide you, but you have to be willing to leave behind the way of life that wasn't working for you. You must be ready to live out your purpose—being connected to others, serving humankind, and letting your own light shine. The world needs more light. If you go about your life consuming material goods, frittering away time in unimportant activities that do nothing but fill empty hours, you are not resolving your karma or living according to your dharma. It's as if you are playing hooky from school!

If you do not know why you are here or where you are going, if you feel aimless and do not know what you are meant to do, be kind to yourself. Remember that the answer to "Why am I here?" lies at the heart of spirituality. Your discomfort with your life is pulling you toward the light of the Divine, where you will find comfort, strength, and faith.

Even the most well-meaning people, doctors, and therapists can unknowingly encourage sadness, isolation, and self-absorption by validating people's image of themselves as sufferers. What many people do not understand is that yes, of course, we have to get in touch with our pain and our problems, but we cannot become stuck in them. We must move through them, resolving our karma. The only way to do this is through dharma.

The way to discover dharma is to stop becoming absorbed by negative feelings and thoughts and start listening to where your heart takes you. Appreciating the love that is all around you can empower you and help you heal. There is help everywhere, but you cannot see it if you are in the heavy darkness of fear, anger, sadness, jealousy, or shame, which lowers your vibration. You have to allow these feelings to go away as you consciously create healthier beliefs.

Let's say that as you become introspective and face your karma, you discover that you are in a financial mess because you made some bad decisions in the past. If you let that take you in the direction of negativity and low-vibration thoughts and feelings, you won't resolve your karma. You must accept what happened in the past, create a new, more positive attitude, such as, "I'm going to learn how to better manage money and make better financial decisions," and create feelings of confidence and hope. Then you can use your dharma to change your karma. Maybe you don't have a talent for managing money, but you are an extrovert with a natural talent for meeting people and making friends. You can use that proclivity to lead you to people who can help you learn better money management. One of my clients told me she learned all about balancing checkbooks, 401Ks at work, and managing credit card debt from a coworker who was very knowledgeable. They became friends because she reached out to her coworker when the woman was going through a bad breakup. My client's compassion and her natural ability to listen and be supportive brought her closer to this new friend, who then felt a desire to help her out by sharing her own money management knowledge.

Finding your dharma and following the path out of darkness and suffering starts with small steps and small acts of courage that are extremely significant. When you say to yourself, "I know it is scary, but I'm going to make that phone call to the person my friend said might be able to help me with my problem," and you follow through, that small act is a step out of the woods. When you are at a gathering and you turn to the stranger next to you and start a conversation, you are taking another small step out of isolation. When you allow yourself to say, "That was hard for me to do just now, but I did it anyway," and feel pride and strength, you take another step forward into the light as you make progress toward healing your karmic issues. And when you say, "I'm pretty good at doing things like this. I think I should make a point of doing this sort of thing more often, because it helps other people and makes me feel as if I can make a difference . . ." you know you are on the path of your own dharma. You are doing what you are meant to do.

Step into the light of divine love and reunite with the world around you, connecting to others and sharing with them your talents as they share yours. Every last one of us has something vitally important to offer others, and when we give to the world, we give to ourselves. This is how we heal the world and fulfill our sacred duty.

THE ELEVENTH ETERNAL PRINCIPLE:

The Law of Infinite Possibilities

We can defy the laws of time and space, and participate in the co-creation of the seemingly impossible.

Physical reality contains many things we can measure, contain, count, and limit. Our minds perceive a separation between water and air, our bodies and the earth, our country and another country. It seems obvious that two things cannot occupy the same space at once, but Bell's theorem, put forth in 1965, states that locality does not exist. An electron has the ability to influence another quantum particle or entity over any distance despite there being no exchange of force or energy. It's as if the two particles are in exactly the same spot, experiencing exactly the same thing at the same moment.

We develop the perception that there are limitations and separations everywhere, because we long to make sense of the world. We feel that if we can understand the nature of things and how things work, and predict what will happen, we won't feel frightened and powerless, and we will have a better chance for survival. In physical reality, we need to see air and water as different and separate because we can breathe one and not the other.

However, we assign too much importance to the world we perceive with our senses and the boundaries and limits we see. We believe that we have limited possibilities because in the physical reality we have created, that is true. But the realm of the Divine is beyond the limitations of time and space. When we allow that reality to come into the physical realm, new possibilities come rushing in and physical reality can be radically transformed.

In the reality of infinite possibilities, all is one and ever changing. Nothing is fixed, not form, space, or time. Past, present, and future are all occurring at once. An object can be in two different places at once, and two particles can communicate with each other across a vast distance instantaneously, far faster than the speed of light. What I'm describing is not an abstract idea about what the divine realm is like, but the nature of reality according to quantum physics. It's only when we are operating at the level of the physical world that we start to perceive that creatures, objects, and energy always behave in predictable, ordered ways. At the quantum level, reality is far more unpredictable, and the possibilities are innumerable.

Timelessness versus Time

Time is a construct of the human mind. Humankind invented the concept of time, of a past, present, and future split into increments, when we looked into the sky and noticed the predictable paths of celestial bodies. We invented calendars, then clocks. We began to feel we understood our world and had some control over it because the rules of the physical world all work together in a logical fashion: the past influences the future, but the future doesn't yet exist so it cannot influence the past or even the present. What goes up must come down. If we drop an object of a particular weight from a specific height, we can measure its velocity and accurately predict when it will hit the ground a few seconds later. All of these rules are a part of physics, a science pioneered by Isaac Newton in an era when many in Europe were dying of the Black Plague. Not knowing the cause of this disease, or how to stop it, people sought certainty. Science offered a promise of understanding. A new age of logic and reason began to arise.

However, in the twentieth century, we started to discover that the rules of Newtonian physics do not apply at the smallest level of reality. Particles and waves defy logic and all the rules of time and space. Their nature actually changes just because someone observes them. All of this is very unsettling to the human mind. Even Einstein didn't know what to make of it and died hoping that someone would come up with a rational explanation for what he called "spooky action at a distance."

We're now realizing that reality at the quantum level is the reality of the Divine, the reality of infinite possibilities all occurring at once in different dimensions. It is the energy matrix the Chinese called the Tao. In Judaism it is called Elohim, in Hinduism, Brahman, or the Supreme Being, from the Sanskrit word *brh* meaning "to grow," and has a connotation of greatness.

As beings of light, we are part of this matrix, this consciousness, and not limited by the laws of time and space. Our collective consciousness is creating our physical reality. Once we understand this, we can begin to question our long-held assumptions about the material realm and our influence on it.

Opening to Infinite Possibilities

Because I work with the divine reality and all its possibilities, and have experienced the mystery of the quantum realm through precognition, visions of the future, communication with the spirits of those who have passed, and awareness of people's past lives, I have opened myself up to what most would call "the impossible." I have seen into the future and discovered that one person will miraculously heal from a serious illness while another is going to die very young and unexpectedly. So I know how limited our minds are when it comes to perceiving possibilities. The more experience you have in aligning with the Law of Infinite Possibilities, the more you will open up to potential future events that your rational, left brain will think of as crazy.

The physical world seems so real and finite that we cannot fathom an infinite universe or grasp the idea that the Universe has no beginning and no end, or that there are endless possibilities. To better understand how the physical world became so real to us, we need to look to the past and how we developed the idea of a three-dimensional world.

Three Dimensions and Our Perception of Physical Reality

Long ago, the ancient Egyptians built the pyramids as an expression of our three-dimensional reality. The pyramids were based on the ground with three triangular sides that reached into the sky, symbolically uniting the realms of the physical world and the ethereal, invisible world of the Divine. The idea of the trinity was further imprinted in human consciousness in the area around Egypt and the Middle East when Christianity arose and popularized the idea of God as having three forms: father, son, and Holy Ghost.

We perceive three aspects to reality—height, length, and width; past, present, and future; father (Supreme Being), son (divinity present in the physical world), and Holy Ghost (spirit, which unites the father and son, the realm of the Divine, and the realm of the material). However, these ideas of trinity are a creation of our minds that try to make sense of this physical world we have manifested. God may have three forms, but all are unified as God, just as past, present, and future exist all at once. Whatever has form cannot be measured according to length, width, and height, as it isn't actually matter but light energy. It is only in man-made reality that there are three measurable dimensions, rules about time, and the partitioning of the Divine.

If we cannot perceive something with our senses, we have difficulty believing it exists, but the invisible realm is real and we are a part of it. For thousands of years, people did not know about the existence of bacteria, but we still experienced them when they infected our bodies. Once we learned about these microbes, our perception of illness and our way of living transformed. We invented sanitation and developed sanitary practices, which allowed us to live longer and healthier lives. Microbes became real for us, although they had been there all along. Imagine what else we do not perceive that, once discovered, could make a tremendous difference in the human experience. The divine realm has innumerable possibilities we are completely blind to when we devote all our attention to the physical world.

Why We Have to Align Ourselves with the Law of Infinity

We are trapped in our ideas about time and hold ourselves back from its limitless possibilities. When applying time to our personal lives, we say we have run out of time, our time has passed, and time is getting away from us. When we look at the human race, we start to believe we have gone past the point of no return and will destroy ourselves through overpopulation, nuclear war, or global warming. We feel hopeless because we cannot "turn back the hands of time." But God has given us unlimited possibilities. The Biblical story of Sarah, who couldn't believe God when he said that she would have a child, because she was "too old," is a story about our unwillingness to entertain the idea that time is limitless, and that the rules about time are an illusion created by our minds. The Divine doesn't follow these rules!

We also become frozen in time, obsessing about the past or future. We block the flow of possibilities when we insist that because our parents divorced during our childhood, we will never achieve intimacy and security in a relationship ourselves. We cut off a relationship before it can deepen because we focus on all the negative things that can happen: our new partner could be unfaithful or may fall out of love with us, or we could discover that we've married the wrong person, and so on. The more weight we give to the influences of the past and the more certainty we have about a negative future, the more stuck we will become.

Two key events in your life cannot be changed: the moment of your birth and the moment of your death. When I was a child, I became obsessed with the year 2000. I got scared just thinking about it, and I didn't know why. I sensed 2000 would be a turning point in my life. This feeling of dread continued for decades. Finally, 2000 came about, and in November of that year, I lost my mother. I realized that I had been picking up on a set point in time, long before it happened. I could break the rules of time and know that something terrible would happen to me in that year, but I could not prevent my mother's death, which was predestined.

What Happens When We Align with the Law of Infinite Possibilities?

In the realm of infinity, all possibilities exist at once. These possibilities collapse into one outcome in the realm of physical reality when that particular outcome becomes fixed in someone's mind. Once an idea is formed, it starts to take physical shape. Remember, all ideas are energy forms that create neural connections (actual, physical structures in the brain) and inspire emotions (which are biochemical reactions). This is the process of one possibility taking form. You've experienced this process if you suddenly had a breakthrough idea and started to feel excitement in your body as you imagined this new concept becoming a reality.

Whatever your mind's limitations are, they will affect the form that an idea takes when it solidifies in reality. For instance, let's say you have the idea that you want to create a successful blog that educates people on a topic of interest to you. It's an idea that takes shape in your mind, and you then start researching blogs, Web designers, and advertising sponsors. You try to repeat successful blog formulas, which is a very sensible thing to do in the physical world. But how can your idea break out of the limitations of your mind, and current reality, and be truly original? Could you write a blog that is transported directly into the mind of one of your readers? The idea is preposterous because it breaks the rules of time and space. We need computers in order to communicate information like this over a long distance. Or do we? In the quantum, divine realm, anything is possible, including telepathic communication.

Another example of the limitations of our mind, and how we try to explain our experiences in terms of a three-dimensional world, is our ideas about the nature of déjà vu. If you are like most people, you've experienced this phenomenon. You may have thought, "It feels like I've lived this moment before," but because that struck you as illogical, you probably thought, "I must have dreamed this." We experience dreams that are strange and break rules about reality, so it makes sense to assume that déjà vu is somehow part of the dream world. But how could you dream the exact conversation, in that exact place, and be accurate about the scene unfolding before you, right down to every single detail? That would make your dream precognitive, which defies the rules of time and boggles your rational left brain.

Scientists believe that the brain creates perception and consciousness rather than consciousness creating the brain. They say that déjà vu is a misfiring of the brain's hardware that causes a false experience that only *feels* real. What is really happening when we experience déjà vu is that we are breaking the rules of linear time and experiencing the future before it happens. Our consciousness is connecting to the Great Consciousness, or what psychologist Carl Jung called "the collective unconscious."

We can experience the future in the present once we connect with the Divine realm, where time flows in all directions and everything happens at once. Whenever this happens, we do not know how to make sense of it, and the scientists' explanation seems logical, so we dismiss the possibility that we actually foresaw the future.

As many experiences as I have had with breaking linear time, I once ignored all the signals about what was going to happen (and what was happening) because my logical brain couldn't make sense of what my intuition was telling me about a friend of mine. I first met her when she came to me for a reading. I discovered that she was troubled and I felt that as a counselor, I could help her. I pushed aside the little voice inside me that said I needed to avoid this woman, because I felt sorry for her. She seemed very sweet, and she soon befriended me. She loved to bring me presents, tell me how wonderful I was, and do things for me.

Although we'd never met before in this lifetime, I kept having flashes of a lifetime we shared in France. I was an opera singer, and she was my cleaning lady. One day, in a most disturbing flash of memory, I saw her trying to poison me. I saw myself confronting her, and her angrily responding that she was in love with my husband, that I didn't deserve him, and that she wanted me to die. Now, in the current lifetime, she seemed to have no designs on my husband, so I didn't know what to make of these bits and pieces of memory that would come back to me for a few seconds here or there. I saw myself visiting her in a French prison cell and then arranging to have her put into an institution of some sort because I felt sorry for her. I told my husband all this, and he didn't know what to make of it. Then, one night, I came home, my husband wasn't there, and I played my answering machine tape. There was a long recording, made by accident, of this "friend" telling my husband she loved him, that I didn't deserve him. She urged him to run away with her. On the tape, I heard him tell her he had no interest in her and that she needed to leave him alone. I ended my friendship with her, and the last I heard, she was in a mental institution.

Why didn't I believe in these flashes of memory? Because like everyone else, I spend a lot of time dealing with the challenges of the material world, and sometimes I start to believe it is the genuine reality. This woman was so kind to me, I couldn't reconcile the information I was receiving from the realm of timelessness with what my senses perceived.

In fact, the very first time I went to Paris, I got the chills because I knew I had lived there before. I could see a clock on my wall, jewelry I wore, a concert hall where I'd sung. I knew what my name had been, and what I looked like. I also knew the streets without looking at a map, and this convinced me that my memories weren't a figment of my imagination. I am confident that I lived there in a past life.

When we align ourselves with the Law of Infinite Possibilities, we recognize that these types of experiences are real, not figments of the imagination. When we acknowledge their reality, we can look at them more closely and learn what paranormal experiences have to teach us about our relationship to the Divine and to totality. We learn why we struggle with certain issues in our lives, and why other things come to us easily. As a child, I sang with tremendous confidence and skill because of my previous life as an opera singer. As a preteen, my sister took her first English classes one summer in Romania and was such a fast learner that she wrote an English-language novel in a matter of months. At the end of the class, she and her fellow students traveled to England for a few weeks, where she entered her novel in a literary contest and shocked everyone by winning—a little Romanian girl who had just learned English! My sister told me she felt that she'd lived in England in a previous life. I'm sure she had, which would explain her quick grasp of the language.

Our families, friends, and teachers tell us what we should and should not do with their lives. People project their own limited ideas onto us. If you have a strong feeling you are meant to do something, or you've had visions of yourself doing it, pay attention because you are connecting with the infinite realm and being given information about your destiny.

Human beings only use 10 percent of the brain's capacity. If we could awaken the dormant areas, we could align with the realm of innumerable possibilities. We could time travel and enter another dimension. We could return to the past and make different choices. When I first came to America, I met a man on the plane who told me that he wished more than anything that he could go back to the past and fix something he'd done that had ended his relationship with the love of his life. He said he could not stop thinking about the mistake he'd made, but he had no way of making amends in this lifetime, because the woman he'd wronged had died. I got to know him after we both immigrated, and one day I was shocked to hear that he'd died in his sleep. He was only in his early thirties, and no one could explain what happened. As soon as I heard the news, I knew that his longing had allowed him to awaken an area of his brain that gave him the power to break time. He'd gone back to that past moment that still existed in the invisible realm, and righted his wrong.

Healing the Past by Using the Law of Infinite Possibilities

Healers and shamans who have learned the ancient art of breaking the rules of time and space are able to travel into the past as well. A medical intuitive and healer I know and have worked with, John Sweeney, leads his patients into astral travel. Their bodies remain in time, in the physical world, but their consciousness goes back into the past, before they developed their illness, when it existed only as one of many possibilities. Once there, they can choose a different outcome than the illness they're experiencing in the present.

Even if you do not have a healer or shaman to work with, you can still heal your past by using hypnosis or dream work to retrieve it and bring it into the present. The memory of everything you've ever done still lives within you, in total clarity. Your subconscious is connected to the infinite where the past, present, and future are all happening at the same time. Consciously, you may remember nothing about a trauma in your childhood, or one that occurred in a past life. Many phobias are based in past-life traumas. By working with a hypnotist, you can bring these memories back into your conscious mind and remove its emotional charge, healing your karma.

I worked with a gentleman on his fear of flying by hypnotizing him, bringing him further and further back into his memories until I found the origin of his phobia: He had been a pilot in World War II and died when his plane was shot down by the Germans. After the session in which he retrieved this memory, he no longer had any fear of flying. What's more, he finally understood why he had worked at airports all his life, and yet had always been too terrified to use his employee discount to fly. On an unconscious level, he was trying to face his fears about airplanes by being around them, but he needed to remember his death in a plane crash in order to overcome his phobia.

How to Align with the Law of Infinite Possibilities

As long as we have unresolved karma and our souls are connected to our bodies, we will never completely do away with man-made law and be able to live outside of the physical realm. We would have to change our very nature to do that. What you can do right now is try to align yourself more closely with the Law of Infinite Possibilities and open yourself up to a range of opportunity that has no boundaries. You have to develop what the Buddhists call "beginner's mind," a sense of openness and curiosity that children often experience but that we experience less and less as we get closer to adulthood and conform to society's ideas about the limitations we face. Children have a much looser sense of reality and time, while adults have very specific ideas. This is why it is very important to monitor the media children watch. At early ages, they do not understand the difference between what they see on the television screen and what is real. If they see the same film clip over and over, they think that event occurred multiple times.

Indigo children are young people who are especially skilled at going back and forth between the physical reality and the infinite, divine reality. They are able to have psychic experiences because some areas of their brain (that are dormant in most people) are active and able to easily communicate with divinity. However, all children are more facile at breaking the rules of time and space than we adults are.

As we get older, we begin to see limited possibilities instead of infinite possibilities. Too soon we fully believe the man-made ideas about what we can and cannot do. We find a sense of security in the predictability of life, even if it angers or frustrates us. The familiarity of the same problems, day after day, gives us a certain comfort. We rely on our logic and left brain to figure out how to address our problems instead of envisioning something entirely different. The brain can have some great ideas, but the challenge is to open ourselves up to a wider range of possibilities than our brains can invent.

Using Visual Imagery to Work with the Law of Infinite Possibilities

If you have visual images come to your mind and you cannot make sense of them, do not dismiss them as unimportant and forget all about them. You may be breaking the rules of time and space and aligning with the Law of Infinite Possibilities. Retain the memory of the vision, meditate on it, or undergo hypnosis so that you might understand it better. Many times, my knowledge about the future comes in the form of a vision I cannot explain when it first appears. But I have learned to value the information I get and analyze it if I can. I was once interviewed by Telemundo, the largest Spanish-language television network, to get my predictions about celebrities. Toward the end of the interview, almost as an aside, the young woman reporter told me she was from Ecuador and said everyone there was wondering who their next president would be. She asked if I knew, and I said no, I couldn't venture a guess. I wasn't even sure I could find Ecuador on a map! But the young woman was persistent, so I took a breath, cleared my mind, and it came to me. As if I were watching a movie, I saw a clear picture of a tall man with a nice smile, green eyes (unusual in Ecuador), in his forties. Although I didn't get a picture of them, I somehow knew he had three children and the initial R.

Because I knew nothing about Ecuadorian politics, I forgot about this prediction until my phone rang two years later. It was the reporter from Telemundo calling to tell me that a dark horse in the presidential race was starting to gain momentum. She had remembered my prediction and wanted me to look at a photograph of Rafael Correa, the former professor turned politician. Correa was the man I had seen in my vision. For weeks, my phone rang off the hook as people from South America called to ask me if he really, truly would win despite the odds against him, and I kept saying yes, he will—and he did.

The future is not fixed, even if we are able to access it by breaking time. My predictions are based on visions and my inner knowing about the most likely future, the direction we are headed in. We can influence the future as individuals, and Divinity can change our course in order to aid us in healing our karma. If you have a vision, do not assume that it absolutely must come true—or that it is a factually accurate memory from the past. Pay attention to the symbolism and consider all the possible interpretations of that image. Learn what you can from it and be willing to change your present course. You can do this by resolving your karma so that you do not have to experience a future crisis.

There are many ways in which we can break the rules of time and space. If we understand them, we can learn to work with them.

Learn from Your Dreams

The left side of the brain operates according to the laws of time and space, but the right side does not. Half the day you are in the world of the senses, and when you go to sleep at night you do not know where you are. That's why you can dream about what happened two hundred years ago or what will happen twenty years from now. As a form of therapy, sleep allows the left side to rest while the right side takes over. Danish physicist Niels Bohr, one of the contributors to our understanding of quantum mechanics, said he made his discoveries in an altered state of consciousness in which he was half asleep. Einstein used to say that he had to sleep on his right side to truly understand the law of gravity. What he meant was that he needed to use his right, intuitive brain because his left brain couldn't fully grasp it. Edgar Cayce was called the sleeping prophet, because many of his visions came in a dream.

Every night, your unconscious mind speaks to you in your dreams, but if you do not remember them, you cannot learn from them. Before you go to sleep at night, tell yourself to remember your dreams upon waking, and you are much more likely to do it. Then, in the morning, as you feel yourself coming into consciousness, let your dream replay in your mind. *Do not stop to analyze it.* As soon as your left brain starts trying to interpret the symbols in your dream, your right brain's activity will decrease and you will forget details from your dream. Let it replay in your mind until you feel you are not going to remember any more of it. Then write it down exactly as it unfolded.

To make sense of the symbols in your dreams, a dream dictionary can be helpful, but you must go beyond the limited interpretations you find there. As I've said before, look at how any particular symbol has played out in your everyday life. For instance, if you dream of a bulldog, the most obvious interpretation is that the bulldog represents determination, aggression, or stubbornness. However, if you were with your child watching a cartoon bulldog on television the day before, and laughing at the character's bravado, the bulldog in your dream might be a symbol of arrogance and foolish pride. Actions and images that are positive, such as flying, diamonds, being in the mountains, clear water, or gold, are almost always symbols of empowerment.

Visual images in dreams may be puns, too. Mail might symbolize men (males), for instance. Pay attention to the emotions you experience in a dream, and it will be easier to figure out what message your unconscious is sending you.

Your dream may be warning you about something that is about to happen. If so, you may be able to prevent the event from occurring. Don't be afraid of the power to break time and know things before they happen. The Divine wants to help us know what's to come, but expects us to use this information to fulfill our dharma, not to indulge the needs of the ego. If you were to dream of the winning lottery numbers, it would be because the Divine wants you to use that money to serve humanity, not to indulge in buying luxury items.

Hypnosis

Hypnosis is another tool for breaking time. Nostradamus would stare into a bowl of water at midnight to awaken his right brain and retrieve information from his own unconscious, as well as the collective unconscious, so he could make his predictions. This activity, which has been called "scrying," is a form of self-hypnosis. You can do self-hypnosis or you can work with a hypnotist to break time by allowing your consciousness to enter the realm of infinite possibilities and then astral travel into the past, where you can heal the karma created by a particular event. Hypnotism can sometimes bring you into the future as well.

Hypnosis isn't only for people who have addictions and phobias, although it is extremely useful for addressing those problems. Anyone can benefit from having a hypnotist assist them in bringing into their consciousness long-forgotten memories of trauma. Because the hypnotist is there guiding and supporting you, a part of your awareness remains separate from the experience you relive under hypnosis. The hypnotist will reassure you that you are safe and can explore this painful memory. With this support, you will find the courage to experience the strong, negative emotions that come up for you. Once you come back into conscious awareness and your hypnotist discusses the session with you, you will realize that the memory no longer has an overwhelming, negative emotional charge. You will be able to talk about it and analyze it without being frightened, because you will have healed the karma you created.

Guided Visualizations

There are many excellent guided visualization CDs and MP3 downloads available to help your unconscious mind bring to your conscious mind messages in the form of symbolic images. As with a dream, allow imagery to enter your awareness without thinking about it or trying to analyze it until after your session is completed. In this way, your left brain won't shut down the activity of your right brain.

Visual imagery is a powerful tool for communicating with the unconscious, which is connected to the collective unconscious. You can use the imagery to "talk" to your unconscious mind. Neuro-linguistic programming (NLP) techniques, such as envisioning yourself successfully managing a conflict and persuading the other person to back off from their hard-line position, are effective because they allow your left brain and right brain to work together to create the future you desire.

How the Law of Infinite Possibilities Works with the Other Eternal Principles

All of us are connected in the realm of the divine. The Law of Infinite Possibilities allows us to access information about other people, across long distances and even across time. It reminds us that our separateness is an illusion we've created. Using the Law of Infinite Possibilities with the Law of Totality, I have been able to learn that someone is going to get pregnant and have a baby boy, or that someone else's parent is going to come through surgery just fine, or that two hundred years ago, someone's spouse was her political rival. By using these two divine laws, I can even access this information when I am doing a reading with someone over the phone, from thousands of miles away.

The Law of Infinite Possibilities also works with and enhances other Divine Laws because all of the Eternal Principles work together. Working with the Law of Karma, it allows us to go back in time and heal our karma. Understanding the Law of Infinite Possibilities helps us to be wise and accept that we are not in control of every outcome, even as it gives us the courage to dream big, to believe in the impossible, and to change our lives for the better by breaking the laws of time and space.

It is easier to love ourselves unconditionally when we recognize there is always hope for emotional healing and the resolution of karma. We may not experience this healing in our current lifetime, or be able to bring it about, despite our best efforts, but it is possible that we can achieve extraordinary healing by breaking the rules of time and space. However, we must work in harmony with all of creation and with our destiny rather than trying to force the Universe to meet all our expectations.

There is no limit to the abundance we can attract and manifest, and no limit to the level of evolution we can achieve, as individuals or as a human race. History is full of examples of huge leaps forward in human consciousness that we take for granted today because we do not stop to think about what it was like to be living a thousand or ten thousand years ago. Finally, the Law of Infinite Possibilities works with the Law of Dharma by providing us endless opportunities to resolve our karma and serve the world.

The Lesson of the Law of Infinite Possibilities:

Patience and infinite possibilities are divine.
Worry and obsession about the past, present, and future
are man-made.

When we are caught up in the world of our senses, it is very difficult to stop worrying about the future or obsessing about the past. In the physical world, we know we cannot change the past or predict the future, and that frustrates us to no end. However, if we align with the Law of Infinite Possibilities, the anxiety, fear, and frustration fall away as we join the Creator and all of creation in manifesting what we desire.

The keys to working with this divine law and letting go of the limitations of the man-made world: breaking time and space by using the laws of quantum physics and patience.

If you can, work with someone who is skilled at using her right brain and can access the realm of infinite possibilities—a healer, an intuitive, or a hypnotist. Not everyone has the skill to easily access the realm of infinite possibilities, but every one of us can develop it to some degree. I had to devote much time and energy to developing my metaphysical gifts. In this chapter, you have learned some of the ways in which you can work with your intuitive knowledge and access the great wisdom of creation. No matter how difficult it may be to believe that you can break the rules of time and space, you can do it, in small ways at first, even now.

Prayer, for example, is a way of working with the Law of Infinite Possibilities and bringing about "the impossible." One of my clients was recently upset about her sister's state of mental health and was praying her hardest for her recovery. In the chapel at the psychiatric facility where her sister was a patient, she found a box set up by a local prayer circle and a note encouraging people to write down their prayers and put them in the box. She asked this group of strangers to pray for her sister to regain her will to live and her mental health. Three days later, her sister, who had been in a deep depression for over a year, suddenly came out of it, without any change in medications. Miracles like this happen every single day as a result of working with the Law of Infinite Possibilities. We actually are able to communicate with another person over a distance and affect them at an energy level, which affects them physically.

Remember, though, that it can be difficult to influence the physical world through consciousness. It can take enormous energy, and physical reality is affected by the consciousness of everyone, not just of one person. We are co-creators, not solo creators.

When you hope for a particular outcome, being patient can be difficult, but you must let go of needing to know how and when the changes you want will take place. The big break you've been awaiting may seem very small when it comes; it is only afterward that it is clear you experienced a turning point. People often meet their future spouse through what seems like pure chance, or a seemingly minor opportunity turns out to be the door to a major friendship, career break, or fundamental shift in your life. You might meet a stranger on the bus or while waiting in line, strike up a friendship with the person who happens to have the cubicle next to yours at work, or make a decision one winter day to stop into a coffee shop to warm up and you meet the love of your life as a result. Maybe your big break has already come, and you don't realize your dream is unfolding even now.

Although "happy accidents" happen all the time, we are stuck in the thinking of the man-made world that tells us these occurrences are not significant or predestined. We try to force the world into giving us what we want and become impatient when we cannot change people's opinions or our circumstances. By shifting your perspective and recognizing that the Universe is orchestrating events, you can open yourself up to opportunities that await you and work with the flow of the Divine, who wants you to have all that you desire. You will stop overlooking all the many possibilities for changing your life that show up every day. Too often, people will say things like, "I met this person and he told me to call his friend who could help me, but I never got around to it and lost the number." Or, they will talk about a time when events lined up in a such a way as to create an opportunity that seemed extraordinarily rare, but they had some excuse for not following through on it, and now they wonder if it will ever come up for them again.

Patience means trusting in divine timing, being open to the opportunities that come to you instead of clinging to preconceived notions about how your life is supposed to unfold, and allowing Divinity to be a co-creator with you. Very often, situations take care of themselves in time. The coworker who's been making your job difficult is transferred or your child matures and the behavior that's been upsetting you finally disappears.

Globally, situations change as well. If you look back ten, twenty, or thirty years, it is astonishing to see how problems we thought were overwhelming and would take many years of hard work and focus to fix were solved almost magically either by technology or a shift in awareness that led to big changes.

When we are in sync with the Divine, we do not constantly hit roadblocks. If we do, we are meant to question whether we are on the right path and to honestly assess our course. Years ago, I was having a very difficult time getting any jewelry merchandiser to understand why I wanted to create jewelry with spiritual symbolism. It seemed to take forever to launch my jewelry line and there were days when I was ready to give up, but then I looked inward and reconnected with my passion. As I did so, I knew I was on the right path. I needed to be patient and open to how this dream of mine would manifest. Eventually, I met with the people at QVC who put me on the air, and my jewelry finally began to sell to the public.

There have been other times when I realized that I was not going to be able to bring something into physical reality in the form and timing I expected. It's not that I gave up on these dreams, but I have set them aside because I understand that this is not the time for me to pursue them. I know that if I try to live according to the Eternal Principles, I will be open to the signals from the Universe to bring those projects back to the forefront of my awareness because the timing will be right at that point.

Every day, more people are aligning themselves with the Eternal Principles, listening to the wisdom that comes to them from their unconscious mind, and tapping in to the great collective unconscious. We are rapidly approaching a tipping point, when we all awaken to our abilities to work in harmony with the Divine, breaking the laws of time and space. The Principle of Infinite Possibilities lets us know that we can instantly share with others any information we possess, without using technology to communicate. The more you open yourself up to infinite possibilities, the more likely it is that you will connect with this ancient, divine wisdom that is available in the collective unconscious. Be patient, and be alert to every opportunity you have to learn, grow, live out your dharma, and evolve. The doors are opening. You have the chance to walk through them into a new way of living. Happiness, peace, and health are your birthright. Do not be afraid to claim them.

WHERE ARE WE GOING?
APPLYING THE UNIVERSAL PRINCIPLES

What is the response of the Divine Consciousness to the way we humans behave? I imagine God watching over us from above, like a parent determined to guide us but also to give us the freedom to learn in our own way. We're like a teenager insisting that we have plenty of time to study so we do not have to do our homework right now, or claiming we do not need to bring a jacket in case the temperature drops. Instead of arguing or pleading, God simply says, "Okay, but you are going to flunk the test and end up having to do extra work to bring up your grade, and you will be cold tonight and have no way to come home early." The Divine knows that we are stubborn and immature, and sometimes we have to learn by doing. Then, we will truly understand the lesson.

I think God chuckles at our foolishness and pride, but is there to help us out at the last minute, sending us signs, guidance, and opportunities for changing our situation and rescuing ourselves from the disasters we create. Meanwhile, like adolescents, we become lost in our personal dramas and forget what is really important. Like teenagers who become upset over who got picked for the school play, we get emotionally caught up in trivial matters. Take a look at the television news and see if you don't agree! When we begin living according to the Eternal Principles, we can look back at what we were obsessed with before and laugh, and ask ourselves "What on earth was I thinking?" Our priorities change, and we stop creating so much suffering for ourselves.

Most people aren't bad or hopelessly selfish. They are only asleep, caught up in a dream world of materialism, power, and pleasure. They are doing their best to avoid pain. Humanity can open its eyes and awaken to a less reactive, more productive way of living—in harmony with the Divine.

We do not need a huge number of people to dramatically change the way they perceive. A small number will make the key difference. From this group will emerge new leaders who aren't concerned with power and serving their egos, but with helping to lift up the consciousness of everyone.

Change is happening, but we do not always notice it. When you put a saucepan full of water on the stove, it seems to take forever to boil, but suddenly a few small bubbles break the surface and in no time, it is boiling furiously. Transformation of consciousness happens in a similar way. If you are paying close attention, you can sense that the bubbles are just about to break.

In 2012, a huge shift in consciousness will seem to happen out of nowhere, and then, in 2033, we will complete the cosmic passage from the Age of Pisces into the Age of Aquarius, beginning one thousand years of peace as predicted by Nostradamus. The energy of Aquarius, of pioneering change and brotherhood, will be in full force.

A Shift of Consciousness

To get an idea of what this shift of consciousness will be like, and how different our lives will be, imagine knowing all that you know and traveling back in time 100 years. How would you describe what your life is like to a person of that time? They would probably be shocked at what you are wearing and have no clue what you are saying when you try to explain shopping malls, mass production, employee benefits, or credit cards. If you talked about going to a therapist, the threat of global warming, or using the Internet, they'd look at you in confusion. If you used terms like "our culture," "positive thinking," "self-esteem," or "consciousness," they'd just stare. Or they might lock you up in a mental institution. It's not only our technology or daily lives that have changed dramatically in a century. Our very way of perceiving the world, our interactions with others, and humanity itself have transformed.

We know that technology is changing faster than ever. One day, we see a television news report about some new device and the next thing we know, every college student has one. It quickly becomes an integral part of their lifestyle. Something like YouTube comes along, and a few people have fun watching videos. Suddenly presidential elections are influenced by clips from the past that someone has dug up and uploaded onto YouTube. We start talking about having our own "YouTube moment" or something "going viral like a YouTube clip." Our technology influences our way of thinking about ourselves and our interactions with others.

The speed at which our lives change, with new technologies and ideas coming more and more quickly, is only going to increase. Thanks to technology and communication, the kinds of changes in our experience that used to take place over ten or fifteen years will happen in three or four years.

If this seems unrealistic, think back to when yoga was an exercise form that only a few people in California practiced—now, coaches on high school sports teams in the Midwest lead their young players in doing yoga moves to warm up. Scientists first began to talk about global warming years ago, but then Al Gore's documentary film *An Inconvenient Truth* came out and, almost instantly, every magazine had a feature on green living, and every local hardware store had a section devoted to green building supplies. You blink, and something you vaguely remember hearing about a few months ago is now part of the mainstream American lifestyle.

When you are trying to live according to divine law, but lose faith that our troubled world will awaken from its unenlightened ways, be patient, and remember that it takes time for water to boil, but when it is ready, it boils furiously.

We are only a few years away from 2012, when the tipping point will occur and suddenly, a huge amount of people will recognize that our man-made laws aren't working for us, and that we have to embrace the divine laws. Higher consciousness will burst forth, seemingly overnight.

We're seeing the signs of this great upheaval now. In the past, we allowed kings and religious leaders to be wealthy and powerful while most people struggled to survive. Now, we are waking up to the fact that we have a new economic ruling class that has no interest in distributing its wealth so that ordinary people do not have to suffer and struggle. We understand that this old system has to change. We're realizing that force doesn't solve problems, that war doesn't fix anything, and that we've drifted away from the grand visions of the past. We're seeing that American democracy has transformed from what the founding fathers designed and from what good people worked hard to support over our history. The ideals we claim to hold have been perverted by greed and fear.

People who never used to think about the connections between their experiences and the trends that affect people around the world are beginning to realize that their financial troubles are not a result of their personal irresponsibility or bad luck, but the natural outcome of a broken financial system that is affecting everyone. They are questioning where the objects at the mall or the grocery store are coming from. They want to know who is involved in bringing them to the marketplace and how the process affects the farmers, truckers, or factory workers. They are awakening to the Law of Totality.

We are realizing that it is time to discard the belief that as long as we amass enough money and power, we will be okay. We're realizing we need to be concerned about more than our own comfort, and we are rejecting the man-made laws that have divided us and confused us.

Humankind is at the end of an era. Systems we took for granted have become obsolete. It's bewildering to see that globally, our old ideas about money and trade do not work any more. It's dawning on us that we have to reconnect with our ideals and create a new vision. We're stepping back and looking at things we've been ignoring for many years, because we sense that we are not just facing a few changes, we are facing a transformation bigger than anyone living can remember.

Then too, the idea that our minds affect physical reality, that we can create psychosomatic illness and attract and manifest what we desire, is still very new to many of us. We are struggling to believe we have that power. Yet these are not twenty-first century ideas. Half a century before Christ was born, the Buddha said, "The mind is everything. What you think, you become." Ancient wisdom teachings from traditions all over the world have been forgotten and need to be rediscovered. We do not have to keep making the same mistakes humanity has made for centuries.

The changes are already happening. There's much talk about a Great Depression happening, but we won't have long bread lines filled with homeless people. We're going to make changes in the financial infrastructure and pull ourselves out of this economic crisis by the year 2018. We are on the verge of inventing a new form of remuneration. We have to start from scratch and rethink how people get paid and pay each other because the old system crashed like an overloaded computer.

We've built up to this tipping point, and though it may be hard to believe, we are going to experience dramatic changes in a very short period of time as people in great numbers shift their consciousness upward and start creating new visions for how we can live together in harmony. Fundamentalist extremists will begin to disappear, and identity politics—the old idea that "my group is right and yours is wrong"—will cease. We do not have to wait for the next generation to do a better job than we have because we will make a quantum leap in awareness.

The problem of large numbers of people struggling to live sustainably on the earth will be solved. Very quickly, thanks to technology, we will be able to rely on renewable wind and solar energy. Food and water shortages will be solved, and we will go back to eating the way we used to, consuming unprocessed food. As a result, we will be far healthier and we will live longer.

It's as if we are going through a divorce, leaving behind the old way of life. But divorces take time, so we won't complete this transitional phase until 2033, when our ambivalence will finally fade and we will all totally accept this new world with its new monetary system, transportation, technology, and spiritual belief systems. Imagine how impossible it would have seemed to someone in the years before Christianity took hold how tremendously that belief system would affect humanity, and you will get a sense of the magnitude of this shift in human experience.

After 2033, we will enjoy a thousand years of peace, according to Nostradamus. I actually think it will be more like sixteen hundred years. Free from war and poverty, we will be able to focus on bettering our lives. We'll eliminate karmically caused diseases and live for hundreds of years. We will begin an era of exploration, using technologies for communication and transportation that are based in quantum physics. This will allow us to travel to other planets, such as Eris, the new tenth planet, and establish new civilizations. We'll meet with other sentient beings from other planets and be able to communicate telepathically. Meanwhile, our relationship with the planet earth will be very different. Instead of angrily rebelling against us and our abuse, earth will embrace us and natural disasters will be rare.

A Shared Positive Vision

We do not have a vision of tomorrow, of what we want our world to be. Without a vision of the future, we are merely existing: moving around without moving toward anything. Living this way leads many people to become trapped in their suffering of the moment.

Not every common vision is a good one. Hitler's vision for Germany inspired many people to do great evil, for instance. His vision was based in ego, in achieving power for himself and encouraging his countrymen to see themselves as superior and worthy of living a prosperous life at the expense of other people suffering. What we need is a vision that is in alignment with the Eternal Principles and focused on resolving global karma and fulfilling global dharma.

When you find yourself feeling hopeless or cynical, close your eyes and imagine the impossible: a world where no one goes hungry, where everyone who is ill has access to healers who can help them, where people resolve their issues through dialogue instead of violence. If we cannot even envision such a world, how will we bring it about? When President John F. Kennedy shared with America his vision of going to the moon before the end of the decade of the 1960s, there were certainly people who scoffed at the idea and said, "That's preposterous." At the time of the first moon landing in 1969, we didn't even have microchips. The indicators on the control pane of the space capsule were mechanical, not digital. When we consider the technology available to us today, it can seem those astronauts were completely crazy to trust in their spacecraft and the engineers in the control center! What gave them courage was a shared vision that allowed everyone to overcome their fears and the limitations of the mind, which is always quick to say, "It cannot be done."

Our collective vision for the future needs to be in alignment with the Law of Infinite Possibilities, the Law of Totality, and all the other Eternal Principles, so that we may all work together to uplift everybody. Originally, religion's purpose was to bring people together and help them achieve higher states of consciousness. The word "religion" comes from a Latin root, *religare*, meaning "unity," but in too many cases, religions have become too caught up in amassing power and influence in the material realm. Government, laws, educational systems, and religions all need to transform so that they can be in alignment with divine purpose.

All around the world, people are developing an interest in the future of all humanity, not just of their countrymen. I see this when I travel to Europe and meet people from around America. I hear the same question over and over again, "Where are we going? What's going to happen to all of us?"

As different as our lives and belief systems may be, people everywhere have more in common with each other than they realize. When we acknowledge that we are all in this together, we can start working with each other, tapping into the wisdom of all consciousness.

Social Upheaval

The near future will bring great social upheaval as people begin to think and perceive differently. Those of lower consciousness will be very frightened by the changes happening all around them and rebel with great force. However, people of higher consciousness will prevail, and by 2033, humans across the globe will have given up many of the most basic low-level patterns of thinking, feeling, and behaving. The people who are greedy and manipulative will come to realize how useless and unsatisfying it is to hoard their great wealth while others suffer. Our increased ability to communicate, to know what is going on all around the world, will help them to awaken because it will be impossible for them to be ignorant of all the tragedies happening around them and the incredible joy that people experience when they use their power and talents to alleviate suffering. The story of one brave person sacrificing for others is no longer passed along by oral tradition over many years, but broadcast on the Internet and television to the most remote areas of the world. Inspiration is everywhere.

Our new awareness will cause us to discard many of our old institutions and systems, because we will no longer need them. We take for granted that we have to have money, banks, and a stock market, but after 2033, none of these will exist. So much of what happens economically is based on fear, hope, and speculation instead of what has real value. As we align ourselves more with divine law, our ideas about abundance will change and our system of value and exchange of value will transform.

The distribution of wealth will be more equitable, and we won't see such extremes between rich and poor. When someone is aligned with divinity, they do not feel rich when they've got more money than they can count but they live in a community where people cannot afford healthy food. Those with money will alter their way of living because what they'll find most rewarding is putting their wealth back into the economy, channeling it so that it can improve the world. Right now, too many people have a distorted idea of what they really need. As we come to better understand our needs, we will understand that nothing we can purchase is going to fulfill our need for companionship or a sense of emotional security. We'll achieve more of a balance of wealth, taking care of our deepest needs as well as others' at the same time.

To achieve harmony and balance, we will have to eliminate injustice and rethink our forms of government and law enforcement. We won't need militaries or police in the future. More than one community in the United States is taking an innovative approach to eliminating crime in lower-income neighborhoods. The district attorney in that city gathers all the evidence he needs to prosecute local drug dealers, then confronts them with a proposition: They can go to trial or they can go to a meeting where local community members will see videotapes of them selling drugs and be able to confront them about their frustrations. After that, local businesses and governments will offer them opportunities for work, and as long as they do not commit any more crimes, the D.A. won't press charges for their drug dealing. This approach has been effective in many cities. The money spent locking people up, postponing their criminal activity for a short time until they get out onto the streets again, is used instead to give them a chance to become working members of the community. We'll see more programs that are in alignment with the Eternal Principles instead of man-made laws, which are based on punishment, power, harsh judgment, and everyone trying to get his piece of the pie.

Every religion teaches that we are supposed to take care of each other, every last person, and we are just beginning to do that. As we start working together to help one another, new leaders will emerge, and the old ones, who are more interested in serving their own egos, will be swept out of power.

Leadership

When people start to think of themselves as victims, they long for a rescuer. The world has many problems, and a lot of people wish there were some politician or leader who could serve as a father figure and make everything better. Our desire for a messiah or savior to right all the wrongs will start to fade as we begin to take responsibility for our part in saving not just ourselves but everyone. The Divine has given us plenty of tools to address our challenges, but it is up to us to use them instead of wishing that someone would do it all for us.

Jesus urged people to understand that we have the power to transform our lives and our world. He said, "The one who believes in me will also do the works that I do and, in fact, will do greater works than these." (John 14:12). Jesus explained that the woman who healed herself by touching the hem of his cloak did so through her own belief. We think we aren't capable of miraculous acts, but we are. The moment we shift our awareness, raising it to a higher level, we open ourselves up to a wider range of possibilities.

Raising Up People with Lower Consciousness

People in some areas of the world have the consciousness of the Middle Ages. They are not just living according to man-made laws, they're obedient to man-made laws from another time. They have completely different ideas about right and wrong and what the Divine expects of us. When we hear a woman speak proudly about sending her little boy out onto a minefield on a suicide mission to clear the field of landmines so that her country's soldiers can win their war against their neighbors, we are horrified. But we need to try to understand this mother's perspective and be compassionate. It is the only way to influence someone of such low consciousness and actually help prevent other children from suffering the terrible fate their culture will impose upon them.

We have to break down the wall that stands between people who live in this mentality and those who live in the modern world, who are more evolved. We're learning more and more how to help people who are distorted and destructive in their thinking. It requires great patience and love, and even then, we may not be able to raise the consciousness of everyone. All around the world, we will be challenged to set aside our indignation and help these people. The issues of racial, national, and religious identity must be faced in each of our communities. We have to dissolve the barriers between people so that we all feel a part of the whole, instead of part of our own, small group. As we build bridges toward these people who are separating themselves from the whole in a way that is not healthy, we break down our walls, and start perceiving that we, too, are too quick to embrace our own tribe and see other people as different, bad, or wrong.

Light Healing through Raised Consciousness

Our raised consciousness will also bring about a huge revolution in medicine. We'll stop looking for magic pills or surgery to fix our health problems and will think more holistically. Rather than treating a disease by trying to kill it while not harming the body, we will ask ourselves questions such as, "Why is my body attacking itself, creating this autoimmune disorder? What's the source of discord?"

Medical researchers are now discovering that many diseases and illnesses are not rooted in a microbe or virus, but in destructive behavior at a cellular level. If one molecule is destroying another, we have to address that. Cancer involves some of your cells battling against other cells, and the bad cells refusing to die off and surrender to the needs of the greater group (the body). Knowing this, scientists can work with what they call a "disease mechanism" and fight the disease differently. What we as patients can do is ask ourselves, "In what ways am I sabotaging myself, and putting my desperate need to survive at all costs ahead of my need to truly live?" When we are able to see what is best for us in the long run, and what our priorities ought to be, we recognize we have to let go of certain survival mechanisms, like being competitive to the point of ruthlessness, being greedy and materialistic, or being prideful about our reputation.

Our consciousness, individually and collectively, creates illness or health in our bodies. Anger is like a fire, inflaming our mind, stirring up fiery emotions, and causing diseases of inflammation, such as rheumatoid arthritis, fibromyalgia, stroke, pulmonary fibrosis, heart disease, and cancer, by inflaming our cells. Anger causes wars and conflicts throughout the world, disease, and even violent acts of nature. Although we cannot pinpoint the specific cause of most tragedy, we can ask ourselves how our emotions might be affecting a situation, which will lead us to a higher consciousness and toward the ways of the Divine.

In the future, our understanding about disease will allow us to address it more effectively. We are beginning to recognize that the key to fighting genetic diseases is through understanding why certain genes express themselves and others do not. In the future, we will be able to have great influence over the expression of our genes.

Thanks to psychology and spiritual practices, we have learned how to bring into our awareness the memories of the past that have a negative emotional charge. We then work to accept these difficult memories and learn from them in order to dissolve the anger, sadness, or resentment that is attached to them. In this way, we both live with our negative karma and work at resolving it, allowing ourselves to be closer to a state of purity. In a similar way, we will learn how to make our peace with microbes, viruses, and destructive cells, acknowledging them, accepting them, and containing them so they cannot wreak havoc on our bodies. Medical technology and medicine will be based on these new understandings of how to deal with disease.

We will also do more healing using energy and light. Radiation and laser surgery involve focusing a certain type of energy, and acupuncture involves manipulating vital energy along meridians. We will expand on these ways of healing, working with the energy field of a person who is ill instead of bombarding their body with chemicals or cutting into it with surgical knives. We will also break time and space, and be able to have our consciousness go back into the past where it can heal our ailment before it takes physical form.

Restoring the body back to balance will be a core focus of healing and the basis of breakthroughs in achieving longevity.

Longevity

Instead of ignoring our bodies until we get sick and then working with a doctor to try to fix ourselves, we will support our health at a cellular level. We will be able to manipulate cells so that they return to a state of health and good functioning, and reprogram our DNA. We'll shut off the mechanisms that tell certain genes to activate and create the diseases that have been passed down by our parents and grandparents. We'll reprogram cells so that when they regenerate, the new generation of cells will be healthier than the previous generation. This will lead to greater longevity, but also to better health as we age.

We'll be able to use injections to bring back to life organs that have failed, actually reviving them at a cellular level. We'll be able to extend our cells' ability to replicate, so if a cell would normally only generate fifty times, we will extend that to five hundred times. Eventually, we will discover how to make our bodies live forever.

We'll work at a cellular level to reverse the oxidation process that causes deterioration of the body (oxidation is the same process that causes a cut apple to turn brown or steel exposed to water to rust and break down).

We'll enhance the movement of energy within the body, bringing light energy into healthy cells so that they can flourish and replicate, outnumbering the cells that are toxic. We'll grow new organs and new skin. Stem cell technology and cloning will give us many options for replacing body parts. We are already discovering how to make mature cells behave like embryonic stem cells. This is just one of the many ways in which we will turn back the clock and return cells to an earlier state.

We'll understand that everything that happens to our physical body is connected to emotional issues and begin clearing our karma and cleansing our body fluids, which carry our anger, sadness, resentment, jealousy, and fear through our body. In this way, we will be able to eliminate tumors and inflammation (a collecting of fluid). We describe a bad rash as "angry" because instinctively we associate the red bumps with the building up of anger. I had a client who told me that any time she got mad at her mother she would develop a rash on her face. I have also had many clients develop breast cancer after ending a relationship or while struggling with issues about motherhood, sexuality, and nurturing. The more we understand the mind/body/spirit connection, the more we will be motivated to change our emotions to lighter, less dense feelings that promote health.

Technology

As amazing as our technological advances have been in the last fifty years, they will take a quantum leap forward. Remember on the television show *Star Trek* when people and objects were "beamed" from one location to another? One day we will have the capability to transform the particles in our bodies to waves, send them energetically through space, and turn them back into particles, regaining our mass.

We will have cars that can fly at the push of a button and are powered by wind and solar energy that create no toxic by-products. We will have the technological means to clean up the pollution in our environment. As with medicine, we will be able to return our water, earth, and air to its previous, clean state.

We'll no longer need money and banks and will wear something like a ring or necklace that carries a great deal of information we can access at any time. Bar codes, fingerprints, and photographs of our eyes will serve as identification rather than ID cards. Satellites will be a big part of new technologies for communication. Our watches will also be picture phones. Our airplanes will operate according to our understanding of quantum physics and will fly at amazing speeds. We'll be able to travel faster than the speed of light and visit other galaxies, and take up residence on other planets. We'll also learn how to levitate. Some monks are able to do this already, and defy other laws of physics. Scientists have recorded evidence that there are monks who can meditate on a snowy mountaintop and yet despite thin clothing, have skin that is warm to the touch and a normal internal body temperature. As we come to accept, learn about, and work with the power of higher consciousness, we will easily be able to perform similar feats.

How We Will Interact with the Planet

Some illnesses and diseases are caused by toxins in the environment; our personal karma may have nothing to do with manifesting them. But because we share karma with others, we can be affected by the toxins manifested by another person's consciousness. As long as humanity feels disconnected from the earth and the environment, we will continue to treat it as separate from us, polluting the water, air, and ground because we figure "out of sight, out of mind."

To some extent, we can get away with polluting our land, water, and air. Our bodies have the ability to cleanse themselves of some impurities, but there are so many poisons we ingest through breathing, eating, and drinking, as well as through our skin, that we cannot keep up with it all. In the future, we will have fewer toxins to deal with and we will incorporate purifying activities into our lives. We'll live much healthier lifestyles because we won't be tempted to hide from our emotional issues by overeating, drinking, or taking mood-altering substances.

We are just beginning to wake up to the idea that when we take care of the earth, we take care of ourselves, and vice versa. We are realizing that the way we've treated planet earth, the plants and the animals, and ourselves has to change. We have been fouling our own nest, creating diseases and disasters. The planet is rebelling with stronger hurricanes and increased earthquakes, tsunamis, and fires. We are beginning to see that each of us must take responsibility for decreasing our individual and collective carbon footprint. When we live according to the Eternal Principles, we do not make excuses for serving our ego. We do the right thing for ourselves and others regardless of how much we have to sacrifice.

In fact, we do not have to sacrifice as much as we might think in order to save the planet. We've forgotten that many people making a few small changes can have a powerful effect. As we raise our consciousness, we focus on our own power to support the earth and help others.

From Superpowers to the Supreme Power

People often wonder if China will take America's place as the greatest superpower, or if the former Soviet Union will somehow regain its foothold and become a superpower again. The only real superpower is divine energy. The more we align ourselves with divinity, the more we will realize that we do not need to dominate other countries or pressure them to live the way we live. There is room for diversity. We'll have to work with other countries to alleviate the real threat, which is people who want to take power for themselves or for their small group, using terrorism.

I have always felt that the world underestimates how much of a threat Russia will be to other countries in the future. We get so focused on the Middle East and do not think about the leaders in Russia who have a low level of consciousness and are capable of very destructive behavior. The Middle East will continue to struggle with issues of power, land, and religion. According to archaeologists, human life and civilization began in this area of the world. Our biggest challenges—terrorism, fossil-fuel based energy problems, religious clashes, tribalism, and global warming—all draw our attention to the Middle East. We are meant to examine the negative karma created in that place, which goes all the way back to the beginnings of human greed, selfishness, and cruelty—behaviors that arose after we chose to take human form. The three Abrahamic religions—Judaism, Christianity, and Islam—began in this region, and we've allowed them to become dogmatic and divisive rather than follow the spiritual teachings at their heart. By examining how we got here, we can begin to resolve our global karma and find solutions to our global problems.

Although many are fearful about the possibility of a nuclear war, either launched by a rogue nation or by the use of weapons that have gotten into the hands of terrorists, I do not believe we will see any destruction caused by nuclear weapons. Humanity faced the possibility of perishing by fire when we discovered the atom bomb, which, as I said, was the result of Pluto's warlike energy affecting us. The discovery of Eris, the tenth planet, with its energy of harmony will protect us from nuclear holocaust. We will be able to invent technologies that prevent or avert such disasters, or minimize their damage.

If many people do die in natural disasters, it will be water that takes their lives, either due to tidal waves or hurricanes or changes in weather patterns caused by global warming and/or the shifting of the earth's magnetic poles. I do not feel we will be facing great destruction, however, despite the doomsday predictions of some.

The Possibilities We Haven't Considered

While we can look forward to new technologies, better health and quality of life, and the end of human suffering, we will also be able to answer some of the greatest mysteries of life and death as we move into the future. The discovery of DNA and its code was one of the most amazing breakthroughs of the last century, but it will pale in comparison with all we will come to know about birth, life, and death.

As we live longer, we will recognize how to live more efficiently and sustainably, in harmony with each other and with the earth. We know that as a population becomes wealthier and more educated, their birthrate decreases. People will no longer have children out of a need to ensure their own survival. Some people will choose to have children and some won't, but our choices about whether to give birth will be based in love, not fear.

I can see into the year 4823: We will be living in a world with lush vegetation, huge trees and flowers, and lakes—no oceans or continents. The weather will be a constant, pleasant temperature. We will be lighter than we are now and very tall, wearing metallic garments and living in houses that look like glass. There will be no technology—no cell phones, no computers. Creatures from other planets will live on our world with us, and we will live on theirs. Our lives will be very long because we will not suffer from disease. We will have demystified the concept of death and be able to live peacefully, without fear, moving easily throughout the Universe at an unimaginable speed, experiencing no boundaries or walls, no wars or conflicts.

* * *

By raising our awareness, we have already dramatically changed the human experience over the course of years. Our consciousness has allowed us to make quantum leaps forward in technology and in our imagination. In the future, we will use our free will to live very differently, changing the very nature of our bodies, the way we communicate, and our relationship to our environment. We'll embrace what George Bernard Shaw once said: "You see things and you say why, but I dream things that never were and I say why not."

These changes are happening even today. We can look ahead in excitement, but even so, we must look at ourselves today and ask, what can I do today to usher in this future? The opportunities are right in front of us. I hope you will take hold of them and make the most of them, as you align yourself with the Eternal Principles that promise to make our lives joyful and abundant.

INDEX